D1609777

CLASS, IDEOLOGY AND THE NATION

A THEORY OF

WELSH NATIONALISM

CLASS, IDEOLOGY AND THE NATION

A THEORY OF

WELSH NATIONALISM

David L. Adamson

CARDIFF
UNIVERSITY OF WALES PRESS
1991

British Library Cataloguing in Publication Data

Adamson, David L.
  Class, ideology and the nation : a theory of Welsh
  Nationalism.
  1. Nationalism   2. Wales
  I. Title
  320.5409429

ISBN 0–7083–1082–6

Typeset by BP Integraphics, Bath
Printed in Great Britain by Billing and Sons Limited,
  Book Plan, Worcester

CONTENTS

ACKNOWLEDGEMENTS

I have incurred a number of personal debts in conducting the research leading to the publication of this book and should like to thank all those who knowingly and unknowingly helped me achieve my objectives. David Berry supervised my postgraduate studies at the Department of Sociology, University College of Cardiff, with a willing ear and regular commentary as the work unfolded. Viv Thomas and Mary Darmanin provided discussion and critique which became lasting comradeship. Hughie Mackay read early drafts with great attention for detail.

Finally, but most importantly, I must acknowledge the sacrifices made by my family. Betty has provided a foundation only I know and appreciate and is the source of inspiration for this and everything else I do. Nia and Elin in turn sat on my knee as I worked, a constant reminder of the need to change the world not just understand it.

INTRODUCTION

The research leading to the writing of this book began in 1981 when the British political system appeared to have moved into a new era and the ethnic and regional politics of the 1960s and 1970s had subsided. A firmly centralist, Conservative government held office and the results of the 1979 referendums on devolution in Wales and Scotland were taken as a mandate for a centralist perspective by both major parties. The nationalist aspirations of *Plaid Cymru* and the Scottish Nationalist Party had failed to maintain any mass basis of support and the general climate was one which saw politics in a British context more than at any time since the early 1960s.

Yet, only two years previously, the major political debate had been over proposals for major constitutional reform which would have devolved major central government powers to regional assemblies in Scotland and Wales. The proposals were indicative of a long-term process in which increasing attachment to national identities in those regions had seriously threatened the ability of a Labour Party to acquire power in Britain. The reliance of the Labour Party on Scotland and Wales for a substantial proportion of its support had eventually forced party leaders to recognize the threat of rising regional and national consciousness (Jones 1983).

These conditions were reflected in academic analysis of the period, which, since the mid 1970s, had been preoccupied with what became known as the 'break up of Britain thesis' (Nairn 1977). Academics writing from a range of perspectives were attempting to explain the importance of ethnic cleavages and their effects on British politics. The predominant view predicted a gradual transformation of the British state to a federal form which gave full recognition to the seperate national identities of the Celtic nations of Great Britain. Academic endeavour was also spurred by the importance of ethnic struggles in Europe and throughout the Third World. For a time it was possible to argue that ethnic struggle had superseded class struggle as the primary social cleavage in developed capitalist societies.[1]

Explanations of the 'new nationalisms' varied considerably, from general theories of modernization (Smith 1971), to Marxist (Nairn 1977) and neo-Marxist (Hechter 1975) analyses. One concept in particular caught the imagination of writers and had the advantage of being capable of informing Marxist and non-Marxist theory. This was the concept of 'uneven development' which, although it had its origins in Lenin's theories of imperialism, had been applied, with considerable effect, by Gellner (1964) within a generally functionalist theory of modernization (Orridge 1981). In the Welsh context the work of Hechter (1975) had been particularly influential. Hechter's central argument was based on the process of uneven development and his adoption of the core/periphery distinction from Latin American theories of underdevelopment (Frank 1969a, 1969b). In this model, Wales was a deliberately underdeveloped 'internal colony' of England. Furthermore, the Welsh people were discriminated against by the development of 'a cultural division of labour' which placed English personnel in command positions in Welsh society. Such a theory had major ideological value to Welsh nationalism itself (Lovering 1978), but was of more dubious theoretical value as an explanation of nationalism in the Celtic fringe.[2] Similarly, Nairn's (1977) explanation of nationalism as a feature of the changing dynamic of British imperialism was judged less successful at explaining Celtic nationalism than English nationalism (Hobsbawm 1977).

The primary value of Hechter's analysis was its promotion of a self-conscious sociology of Wales which attempted to engage Welsh issues with wider sociological and political perspectives. Of key importance was the work of the British Sociological Association, Sociology of Wales Study Group, which focused research on the key areas of economic and class restructuring.[3] Explanation of contemporary Welsh nationalism was sought in the internal social relations of Welsh society, necessitating an increasingly historical analysis of earlier expressions of nationalism (Day 1981, Day and Sugget 1983, Adamson 1984).[4] Increasingly, analysis of Welsh nationalism became distanced from simplistic explanations which referred only to cultural phenomena. It was recognized that economic relations between classes were a necessary element of the explanation of historical forms of Welsh nationalism and of its contemporary expression (Williams 1981). Consequently, this study was commenced at a time when it was apparent that the most fruitful search for an explanation of nationalist resurgence would involve an assessment of the link between ethnicity and class.

This strategy was also indicated by developments within Marxist theory which had begun to challenge economic reductionism through the development of increasingly sophisticated theories of class and ideology. Central to these developments was the work of Louis Althusser and his attempts to shed the reductionism of Marxist theory during the Stalin years and to provide a theory which could accommodate the complexity of social formations (Benton 1984). Furthermore, the elaboration of his ideas by writers such as Poulantzas (1973, 1974, 1975) and Laclau (1977) pointed directly to ways in which theories of class and ideology could be applied to an analysis of nationalism. However, the greatest potential for the development of a Marxist theory of the national question was presented in the work of Gramsci (1971, 1977, 1978) which, by the early 1980s, was receiving increasing attention in English-language sociology. Gramsci's identification of the concept of hegemony and the role that national identity played in the creation of hegemonic and counter-hegemonic social movements presented a means by which the class alliances associated with nationalism could be theorized.

These developments in Marxist theory pointed the way to an analysis which recognized the role of social classes in the political process, but which did not attempt to reduce all political practices to a direct correspondence with class interests. The complexity of social formations could be recognized and the role of political and ideological elements, with their origins outside class relations, could be given full status in Marxist analysis. The study of nationalism was clearly an area where these developments were of crucial significance.

Consequently, the general framework of this enquiry into Welsh nationalism arose out of the debates and discussions of the period and reflects an attempt to place the analysis of Welsh nationalism in the major theoretical developments which followed the publication of the work of Althusser in the English language.[5] Given these origins, this study is primarily a theoretical exercise in that it attempts to develop an explanation for the emergence of Welsh nationalism in the nineteenth century and its resurgence in the twentieth, by employing the concepts and principles of contemporary social theory. Its empirical content lies in the application of those theoretical tools to the analysis of a 'real concrete' (Althusser 1969) social formation and the relations between various elements and classes within it. I have engaged in a historical analysis in the belief that any attempt to understand political and social movements must include a thorough understanding of the precedents and antecedents which shape the particular character of any social practice. Nationalism in contemporary Wales differs, in many ways, from its nineteenth-century expression, but cannot be understood without reference to the social forces which existed then, and continue to have effect. Thompson's (1978) attack on the theoreticism of Althusserian sociology justifies the historical method, and his distinction between 'empirical' and 'empiricism' is useful in avoiding the tendency to reduce all theory to verifiable facts, which has characterized much of British sociology.[6]

The emphasis in this study is on an attempt to develop a theoretical framework capable of explaining nationalism as a social and political practice in the Welsh social formation. It is also hoped that the results will contribute to the analysis of nationalism as a political and ideological phenomenon evident in all political discourses. The first chapter reviews some of the theories of nationalism which have been influential in the post-war period. The first writer considered is Elie Kedourie as an example of 'conservative' (Smith 1971, p. 40) attempts to explain nationalism and is followed by an examination of the writings of Ernest Gellner and, finally, Anthony D. Smith. In the work of these writers we find opposing characterizations of nationalism. For Kedourie, nationalism is the 'spirit of an age', the brain-child of philosophy and independent of the material world. In contrast, for Gellner and Smith, nationalism arises out of the material conditions of social relations and is the product of the process of modernization and the problems and solutions it engenders.

The value of this sociological analysis of the national question identifiable with Gellner's work is developed further in Chapter 2 by a consideration of Marxist contributions to this area. In spite of recognizing the difficulties of placing the nation in the class-dominated concerns of Marxism, a paradigm will be identified which places the national question centrally in Marxist thought. This paradigm is recognized most easily in the work of Antonio Gramsci. In Chapter 3 the insights developed from Gramsci's writings are placed within a discussion of ideology in an attempt to discover the links between classes and ideologies. Nationalism is examined as an ideological element of the process of class struggle.

In Chapters 4 and 5 the theoretical arguments developed in Chapter 3 are applied in an empirical investigation of nationalism in nineteenth-century Wales. The argument developed is that nationalism provides an ideological cement which binds classes together in a complex social formation, characterized by the articulation of a feudal and a capitalist mode of production. In Chapter 6 the study turns to an investigation of nationalism in twentieth-century Wales and gives a brief account of the resurgence of nationalist political practice in the 1960s and 1970s. Chapter 7 reviews contemporary theories of class before suggesting that the nationalist resurgence can be explained by reference to changes in the class structure of post-war Wales. This claim is then assessed in Chapter 8 by examining economic reconstruction in Wales and its political consequences.

Throughout this book the terms ethnicity and nationalism have been used to describe a particular ideology and political practice. Numerous definitions of these terms exist in the literature surveyed by this research and it is proposed to state here the assumptions which underlie the application of these terms in an attempt to eliminate any ambiguity of meaning and usage. Ethnicity is based on the recognition by elements of a social group or collectivity that there exist certain features or characteristics shared by all members of that group. The characteristics are employed as criteria for identifying group membership and constructing a group identity. The criteria most commonly adopted include language, culture, religion, common history and residential patterns (Bottomore 1979). Whilst racial characteristics may not feature visibly in the construction of an ethnic identity there is a general assumption that members of an ethnic group have a common ancestry and cultural inheritance (Nyström and Rönnquist 1982). Subjective criteria are crucial in the construction of ethnic identity; frequently, the perception of common characteristics is not an objective conclusion but the consequence of subjective interpretations of history.

> The experience of post-1917 history also shows us that the nation is not simply a collection of abstract external criteria. The subjective element, i.e. the consciousness of national identity, a national political movement are no less important. Obviously these 'subjective factors' do not come out of the blue; they are the result of certain historical conditions — persecution, oppression etc.
> (Lowy 1976, p. 98)

An additional feature of ethnicity is that the perception of shared identity is not necessarily experienced by all members of the social group.

Nationalism is a direct consequence of the existence of ethnicity and reflects attempts by ethnically conscious groups to secure or preserve the cultural and political integrity of the group. Few ethnic groups inhabit territories which coincide with the national boundaries of the modern nation states (De Marchi and Boileau 1982). Nationalism occurs where an ethnic group elevates its sense of shared identity to the status of nationhood and mobilizes the achievement or maintenance of sovereignty as a political objective. The characteristics that define group membership are expressed as a national identity. Such identities are employed by groups to create pressure to secure nationhood and to ensure the survival or enlargement of existing nations. There can be little improvement on the definition of nationalism offered by Louis Wirth in 1936:

> Nationalism refers to the social movements, attitudes, and ideologies which characterize the behavior of nationalities engaged in the struggle to achieve, maintain, or enhance their position in the world. (p. 723)

Having established such a definition of nationalism, it is possible to go further and identify stages in the development of a nationalism, or specific types of nationalism. It is proposed to avoid this practice here for reasons given in the opening chapter.

This study attempts to illustrate that the apparent independence of nationalist ideology from class politics cannot be taken for granted. Instead, it is argued that the concepts of nation and nationhood are articulated with the class struggle and given specific meaning by the terms of that struggle. National identity and the concept of the nation can have many expressions. Definitions of nationality and the nation are the subject of negotiation between competing social groups. The struggle between classes in society is reflected in the expression of national identity and the definition of the nation and the national interest is only understood by referring to its articulation with class and class fractional ideologies.

> The nation cannot be defined as a fixed or static entity, but must be analysed historically, since 'national character' changes according to the changing conditions of material life. (Vogler 1985, p. 62)

CHAPTER 1

THREE THEORIES OF NATIONALISM:
A REVIEW AND CRITIQUE

Any attempt to explain the emergence and persistence of the ethnic and nationalist dimension of Welsh politics must begin by recognizing that Welsh nationalism is but a specific expression of a universally occurring political doctrine. There is nothing wholly unique about Welsh nationalism and, consequently, a search for explanation must look outside the particular context of Wales and engage with the many and wide-ranging theoretical analyses of nationalism that have emerged, especially since the Second World War. In this and the next chapter such an exercise will be undertaken in an attempt to arrive at a theoretical position from which nationalism can be explained.

However, moving out of the limited context of Welsh cultural and political life opens the door to a bewildering array of definitions of nationalism and to the analysis of many cultural and political movements to which the labels nationalist or ethnic have been applied (Bottomore 1979). The diversity and considerable number of such movements have been matched by a parallel development of theoretical frameworks seeking to explain them, drawing from a wide range of disciplines including history, sociology, psychology and political theory. The complex diversity of movements which have been perceived as nationalist or ethnic produces major difficulties in the construction of theory and militates against the development of theory which is universally applicable. The diversity of form which nationalism takes is illustrated when it is considered that in various contexts the doctrine displays conservative and reactionary, liberal and progressive or even socialist and revolutionary ideologies (Kamenka 1973a, Minogue 1967).[1] The problems involved in the construction of adequate theory are self-evident.

Often in the search for a theory of nationalism students of the movement have presented little more than typologies in the attempt to describe the many forms nationalism takes.[2] Such strategies revolve around the identification of 'ideal typical' features which nationalist movements can be shown to display. Whilst the working out of the variations that the doctrine has manifested is a useful contribution to understanding the phenomenon of nationalism it cannot be a substitute for developing an explanation of the forms nationalism has taken and the apparent universality of the doctrine. Additionally, the creation of typologies and taxonomies, no matter how accurate, presents a number of methodological limitations which it is useful to consider before attempting to venture into the arena of theory creation.

Firstly, the placing of a political movement in one or other category of a formal scheme represents a 'still photograph' of the movement, illustrating its state at a particular point in time. Such an exercise ignores the dynamic quality of political movements and the way in which their policies, ideology and actual membership change through time and in response to the external stimuli of the wider political context in combination with internal disputes and struggles. Consequently, the placing of movements into categories limits the potential analysis of the fluidity of movements and their changing internal structure and position in the wider political context. Such a methodology is at best merely descriptive and, ultimately, is ahistorical. Secondly, nationalist movements often combine various social and economic groups within an 'umbrella' ideology and consequently contain contradictory as well as complementary social forces within their overall structure. Although it may be justifiable to categorize such movements according to the dominant strands of their ideological content, this often results in the obfuscation of important elements which make up the complex whole.

For example, one may be engaged in an analysis of a national movement which is primarily concerned with the cultural and linguistic survival of a particular ethnic group. However, within that movement there may be less powerful factions which translate that objective into economic terms and regard their perceived subject status as the result of economic exploitation. A secondary group of this type might argue for strategy which seeks economic and political autonomy as the most apposite means of guaranteeing the viability of their culture. Comparison with an ideal type is not sufficiently flexible to accommodate this diversity of nationalist praxis even in the limited context of a single movement. The labelling or categorization of the movement would necessarily reflect the primary and most visible terms of ethnic conflict expressed by the movement, in this instance a cultural form of nationalism. There would be little space for considering the relative weighting of the different elements within the nationalist organization. Furthermore, the inability of ideal-typing to respond to changes within the movement is illustrated when it is considered that an alternative faction may at any time achieve ascendancy within the movement, leading to changed strategies and ideological stances which would be lost in an analysis fixed by a previous labelling of the movement as being of a particular type.

As an example, consider the changes which have taken place within *Plaid Cymru*, the Welsh nationalist party, in recent years. A party characterized by a cultural basis of national politics throughout its history (Butt Philip 1975), *Plaid Cymru*, during the 1970s, moved consistently toward an economic orientation in policy. This change reflected internal divisions and struggles within the party leading to virtual control by a left-of-centre group by the early 1980s, a control itself now in decline. The dynamism of the movement can only be appreciated from a broadly historical perspective as opposed to an analysis based on fixed and static ideal-types. With these observations in mind consideration should be given to theories of nationalism which have influenced approaches to the subject in recent years.

Three theories of nationalism

The review of theories of nationalism begins with the work of Elie Kedourie who explains the emergence of nationalism in terms of a re-flection of fundamental political principles first established within Enlightenment and post-Enlightenment thought. As such it is repre-sentative of what Smith (1971) identifies as 'conservative' or 'historical' (p. 40) attempts to theorize about nationalism. The second theoretical model reviewed is found in the writings of Ernest Gellner who puts forward the claim that nationalism is a feature of the complex process of modernization and industrialization of society. Gellner's ideas represent a school of sociological thought perhaps best described as modernization theory and linked closely to structural functionalism. Gellner builds on discussions by modernization theorists of the effects of the modernization process and its central aspect of increasing differ-entiation of social processes.[3] He adds to this a discussion of the effects of uneven development (Orridge 1981). Finally, Smith's prolific work in this area constitutes one of the most important contributions to the understanding of the subject and no contemporary study can deny its debt to Smith and his detailed analyses of European, Third-World and modern nationalisms. The theories discussed in this chapter are re-garded as indicative of the dominant approaches to the study of nationalism which have had considerable influence, each in turn setting the terms of the debate about nationalism for some time following their publication.

Following the review of these theories in this chapter consideration will be given to Marxist theories of nationalism in the following chapter. Marxism has a long tradition of concern with the 'national question' beginning with the work of Marx and Engels themselves. Marxist theories of nationalism represent an alternative approach to the study of nationalism which has traditionally subordinated the study of nationalist movements to a central concern with class struggle.

The theory of Elie Kedourie

Kedourie's theoretical perspective is evident from the first page of his work *Nationalism*, where he writes:

> Nationalism is a doctrine invented in Europe at the beginning of the nineteenth century. (1960, p. 9) [4]

The key word in this quotation is 'invented', for Kedourie is in no doubt that the doctrine is the direct result of the deliberations of specific philosophers of the era. He identifies a school of thought with its origins in Kantian philosophy and its doctrine of self-determination, later developed by Fichte into an organic theory of the state. Fichte believed that each individual could achieve self-realization through service to the state which in turn embodied the self-realization of the nation. The nation for Fichte was a linguistically defined unit of social organization, therefore achieving a combination of language, state and nation in his philosophy (Smith 1971). So, for Kedourie, nationalism is the end-product of a philosophical tradition originating in Kant but finally resolved through the work of Fichte and his contemporary German philosophers.

Kedourie argues that the emergence of nationalism as a universal doctrine in nineteenth-century Europe was dependent on two processes, with an intelligentsia playing a central role in both of these. The first and most crucial factor lies in the low social status ascribed to intellectuals during that period in Europe. Governed by a landed aristocracy and subjected to the decaying and increasingly irrelevant values and social relations of feudalism, they were at the same time faced with the potential for innovative social organization envisaged by Enlightenment thinkers. The intelligentsia sought to establish a new community in which they could practice the ideals of Enlightenment thought and achieve higher status for themselves. Kedourie argues that there existed a serious rupture between the status ascribed to the intelligentsia by their contemporary society and the status they felt was due to them. Consequently they experienced a 'status frustration' which provided the motivation to seek change in society.

The second factor promoting the 'invention' of nationalism lies in the breakdown of the traditional mechanisms for the inter-generational transfer of political cultures and values. Kedourie argues that nationalism had a generational quality whereby the intellectuals renounced the political values of their fathers and formed such movements as Young Italy, Young Egypt and Young Turkey. The erosion of traditional values and the breaking down of society disrupted the transference of political culture between generations leaving a vacuum of political ideas which was filled by the development of nationalism as the political ideology of the new generation. The status frustration of the intellectuals and the failure of cultural transmission between generations represent the sociological elements of Kedourie's theoretical framework (Smith 1971), and to this he adds a somewhat abstract psychological 'need to belong' (p. 101). This need, argues Kedourie, was felt by the intellectuals and it prompted them to envisage a new community in which they did not feel or experience the sense of alienation which they experienced in their contemporary social contexts.

In Kedourie's analysis, key intellectuals arrived at a doctrine of nationalism at the beginning of the nineteenth century. The social and political context of his location of the emergence of nationalism is a Europe reeling from the impact of Enlightenment thought, in which intellectuals sought to establish a social order in which they achieved the status they felt due to them. If for the moment this is accepted as an adequate explanation of the genesis of nationalist thought, an assessment of the ability of the theory to explain subsequent expressions of nationalist sentiment can be made. Kedourie's theory places nationalism in the specific social, cultural, political and economic context of nineteenth-century European society. How then does it make the journey through both space and time to appear as a globally experienced phenomenon in the twentieth century? The answer for Kedourie lies in a process of 'imitation' by other intellectuals finding themselves in similar conditions to those experienced by their nineteenth-century European predecessors. He presents an ill-defined theory of diffusion of the doctrine of nationalism via Western-educated intelligentsia 'imitating' the processes of thought undergone by their historical European counterparts. By this process nationalism spreads 'virus-like' to infect the world; Kedourie leaves no doubt as to his negative evaluation of the qualities of the doctrine (Smith 1971).

The major criticism of Kedourie is self-evident: his theory is idealistic with minimal reference to the material reality of the social, political and economic contexts in which nationalism emerges (Smith 1971, Gellner 1983). He creates a framework of explanation based solely on intellectual determinism. His claims rest on the belief in an apparent independence of ideas from the social context in which they emerge. Despite his discussion of intellectuals and their apparent alienation, together with the more general breakdown of an established social order, it is the independent growth of an idea which provides the mainstay of his theory. Nationalism for Kedourie is an independent, self-creating 'spirit of an age'. He offers us no explanation for the breakdown of the traditional communities other than the impact of Enlightenment thought. Nor does he attempt to explain why it is the intellectuals who alone experience the perceived 'need to belong' or indeed why they should choose nationalism as the source of their salvation.

Kedourie makes little concession to the sociological or economic as causal factors in the development of nationalism. In his discussion of the possibility that nationalism is a feature of ideology arising from class conflict he dismisses the view that it can be identified as an ideology of the bourgeoisie. Despite conceding that its German 'inventors' could be described as bourgeois, he denies that other nationalist intellectuals who imitate the doctrine can so easily be placed. Whilst it is possible to agree with his reservations about attempts to superimpose nineteenth-century class models on other societal contexts, Kedourie's analysis is clearly deficient without some consideration of the social class position of the imitative intellectuals to whom he attaches such primary importance. His claim that they are:

> young officers and bureaucrats, whose families were sometimes obscure, sometimes eminent, who were educated in Western ideas often at the expense of the state (1960, p.102)

does not prove his argument. Obscurity or eminence is not a sufficient basis for the analysis of the social origins of the imitative intellectuals. Indeed, in colonial society the above categories often do belong to the bourgeois and petty bourgeois strata of the economic, social and political hierarchies. In his denial of class as relevant to his discussion, he is simply confirming the idealist quality of his theory. Kedourie has created an ideal-type for which the model is nineteenth-century European nationalism and he proceeds to apply that ideal-type without discrimination or qualification. The following criticism of Kedourie appears apposite:

> The ideal type base line is too narrow to support the weight of the overall theory, and the comparison of empirical cases too mechanical. (Smith 1971, p. 39)

Kedourie has failed adequately to explain the genesis of the nationalist doctrine in the European context. He does not explain how the doctrine established such a comprehensive social base in European society that it was able to spread throughout the world. He carries the determinism of an intellectual tradition far outside its potential sphere of influence both spatially and temporally.

Kedourie's failure lies in his belief, like that of conservative historians, that social change occurs through the actions of key individuals in the historical process, acting independently of their material conditions of existence. Their revolutions in thought are seen as actual revolutions in the social formation. He fails adequately to explain nationalism because he fails to grasp the complex interplay between social, cultural, political and economic factors present in nineteenth-century Europe. The interdependence between ideas and material reality is something which Kedourie rejects in favour of an emphasis on the influence of philosophical traditions and paradigms. However, political doctrines are not 'invented'; they are determined to the greatest extent by the relationship between specific circumstances and processes of thought structured within a given material existence. To prove effective a theory of nationalism must possess more than an intuitive feel for the 'spirit of an age'. It must be capable of assessing the diverse factors which come to bear on individuals and societies and which shape the development of political ideas and systems of thought. If we are to arrive at an adequate theory of nationalism we have to be more sociological in our analysis than Kedourie. The last word is given to Ernest Gellner who writes of Kedourie's analysis:

> There is something bizarre in the suggestion that a force so widespread and pervasive, a flame that springs up so strongly and spontaneously in so many disconnected places, and which needs so very little fanning to become a devouring forest blaze, should spring from nothing more than some extremely obtrusive lucubrations of philosophers. (1983, pp. 125–6)

The theory of Ernest Gellner

If the major deficiency of Kedourie's theory is a lack of sociological analysis, Gellner's theory more than compensates. Gellner's contribution to this area of study in *Thought and Change* (1964) has had considerable influence on subsequent theories of nationalism and his influence will continue through his more recent publications (1983 and 1987). Furthermore, the concepts he employs have enjoyed some currency in recent theories of Celtic nationalism, especially the related ideas of uneven development and the cultural division of labour.[5]

Despite being a complex and at times unwieldy system of explanation, it raises issues which have become the staple diet of those conducting enquiries into the nature and form of nationalism. Gellner's work can perhaps best be described as modernization theory in that it locates the development of nationalism within the context of processes of modernization and the transformation of traditional societies into modern, complex, differentiated social formations. Nationalism is seen as the product of specific demands placed on societies and individuals experiencing the pressures of modernization. The clearest exposition of his thinking can be found in *Thought and Change* (1964) where the basis of his theory of nationalism is established. Although developed and refined in *Nations and Nationalism* (1983), his theoretical framework remains unchanged and this discussion will refer primarily to the earlier work.

Gellner's initial priority is to dismiss the implicit belief, shared by both proponents and opponents of nationalism, that there is something both natural and inevitable about nationality and consequently nationalism. He does so by identifying and criticizing what he regards as the 'contingency of nationalism'. He details three central tenets of the nationalist belief system which can be summarized as follows:

1) That nationality is a 'physical attribute' of every individual and consequently nationalism is also naturally occurring.
2) That collectivities who share that 'natural attribute' (p. 150) should aspire to exist in a common political unit governed by fellow members of the collectivity.
3) A belief in the desirability and legitimacy of that aspiration.

Gellner argues that there is nothing natural or inevitable about nationality or nationalism. Indeed he presents a convincing case for the view that rule by alien authority has historically been the norm and has performed a clear integrative function in many societies. Consequently, Gellner maintains that the central tenets of nationalism, outlined above, are false. He continues by describing the processes which have led to the development and apparent universality of these beliefs. He is concerned with the ways in which the process of modernization produces what he describes as the 'negative' and 'positive' causes of the emergence of the nationalist doctrine.

The negative cause

This cause lies in the transfer from the primacy of 'structure' in traditional societies to the primacy of 'culture' (p. 153) in modern societies. In a primarily Durkheimian analysis, Gellner argues that traditional society ascribed roles to individuals which were located in and defined by the kinship network. That role network constituted a social structure which gave identity to the individual. The role of culture in this context was limited to dress and ritualized behaviour. In modern societies, however, social structure is primarily defined by institutional and bureaucratic systems. Many role locations exist outside of these structures and consequently have to be defined by cultural practices. Their effectiveness is dependent on their ability to be communicated through a shared language. In modern society, citizenship depends on cultural identification, not ascribed membership of tribe or clan. The importance of ascribed characteristics is eroded within a more complex and differentiated social system and, as a consequence, individuals have to carry their identity with them into social interaction. For Gellner, therefore, the individual is classified by others in interaction by the key cultural attributes of language and nationality. Nationality then appears as a 'natural and merely physical attribute'. This, for Gellner, is the 'negative cause' of nationalism.

The positive cause

Here the process of analysis is more complex and demonstrates more clearly its structural-functionalist roots. Gellner identifies a requirement of all societies to produce 'effective' or 'full' (p. 159) citizens. In the past, small social units have performed this function producing 'effective' citizens capable of performing their limited, ascribed, roles. However, in modern, complex and increasingly technological society the minimum condition that has to be satisfied in order to produce 'effective' citizens is literacy. The need arises for a system of education to promote literacy and 'technological competence' (p. 159). Such a system can only be created and maintained by the nation as the primary social and political unit. For Gellner the state becomes the only effective agency for the overall provision, maintenance and monitoring of a viable education system. Furthermore, the role of the education system is to promote the creation of 'substitutable' final products; it must be capable of providing people who can move relatively easily between the complex differentiated roles of the modern social formation. It is the possession of a common language and cultural pattern which makes individuals 'substitutable'. The educational system promotes a single linguistic medium and the state becomes intimately involved with the assertion of a particular language and culture. The nation and the state are brought inexorably together in the process of industrialization.

In the later work (1983) Gellner stresses the central role of the idea of 'permanent growth' in industrial society. Constant innovation produces an 'ever-growing, ever-progressing society' (p. 23). The consequence is a correspondingly complex division of labour which is in a state of flux, permanently re-defining and re-creating social roles. A highly mobile society results in which individuals adapt to an ever-changing division of labour. It is this situation which gives birth to the nationalist doctrine. The new division of labour is characterized by a specialization of occupations. However, it is a 'complementary specialisation' in that there exists a shared set of minimum or core skills, shared by all and underpinned by 'generic training':

> the major part of training in industrial society is *generic* training, not specifically connected with the highly specialised professional activity of the person in question, and *preceding* it. Industrial society may by most criteria be the most specialised society ever; but the education system is unquestionably the *least* specialised, the most universally standardised that has ever existed. (Gellner 1983, p. 27 — author's emphases)

In short, it is the education system that produces the easily substitutable effective citizens identified in the earlier work. Such a task cannot be achieved at the local level and becomes the responsibility of the state. A 'national' education system ties the state to the maintenance of a cultural framework which reproduces a common language of communication within the new complex division of labour:

> The imperative of exo-socialization is the main clue to why state and culture *must* now be linked, whereas in the past the connection was thin, fortuitous, varied, loose and often minimal. Now it is

unavoidable. That is what nationalism is about, and why we live in an age of nationalism. (Gellner 1983, p. 38 — author's emphasis)

Thus nationalism has its origins in the complexity of the division of labour and the need for the state to involve itself in the provision of an educational system which promotes and facilitates the mobility identified by Gellner as the central characteristics of the division of labour. Effective communication is guaranteed by the reproduction of a homogeneous culture and language. The state is identified with a specific culture, and nationalism results. A more detailed but largely unchanged explanation of the emergence of nationalism is offered by Gellner in his recent work.

Within this element of his theory there are two results of the development of the doctrine of nationalism. Firstly, it will promote the cohesion of single-language groups into national socio-political units as these are the most clearly viable basis for nationhood and the creation of effective citizenship. Secondly, it will tend to dissolve ancient regimes and empires founded on other criteria such as religion. These larger units, characterized by cultural and linguistic diversity, would be incapable of producing easily substitutable effective citizens. The effect of the development of the nationalist doctrine can thus be seen to have both divisive and integrative consequences.

Up to this point Gellner offers us a primarily sociological explanation for the genesis of nationalism and the nation-building evident in nineteenth-century Europe. He continues by considering the differing reactions of social groups within developing and emergent nation states. Why do some groups accept the majority language and culture and actively seek effective citizenship through education in the majority linguistic medium, whilst others reject that path and develop an oppositional nationalist doctrine? The answer, for Gellner, lies in the nature of the modernization process itself. It is the unevenness of the spread of modernization which provides the real dynamic of nationalism. Gellner argues that modernization spreads in the form of a wave, but with an uneven front.[6] Those first affected by its arrival achieve modernity and social maturity early and become reluctant to share the benefits of modernization with those yet to experience it, or those still locked in what Gellner describes as the 'destructive phase' of modernization. Thus, in a given political unit, there may exist a duality of social groups, the one already modernized, the other considerably behind in the process. The first group, seeking to preserve the benefits of modernization for itself, denies effective citizenship and its associated advantages to the second group. Where that less privileged group is culturally, linguistically, racially or religiously distinct, the distinguishing factors will be utilized as the criteria for the exclusion of the group from the full advantages of modernization. The criteria on which exclusion is based provide the means by which the disadvantaged group becomes conscious of its exclusion and articulates its demand for full citizenship.[7] In short, the exclusive nationalism of the dominant group is matched by the development of a reactive nationalism on the part of the excluded group.[8]

Crucial to the development of reactive nationalism is the role of the minority intelligentsia. Like Kedourie, Gellner regards the period of modernization as a period of crisis for the intelligentsia. As members of the subordinate social group they are not regarded as effective substitutable citizens, but as second-class citizens denied the status they could otherwise expect. However, because of their educational achievement and their correspondingly higher aspirations, they do not accept their position of inferiority. Consequently, rather than seek position and prestige within the dominant culture, paying the heavy price of forfeiture of their cultural heritage, they instead seek to establish a national unit based on the criteria utilized against them in the practise of exclusion. Gellner writes:

> For the intellectuals independence means an immediate and enormous advantage: jobs, and very good jobs. The very numerical weakness of an 'underdeveloped' intelligentsia is its greatest asset: by creating a national unit whose frontiers become in effect closed to foreign talent . . . they create a magnificent monopoly for themselves. (1964, p. 169)

Here, for Gellner, lies the motivation for the intellectual to seek the establishment of an independent socio-political unit based on the very identity created by the process of exclusion engendered by the uneven spread of modernization. Gellner continues by arguing that the intelligentsia represents only one element of the 'two prongs' of nationalism (p. 168). Of equal importance to a disaffected intelligentsia is the existence of an urban working class. Although this working class is likely eventually to become disillusioned, he claims it willingly exchanges 'hardship-with-snubs for possibly greater hardship with national identification' (1964, p. 172).

For Gellner, the transition to modernity brings into existence a large body of industrial workers who, displaced physically and mentally from their traditional location on the land, seek their identity and future in a national context identified for them by the intelligentsia. A common culture and language, as the media of communication, become of crucial significance in such a context.

Gellner has progressed considerably further than Kedourie in the attempt to provide a theory of nationalism. Although both theories locate the emergence of the doctrine in nineteenth-century Europe and both credit the intelligentsia with a major role in the development of the doctrine, there the similarity ends. Gellner's theory is grounded in the context of modernizing societies. It sees nationalism as the product and even concomitant of the definable and universally identifiable social process of modernization. It recognizes not only the importance of language and culture but also the significance of economic interest and the striving of diverse social groups to improve the conditions of their economic and cultural existence. Perhaps the most significant improvement over the work of Kedourie is the explanation offered by Gellner for the transmission of the doctrine and its development as a global phenomenon. Rather than there being a vaguely defined process of 'imitation', Gellner asks us to recognize nationalism as an inevitable component of the modernization process wherever it occurs. Of particular importance to the development of nationalism is the uneven progress of modernization and the consequent practices of exclusion or 'social closure' (Parkin 1979, p. 44).

To summarize, for Gellner nationalism arises in the first instance from the need of modern society to produce effective citizens — a need which necessitates the growth of a national educational system operating through the medium of a common language and regulated by the state. Additionally, it arises from the need of individuals in a modern mass society to carry with them the cultural indicators of their social identity. These elements of the theory are offered as explanation of the first phase of nationalism recognizable during the emergence of modern European nation states. Gellner continues by explaining the nationalism evident in the contemporary developing world as a consequence of the uneven spread of modernization and the benefits it carries in its wake. In this latter context nationalism is a response to the stratification of society and an unequal distribution of resources, the criteria for which are identifiable differences between racial, religious, linguistic and ethnic groups. Gellner's theory clearly links the emergence of nationalism to the interests of particular collectivities, namely the excluded intelligentsia and the proletariat. This is a fruitful move away from the intellectual determinism of Kedourie toward a more materialist explanation of nationalism. There are, however, weaknesses in his theory.

The first and most significant criticism must refer to the usage of the concept of modernization established by Gellner. He makes little distinction between modernization and industrialization: 'the two are to be distinguished only as narrower and wider aspects of the same phenomena' (1964, p. 171).

Gellner argues that the processes of modernization and industrialization are synonymous. He stresses the importance of the development and application of science in the process of modernization as a watershed in human development. Science, he argues, arises as the only effective form of knowledge; it challenges traditional belief systems and ends the intellectual stability of the old order. He equates modernization with a transformation of beliefs, as well as a revolution in technological methods. Nationalism is a concomitant of the change from stability to uncertainty, from traditional agrarian to modern industrial society. However, a distinction should be drawn between modernization and industrialization. The latter is specifically only an element of the former process. Industrialization is a particular phase of a longer historical process recognizable as modernization.

Modernization in the European context has been a process through which fundamental changes in the mode of production have occurred.[9] In European societies the process was one of change from the feudal to the capitalist mode of production and the crucial factor in that change was the transformation of the social relations of production, a transformation which will be discussed in greater detail in Chapter 4. It is that transformation which initiated the fundamental societal changes of the last four to five centuries. Changes in the social relations of production have had considerable impact on social development and must be distinguished from the more specific, but limited, changes initiated by industrialization, which constituted change in the method of production rather than the actual relations of production. Changes in the relations of production and of the resulting structure of society can be identified prior to the period of industrialization. Whilst there may be controversy as to the exact periodization of the transition, it can be argued that phases of mercantile capitalism are a prerequisite of industrial capitalism in that they provide the period of capital accumulation necessary for the provision of large concentrations of privately owned capital vital for industrial enterprise in the pioneer years of industrialization.[10] Furthermore, during the pre-industrial period of capitalism, changes in the organization of labour occur, establishing the model of the wage labour/capital relationship which is essential for the industrialization of production. These issues will be discussed in greater depth in Chapter 4.

Modernization must therefore be seen as a long-term and continuous process. A demarcation of the actual point of modernization can only be achieved by subsuming the total process of societal development under the limited category of industrialization. Modernization, unlike industrialization, cannot be said to occur at a specific point in time. Rather, in the transition from feudalism to capitalism, societies will at various times display elements of both modes of production but the latter will increasingly come to dominate and eventually supersede the former. Industrialization is distinct from this underlying process in that it represents only a specific phase of modernization, a phase which cannot occur without the preceding emergence of capitalist relations of production. Gellner's failure to make this distinction leads him to conclude that nationalism is a phenomenon derived from the transition to industrial society and as such must be located specifically at the historical juncture which displays the visible indicators of industrialization.

By seeing the genesis of nationalism as peculiar to the industrial period, Gellner is missing the significance of pre-industrial factors leading him to an ahistorical stance which seriously undermines the effectiveness of his analysis. A more accurate analysis would trace the roots of the development of nationalism in the European context in the transition from feudalism to capitalism and in the antagonistic class relations which were brought into existence by that process. If the English context is examined it can be seen that the origins of the nation-building of the eighteenth and nineteenth centuries are found in the mercantilism of the sixteenth and seventeenth centuries. The emergence of a strong tendency toward centralism and unification predates the advent of industrialism by some two centuries (Tilley 1975). The annexations of Scotland and Wales through the Acts of Union were crucial factors in the development of the British nation state.

The consequences of the ahistorical basis of his theory are twofold. Firstly, when applied to concrete situations we discover an ideal-type construct with a base line little wider than Kedourie's. Gellner has created a model of the development of nationalism which is bound within the paradigm of modernization theory. Its ethnocentric basis in the European linear model of development seriously undermines its applicability elsewhere.[11] His equation of modernization with industrialization and his location of nationalism as a feature of industrialization does not stand up to the test of empirical evidence. For example, the Mazzinian movement in Italy cannot be said to have come into existence in the context of the pressures of industrialization.[12] In fact the most active period of nation-building in the European context pre-dates actual industrializaton and in many instances the unification of small states into large national units appears as a prerequisite of industrialization (Vogler 1985).

Similarly, Lele (1980) analyses a pre-modern, or in his terms, pre-capitalist, expression of nationalism in Maharashtra in the seventeenth century. Criticizing Gellner's 'Eurocentrism', he argues that nationalism and its articulation of traditionalism has a universal character and is an element of hegemony which legitimizes the appropriation of surplus labour in pre-capitalist societies as well as capitalist. Nationalism for Lele, also, has two faces, one as dominant ideology, legitimizing appropriation, the other revolutionary, resisting domination.

> The early poet-saints make us aware of the fact that a critique of oppressive institutions, a challenge to legitimation, is not a pre-rogative of the times in which 'every man [is] a clerk formed by the local educational machine using local language' (Gellner 1964, p. 158) but of all oppressed classes at all times. (Lele 1980, p. 207)

Lele's argument previews, in abbreviated form, some aspects of Marxist analysis of the national question which will be considered in the following chapter.

Secondly, Gellner's usage of the concepts of modernization and industrialization as synonymous leads to a failure in the ability of his theory to explain the resurgence of nationalism and ethnicity in contemporary Europe. The location of nationalism in the period of transition to industrial society cannot be made relevant to the contemporary European context. Following Gellner's argument the transition to modernity and fully industrialized society would by now be complete, with the establishment of national education systems and the efficient production of effective citizens sharing a common linguistic base. Furthermore, the benefits of modernization would have been felt by virtually all European citizens through the creation of welfare states and unified education systems, the establishment of national wage scales, and the extension of effective communication and transport networks into even the most remote corners of Europe. Whilst it is possible to identify relatively 'underdeveloped' regions within

European nation states, it is difficult to assert that the benefits of modernization have not been experienced within such regions. Regional and ethnic consciousness, however, does not always coincide with relative underdevelopment and many regions where a nationalist consciousness exists are prosperous areas within the national economy (Orridge 1981). This was the case in Wales in the late nineteenth century and remains true of the Basque region in contemporary Spain.[13]

This inability of Gellner's early work to explain the resurgence of nationalism in the major European states is perhaps forgiveable given its publication before the ethnic revival in western Europe had become significant, although an adequate theory of nationalism should perhaps not be so easily challenged by unforeseen circumstances. However, his recent work (1983 and 1987) was written on the downward turn of the wave of ethnic resurgence which one would expect him to accommodate. Little mention of such movements is made and no explicit attempt is made to apply the theory to the genesis of such movements. Readers are left to their own devices to attempt the application of Gellner's thinking to contemporary European nationalist movements. Two openings exist in his theory for such an endeavour to succeed.

Gellner describes the mobility and openness of the division of labour as 'entropy'. The emergence of groups which present barriers to that entropic tendency can have different origins. Firstly, if an ethnically distinct group with different linguistic and cultural patterns prevents the total homogenization of the society, the problem can be resolved in one of two ways. The group will either a) be assimilated into the dominant culture or b) will raise a new cultural identity in opposition and, if successful, form a new nation.

Repeating the argument of the early work Gellner sees the first situation as likely where there are no substantive criteria for the exclusion of the minority from the benefits of industrialization. However, in the second instance there exists some immovable barrier to assimilation, for example, genetic criteria such as skin colour, or non-genetic factors such as religion and its concomitant social identity — Jewishness, for example. Here the only resolution of this barrier to entropy is succession. However, this option only exists where there is a clearly identifiable homeland or geographical territory associated with the excluded group.

It is clearly difficult to locate the characteristics of contemporary European nationalist and separatist movements in either of these possibilities. The second eventuality, which would give rise to a national movement, depends on the minority movement being recognizable as a homogeneous and universally oppressed and emmiserated group within the overall social and political unit. This, as was argued above, is frequently not the case. Welsh nationalism demonstrates this very effectively. The peaks of both its nineteenth and twentieth-century expressions were in periods of relative affluence within the overall economic framework and in periods when the economy of the region was undergoing considerable reconstruction which was having beneficial effects on key elements of the ethnic minority. Gellner is unable to see the significance of this because he fails to differentiate within the excluded minority element. Gellner sees the excluded group as a unified whole sharing equal, if undesirable, relations with the dominant culture. In reality the excluded group is internally differentiated by class, and different sections of the ethnic minority will have different levels of inequality within the overall structure of the dominant nation state.

Finally, it must be added that those regions of Europe now suffering relative deprivation are not necessarily the subject of practices of exclusion. Indeed, given their integration into the framework of the state they seek independence from, they may be net beneficiaries in economic terms. In poor regions, for example, inward flows of state provisions may outweigh the outward flows of taxation.[14] Furthermore, attempts to improve economic performance and modernize industry through the application of various regional aid schemes, although often only partial and unsuccessful, demonstrate at least an ideological commitment to the resolution of regional economic problems.

The key weakness of Gellner's theory is the lack of distinction between the processes of modernization and industrialization. If Gellner had recognized the far more fundamental and longer-term quality of what has been here identified as modernization, he would have been led to examine the process of change in European society which gave rise to the nationalist doctrine: that is, the development of the capitalist mode of production. It is only through analysing the specific nature of the transformation of the relations of production that we can begin to understand the emergence of the doctrine effectively. Gellner discusses the consequences of uneven development without reference to its causes, thereby divorcing one of his major explanatory devices from its origins in Marxist economic theory, particularly in the work of Lenin and Hilferding (Orridge 1981).

Several crucial ideas emerge if this original framework is taken as the point of reference. Firstly it is possible to explain why the front of the modernization wave is uneven, an explanation Gellner chooses not to attempt. That unevenness can be understood in terms of the uneven development of capitalism and the changing bases of capital accumulation which move forward in both space and time, articulating technology and labour in changing combinations. Theories of the uneven development of capitalism have been applied to European economic regions by Massey (1978). For Massey, capitalism realizes surplus value by creating a spatial division of labour as well as a division of society into classes. The surplus value of labour is appropriated according to changing criteria determined by the falling rate of profit. Strategies to offset the falling rate of profit include technological innovation but, more importantly for this discussion, also include the manipulation of the spatial division of labour. Thus in the early stages of capitalism, capital accumulation is primarily in the extractive and heavy industries. Later stages emphasize production of consumer goods and provision of services, and the heavy industries go into decline. When it is considered that those industries were located geographically according to the availability of raw materials in the early stages of industrialization, the spatial effect of this unevenness can be seen.

The first regions to industrialize are characterized by a specific division of labour associated with a particular industrial process, for example metal manufacture. That localized division of labour becomes organized and resistant to exploitation and to the changes that capitalism requires to maintain a basis for continued capital accumulation. The consequence is that capitalism relocates itself, creating a new and more effective spatial division of labour. When it is considered that the spatial division of labour will, at times, coincide with ethnic boundaries, we can see a potential basis for class divisions to mesh with ethnic divisions.

This process is evident in the context of the European nation states and the way in which certain regions once prosperous and at the forefront of capital accumulation are now relatively underdeveloped enclaves within their host nation state. On a global scale the understanding of the uneven development of capitalism also enables us to explain the pattern of European expansion into the growing world market and economy from the sixteenth century onwards. The same search for conditions favourable to the continuing accumulation of capital ensures an unevenness in the global development of cap-italism. The spatial division of labour spans continents as well as regions. Thus, by reference to the development of capitalism, a better understanding of the uneven character of industrialization can be achieved, as well as of its potential to bring ethnic and class divisions together, an understanding not offered by Gellner.

Secondly, if Gellner had chosen to examine the nature of the development of capitalism, he would have recognized the real basis for the practice of the exclusion of social groups from the benefits of modernization. Mention has already been made of the transformation of the social relations of production involved in the transition from feudalism to capitalism. The most visible aspect of this process is the destruction of the feudal class structure and the bringing into existence of new, antagonistic classes determined by the ownership of capital. At this stage it is not proposed to engage in an exhaustive discussion of class relations within capitalism; it is sufficient simply to state that the class relations of concern here are those created by the appropriation of the surplus value of labour by the capitalist class.

This relationship, it is argued here, constitutes the basis of exclusion from the benefits of modernization. Whilst clearly the working class eventually benefits from the growth of industry, it is also necessary, in order to secure the continued process of accumulation, to maintain large sections of the proletariat at or below the level of subsistence both as a reserve army of labour and as a means of depressing wage levels of those in work. Thus a stratified and economically divided working class is a central feature of the process of capital accumulation. The sectors of the population excluded from the doubtful benefits of wage labour frequently coincide with distinct social and cultural groups. The ability to identify a group by racial, linguistic or religious criteria renders the task of legitimizing exclusion easier.

In nineteenth-century Britain the Irish could be classified as just such a group which, excluded from full integration into the working class, constituted a permanent reserve army of labour. In this context the English working class adopted and participated in the exclusion of the immigrant Irish labourers, seeing in them a threat to their livelihood. Anti-Irish prejudice consequently became an integral part of working-class consciousness.[15] The consequences were a divided working class which was politically weakened by its division. Mensah (1980) argues similarly that the apparent use of ethnic criteria as the basis for exclusion frequently masks the ways in which minorities are defined and excluded on the basis of the economic role they play in the social formation. He suggests that Indian exclusion in African societies since independence arises from their domination of 'petty trading' which constitutes a crucial domain of African economic and social life. The basis of exclusion is an economic role, the ethnic dimension only serving to identify the 'alien' (p. 223) and their illegitimate possession of a particular role.

The point to be emphasized then is that Gellner has overlooked the essential basis of exclusion because he fails to identify the significance of the emergence of capitalism.[16] Whilst the general quality of his conclusions are acceptable, they have been reached by a different path from the one in this study, and the significance of this difference will become apparent when explaining nationalism. For Gellner, nationalism emerges as a response to exclusion from the benefits of modernization, but he offers no explanation of why the dissaffected intellectuals and the proletariat choose a nationalist ideology as the potential solution to their problems. In the case of the minority intellectuals it is perhaps easier to see why nationalism is chosen. Their education in, and celebration of, an indigenous language and culture and the use of these characteristics as the basis for their exclusion from full citizenship is a process well explained by the framework of Gellner's theory. However, in the case of the proletariat the connection is not so easily made. Why, for example, should it choose nationalism before socialism as the panacea for the ills which afflict it? Why should it be motivated more by the affinity for a cultural group identity than by a consciousness of class position? The answer, of course, is that the latter is frequently the reality. The existence of the proletariat as one of the two prongs of the nationalist movement is in fact difficult to substantiate in the analysis of specific nationalist movements.

This point is taken up by Smith (1971 and 1976) as one of his major criticisms of Gellner. Smith concedes the active role of the intelligentsia in most nationalist movements, but calls into doubt the role ascribed to the proletariat by Gellner. He argues that it is easy to overestimate the role of industrial workers and gives several examples of their failure to be attracted to the nationalist banner. This study of Welsh nationalism will support such a view, in that the evidence indicates a direct antipathy between the interests of the industrial work-force and the leaders of the nationalist movement in nineteenth-century Wales. That view is reinforced by the long-term failure of nationalist politics to attract a mass basis of support in the industrial areas of contemporary Wales where the adherence to labour politics remains dominant. Indeed, for most nationalist movements the fundamental problem has been the establishment of a mass popular base (Smith 1971). Ideological appeals founded on language and culture usually fall on deaf proletarian ears. Smith argues that it is usually the peasant and the landless labourer who constitute the foot-soldiers of nationalist movements and that the proletariat only involves itself in the latter stages of the struggle for independence (Smith 1976b).

It has been argued here that, in spite of Gellner's concern with the material conditions of change in society, he, like Kedourie before him, has ultimately failed to explain nationalism. Despite identifying the functions that nationalism fulfils in the process of modernization he fails to integrate those insights into a full account of the emergence of the nationalist doctrine. Furthermore, his concentration on the argument that nationalism is a feature of modernization as a universal process produces problems in applying his theory to many Third-World contexts as well as contemporary European nationalisms.

Gellner has, however, provided us with a recognition of the potential explanation of nationalism by locating it in the struggle for economic and political resources by specific collectivities. Nevertheless the basis upon which Gellner sees the collectivities being determined is flawed; the relations of production within the capitalist mode of production are a more credible basis for the formation of social groups or classes.

In short, rather than analyse modernization it is necessary to analyse capitalism. Rather than seeing nationalism as a political doctrine grounded in the struggle of competing groups for the benefits of industrialization it should be viewed as grounded in class struggle over the relations of production. The struggle is concerned with the pattern of control of the means of production rather than with the distribution of the advantages of modernization. The real significance of this different path of analysis is that to understand nationalism, explanation must centre on the context of the class struggle in which it emerges.

The theory of A. D. Smith

Smith has developed his perspective on the national question over a number of years and in a prolific range of publications.[17] The basis of his theory can be found in *Theories of Nationalism* (1971) and is developed primarily in *The Ethnic Revival in the Modern World* (1981). The majority of his other books on the subject apply his theories to specific contexts in which nationalism has appeared and do not add significantly to the general theory of nationalism that Smith has offered.

In *Theories of Nationalism* Smith identifies the fact that, whilst the form of nationalism varies considerably, there exists a core doctrine which individual nationalisms embellish with 'supporting theories'. The seven elements of this core doctrine largely coincide with what Gellner identified as the 'central tenets' of nationalism and reflect the claims that nationalism makes for itself. Smith summarizes these seven elements in the following passage:

> Fundamentally, nationalism fuses three ideals: collective self-determination of the people, the expression of national character and individuality, and finally the vertical division of the world into unique nations. (1971, p. 23)

Outside of this basic core Smith argues that each nationalism will demonstrate unique features determined by the specific set of social forces at play in the particular society under study. However, for Smith the primary social forces leading to the emergence of nationalism are political and religious and he sees economic issues as very much secondary, only occasionally providing the catalyst which brings the other forces into play. The key to understanding nationalism, for Smith, lies with identifying the role of the development of the 'scientific state'. Echoing Gellner's arguments abut the complexity of modern society Smith describes the 'scientific state' as one which:

> seeks to homogenise the population within its boundaries for administrative purposes by utilising the latest scientific techniques and methods for the sake of 'efficiency'. The rulers use the bureaucratic machine and the fruits of scientific research and technological application to harness resources and mobilize people in their territory. (1971, p. 321)

Again, as for Gellner, language plays a key role, for a single official language facilitates the administration of the scientific state. However, this attachment to a specific language and the use of other homogenizing forces creates what Smith terms 'sociological minorities' (p. 235). These represent groups with a different language or culture who are discriminated against by the scientific state in its quest for homogeneity and efficiency. Again, as in Gellner's model, we find a system of social closure whereby certain social groups, readily identifiable by linguistic or other criteria, suffer disadvantage and oppression.

Central to Smith's theory is the way in which the scientific state begins to dismantle the traditional social order especially through its tendency toward secularization and the attack of science on religion and traditional belief systems. In this respect the role of the intelligentsia becomes crucial in the development of nationalism. Smith claims that this process of modernization both repels and attracts the intelligentsia.

They suffer from the desire to accept the solutions the scientific state offers to the problems of the old order, yet regard the demise of religion as a high price to pay. The consequence is a

> crisis of faith among intelligentsia and the clash between reason and revelation, science and tradition, sons and fathers, which so agitates them. (1971, p. 240)

Consequently, the intelligentsia are faced with 'two sources of authority' in what Smith describes as a process of 'dual legitimation'.

Smith identifies three responses by intellectuals to the crisis of 'dual legitimation': 'traditionalism', 'assimilation', and 'reformism', all with consequences for the development of the nationalist doctrine. Of particular importance is the reformist who, unlike the traditionalist who denies the legitimacy of secular authority and the assimilationist who unequivocally accepts it, attempts to create a synthesis of religious legitimation and the authority of the secular state. The result, Smith argues, is a doctrine of 'providential deism' in which God acts through the scientific state. Only those elements of religion which can withstand the test of reason survive. The end result is a search for the essence of religion which develops into a form of 'historicism', a revivalism which seeks this essence in a previous golden age. Now only one step away from nationalism the revivalist begins to identify with the community of the golden age and ultimately that community and its chosen people become the object of interest and 'value'. Ethnicity is discovered as the belief in the value of a golden era becomes detached from the search for a religious essence and is tranformed into a celebration of the community and its people who kept the pure faith alive. Thus for Smith the 'revivalist heresy' (1971, p. 246) within the 'reformist' response to dual legitimation creates an 'ethnic solution' to the crisis of dual legitimation.

For this doctrine to become an active nationalist movement requires the addition of the final element in Smith's equation. The second response to dual legitimation identified by Smith was that of the assimilationist. This strategy was described as an unequivocal acceptance of the legitimacy of the scientific state and its ideology of progress and rationality. The assimilationists develop a messianic vision of a world state in which all citizens are equal, regardless of race or creed, and the problems of the old order are eradicated. However, the reality of the scientific state with its stratification and élitism destroys their faith in world citizenship, the dream becomes modified and they take on the ethnic solution offered by the revivalist reformers. The messianic belief in a world state becomes a belief in the necessity of an ethnic state. Smith writes:

> The utopian world dream is consigned to arid sterility, and replaced by the more modest single-state messianism. (1971, p. 254)

So, in Smith's model, as with Gellner's, we find nationalism occurring in modernizing societies in which the state becomes identified with a particular language and culture. Intellectuals play a key role by mobilizing the concept and imagery of the nation in an attempt to resolve their own crisis of identity and legitimation.

In criticism of Smith, a number of problems shared with Gellner's approach can be identified. The development of the scientific state represents a process similar to Gellner's conception of modernization. It employs an idealist application of Weber's concept of rationality and his model of the development of bureaucratic states but offers little information about the social processes of which these developments are a consequence. Smith creates a picture of the emergence of the scientific state out of the 'possessive state' without any reference to the historical conditions which produced the new social formation.

His theory is also idealistic in terms of the key role given to intellectuals in the development of the nationalist doctrine. Whilst it is impossible to deny their role in the emergence of the majority of nationalist movements, Smith fails to explain why; he simply tells us that this is the case. Although the crisis of dual legitimation is offered as explanation, Smith gives no reason why the three responses of traditionalism, assimilationism and reformism are the only possibilities available to the intellectuals. Nor does he tell us on what basis individual intellectuals select from these three responses. The reader is left to wonder whether there are social, political or religious reasons for their choice, or whether there are psychological factors which predispose individuals to a particular action. It is quite clear that many intellectuals in the context of a developing secular and 'scientific state' have historically turned to socialism as the primary response to the oppression and prejudice institutionalized by the modern state. Smith, in ignoring economic factors,[18] fails to identify a basis for intellectuals' actions which, as the remainder of this book suggests, are often determined by the class interests with which intellectuals identify themselves.

By virtually ignoring economic relations and in spite of promoting political and religious factors, Smith offers little understanding of the politics of nationalism. Political struggles arise over the distribution of scarce resources in society and from competition for control of those resources. We can derive little sense of the role of nationalism in that process from Smith's analysis. There is little information as to how the individual personal crisis of the intellectual becomes a mass sociopolitical movement. If Smith gives emphasis to the political dimension, he offers few details of its effect. What remains is an idealistic theory which relies heavily on the crisis of religious faith experienced by the intellectuals to explain the formation of national movements.

Finally, like Gellner, Smith fails to identify the class basis of social closure. For him prejudice and discrimination are inherited by the scientific state from the possessive state which was founded on conquest and victory at war, leading to the institutionalization of the punitive treatment of the defeated. Such institutionalized practices become aimed at the 'sociological minorities' created by the homogenizing policies of the scientific state. This represents a far less satisfactory explanation than Gellner's which at least identifies the conflict between collectivities over scarce resources and the allocation of power.

This chapter has discussed three theories of nationalism which have had considerable influence on the study of the subject in the post-war years. The idealism of Kedourie offers little capacity to explain nationalism. The modernization theory of Gellner proved more fertile ground in its identification of nationalism as the struggle between collectivities over the benefits of modernization. Smith, to a lesser extent than Kedourie, proved idealistic and consequently vague about the basis of the actions of individual intellectuals and the development of nationalism as a political movement. The next chapter turns to Marxism and the opportunities it presents for the expansion of the more promising aspects of Gellner's analysis.

CHAPTER 2

THE MARXIST TRADITION AND
THEORIES OF NATIONALISM

Perhaps more than any other aspect of Marxism, the national question cannot be considered without full reference to the work of Engels as well as to that of Marx. Unfortunately, as with other areas of their writings, neither gives a clear, coherent statement on the nation (Lowy 1976). Rather, they demonstrate an ambivalence toward the national question, occasionally supporting, at other times denouncing, national movements. However, their attitude to specific national movements is not as random as at first appears but is determined by their view of a movement's political expediency and an assessment of its role in the contemporary political context. Their models were the 'bourgeois revolutions of 1648 and 1789' (Cummins 1980, p. 29) with their associated centralism and drive for cultural and linguistic unification under a new, bourgeois, social order. For Marx, the successful establishment of a bourgeois state is an essential condition for the full development of capitalism and hence socialism. Consequently, the apparent ambivalence of Marx and Engels on the national question rests on differing assessments of particular political movements and whether or not they accelerate or restrict the development of, initially, the bourgeois revolution and, ultimately, the general movement to socialism.[1] Debray writes:

> So you have to admit national independence is never an ultimate criterion for Marx, but always subordinate to something or other. Subordinate to what? To what he calls the general movement, or the international proletarian revolution. (1977, p. 2)

Central to their assessment of the contribution of a national movement to the general revolutionary process is the concept of 'nations with history' and 'nations without history'. Associated primarily with Engels's writings on central Europe (Herod 1976), the distinction identifies nations as contributing to or inhibiting the general movement. Nations without history have lacked the conditions necessary for the emergence of a bourgeoisie and have failed to develop a centralized state. Their fate is to be assimilated into the nations with history. Non-historic nations would not contribute to the progression toward socialism and, for Engels, would give rise to reactionary or counter-revolutionary political movements (Cummins 1980).

The distinction between historic and non-historic nations has tended to dominate subsequent Marxist writings on the national question, and for most Marxists their view of a national movement is ultimately dependent on its potential contribution to the revolutionary process. Herod (1976) identifies the distinction in the work of 'Otto Bauer, Karl Kautsky, Rosa Luxemburg, V. I. Lenin, Joseph Stalin and Fran Zwitter' (p. 5).

Nimni (1985) argues that the historic/non-historic nation distinction provided Marx and Engels with 'a coherent perception of the national question' (p. 102). For Nimni, only movements which displayed potential viability to be a nation were judged worthy of support by Marx and Engels. Those ethnic groups without sufficient population and with no territorial basis for the formation of a state were to become 'historyless peoples' (p. 102).

Nimni criticizes Marx and Engels for the 'social evolutionist and epiphenomenal' characteristics of their discussion of the national question. He claims that their work was 'capitalocentric' in regarding the nation as an epiphenomenon of the rise of the bourgeoisie in the transition from feudalism to capitalism. Nimni's critique derives from the benefit of hindsight, and he fails to recognize the central charac-teristics of the contemporary context of Marx's studies. It was a period significant for the universality of the transition from feudalism to capitalism in western Europe. Although European societies were in different phases of this process, the central feature of many was a developing capitalist mode of production and the ascendancy of the bourgeoisie within the context of unifying and centralizing state structures.

It is only in retrospect that we can recognize that such developments are not inevitabilities along a linear path of societal evolution (Amin 1980). If Marx and Engels regard nationalism as an epiphenomenon of the rise of the bourgeoisie, it is because the concept of the nation was an epiphenomenon of the class struggle in which the bourgeoisie were engaged, in the transition from feudalism to capitalism. The concept of nation was a key factor in the unification of bourgeois and other fractional class interests in the securing of the bourgeois revolution. Later, Gramsci's notions of the 'historical bloc' and the role of the nation in establishing successful 'Jacobin movements' in the majority of

European countries will be discussed. For Gramsci the emergence of such a bloc was the pre-condition for bourgeois revolution and the creation of a 'national popular will' was the basis of bourgeois hegemony in the capitalist mode of production (Gramsci 1971).

In fact, in identifying some national movements as hindering this process, Marx and Engels are suggesting that nationalism is an epiphenomenon not simply of the rise of the bourgeoisie but of the struggles which characterize society in the transition of feudalism to capital. If merely associated with the rise of the bourgeoisie, all national movements would gain Marx's support in that bourgeois success furthers the revolutionary process. However, his rejection of some movements points to his awareness that the imagery of the nation is also mobilized by groups which resist the revolutionary process and seek to establish regressive and reactionary social movements. Thus nationalism is not necessarily a bourgeois ideology but can be mobilized by diverse classes and class alliances. For example, an alliance between a landed class and a rural peasantry can be sustained by an appeal to their common sense of nationhood. This is an important theoretical insight which is further expanded by Lenin and Gramsci and which will provide the potential basis for a theory of nationalism. Marx and Engels have pointed to the potential 'free floating' quality of nationalist ideology and its potential connection with classes other than the bourgeoisie.

The degree to which the national question has been integrated into the work of Marxist writers has been dependent on the significance of nationalism to the revolutionary struggle in which they have been engaged. The apparent ambivalence of Marx and Engels has given a legacy of competing interpretations of the place of the national question in Marxist theory and praxis. Two dominant strands of thinking have emerged, both grounded in the work of Marx and Engels but emphasizing different aspects of their work. The illustration of these separate traditions can be seen in the work of V. I. Lenin, Rosa Luxemburg and Antonio Gramsci. All three writers demonstrate a central concern with the national question and have contributed significantly to the place it now occupies in Western Marxist thought.

No claim is made that their views represent the only Marxist work on the subject or even that their writings are more illuminating than that of others. Rather they are considered because they have dominated Western Marxism and consequently reflect most accurately the development of Marxism in relation to the national question. Other positions, including that of the Austro-Marxists,[2] will be neglected here, simply because of their failure significantly to influence Western Marxism and its treatment of the national question (Nimni 1985). However, before examining these traditions, the writings of Marx and Engels on the subject should be considered in more detail in order to clarify how such divergent positions can emerge in authors all claiming to develop what they believed to be Marx's position on the national question.

Marx and Engels on the national question

In *The Communist Manifesto* (1967) Marx and Engels are in no doubt of the international qualities of the proletariat.[3] They write:

> The working men have no country. We cannot take away from them what they have not got. (p. 102)

Furthermore, the activities of the bourgeoisie in developing and promoting 'freedom of commerce' and a world market were already eroding national differences through the establishment of a 'uniformity in the mode of production and in the conditions of life corresponding thereto' (Marx and Engels 1967, p. 102). Marx and Engels saw that the victory of the proletariat could only hasten that process. However a contradiction to this view can be found elsewhere in *The Communist Manifesto* where they argue that:

> Since the proletariat must first of all acquire political supremacy, must rise to be the leading class of the nation, must constitute itself the nation, it is, so far, itself national, though not in the bourgeois sense of the word. (p. 102)

Fortunately, some clarification of the ambiguity present in *The Communist Manifesto* is possible by reference to other writings on the national question.

Michael Lowy (1976) identifies three main themes from the writings of Marx and Engels on the national question:

> 1. Only the national liberation of the oppressed nation enables national divisions and antagonisms to be overcome, and permits the working class of both nations to unite against their common enemy the capitalists;
> 2. the oppression of another nation helps to reinforce the ideological hegemony of the bourgeoisie over workers in the oppressing nation: 'Any nation that oppresses another forges its own chains';
> 3. the emancipation of the oppressed nation weakens the economic, political, military and ideological bases of the dominating

classes in the oppressor nation and this contributes to the revolutionary struggle of the working class of that nation. (p. 83)

Marx's views on the Irish question[4] illuminate these basic points. He
saw the establishment of a free Ireland within the framework of a federal British state as a prerequisite of the emancipation of the English
working class (Cummins 1980).

> The oppressed classes in England and Ireland must at least fight
> together and conquer together or continue to languish under the
> same oppression and live in the same misery and dependence on
> the privileged and ruling capitalist class. (Marx and Engels 1976,
> Vol. 6, p. 449)

In short, the abolition of national oppression of Ireland was a necessary
pre-condition for successful proletarian revolution by the English working class. Whilst the British state maintained rule in Ireland, the working
class in England were a party to oppression which weakened its ability
to develop an adequate revolutionary consciousness. Additionally, the
common objectives and exploitation of both working classes were obscured by the relationship which existed and which prevented the
unification of the working-class struggle. Elsewhere, Marx is concerned
to point to the progressive potential of nationalist demands. Of the
Cracow insurrection of 1846, he wrote:

> The Cracow revolution has given a glorious example to the whole
> of Europe by identifying the national cause with the democratic
> cause and the emancipation of the oppressed class. (1976, Vol. 6,
> p. 549)

Thus Marx and Engels were clearly willing to identify nationalism with
progressive democratic demands and recognized its contribution to
working-class emancipation. Their writings on Poland support Lowy's
conclusions drawn from an analysis of their writings on the Irish question. They regarded Polish independence as an essential stage in the
democratization of Germany. This point is made by Herod (1976) in a
detailed discussion of nine articles addressing the Polish question in
Neue Rheinische Zeitung in 1848:

> . . . as long as the German people helped in the suppression of
> Poland; as long as part of Poland was held by Germany; as long as
> Germany was welded to Russia and Russian politics through
> Poland; that was just how long the German people would not be
> able to rid themselves of the particularistic-feudalistic absolutism
> then so prevalent in Germany. The creation of a democratic

Poland with control over the outlets of its great rivers, it was argued, was the first condition for the creation of a democratic Germany. (p. 11)

However, their support did not extend to the national demands of other Slavic groups: only Poland occupied such a pivotal position in the political structures of the day.

In summary, Marx's and Engels's assessment of national movements depends not only on the contribution of those movements to a specific revolutionary rupture but also to the unfolding of the 'general movement'. Their support is contingent upon both an assessment of the role of the national movement in the local struggle as well as its overall implications for the transcendence of capitalism by socialism. Thus Marx and Engels might support a bourgeois national movement whilst rejecting a peasant nationalism which would hinder the full development of capitalism. It is this general theoretical framework that subsequent Marxists have developed in their different ways. Within it, there exist the foundations of two schools of thought. The one regards nationalism simply as a feature of the bourgeois revolution and thus inevitably and permanently linked to bourgeois values and supportive of bourgeois domination. The other recognizes its potential connection with other classes and its ambiguous and contradictory role in the general revolutionary process. The first of these views is associated with Rosa Luxemburg and the second with the work of Lenin and Gramsci.

Rosa Luxemburg[5]

Luxemburg, like Marx, argued for the primacy of the revolutionary struggle, maintaining that the cause of the proletariat should not be subsumed under 'sterile national struggles'. Nettl (1966) sees her case against nationalism as being based on two assumptions:

First, that national and Socialist aspirations were incompatible and that a commitment to national self-determination by Socialist parties must subordinate those parties to bourgeois nationalism instead of opposing one to the other. (Nettl 1966, p. 845)

And the second argued that Russia was 'itself moving into the era of social revolution' (p. 845) and consequently represented a progressive direction of change which would be advantageous for Polish socialism. To Luxemburg the national and socialist causes could not be conducted in parallel: the former could only detract from the latter. She did not believe that the liberation and unification of Poland from annexation and division would be achieved through the articulation of nationalist demands. Rather, Polish restoration was dependent on close co-operation between the Polish socialist movement and socialist groups in the three nations which dominated Poland. For her, Polish nationalism precluded such co-operation and consequently should be fought against (Herod 1976). The objective of Polish socialism should be the formation of a capitalist economy thereby creating the necessary conditions for the transition to socialism under the leadership of the proletariat. In this sense she maintains Marx's and Engels's commitment to the 'general movement' discussed above. Polish separation from Russia would inhibit or prevent the development of capitalism in Poland. Herod (1976) writes:

> While the Polish bourgeoisie was strengthened economically through their close economic interaction with their Russian counterpart, the industrialization of Poland would move steadily ahead accompanied by a growing Polish proletariat. It was only in this manner that the formation of a proletariat capable of revolutionary seizure and the development of a socialist Poland could take place. (p. 85)

Nationalism, for her, was the expression of pre-capitalist and petty bourgeois sentiments and only the peasantry and the petty bourgeoisie had no interests in continued links with Tsarist Russia (Lowy 1976). Both the bourgeoisie and the proletariat had interests in maintaining the relationship of domination. The bourgeoisie depended on the economic benefits of continued links and the proletariat needed the solidarity with the Russian proletariat. The relationship between the two national proletariats was of crucial significance to Luxemburg. Nettl argues that she believed:

> Russian Poland as well as other non-Russian areas in the Tsarist Empire now depended for their release, not on nationalist separation from Russia, but on proletarian revolution within Russia itself. (Nettl 1966, p. 846)

So, in contrast with Marx, Luxemburg saw the cause of proletarian revolution in both Tsarist Russia and Russian Poland as best served by continued imperial rule by Russia. She would not have accepted the argument that the national liberation of Poland would weaken the Tsarist regime and further the cause of both national proletariats. Much of her argument against such strategy was based on what she perceived as the almost total integration of the Russian and Polish economies. She

believed that the Polish economy could not survive without its trade
with Russia and consequently the ideal of an independent Polish nation
was purely utopian.

Furthermore, for her, the whole premise of national self-
determination was based on 'abstract and metaphysical' notions of
rights. She compared such rights with the 'right to work' demands
(Lowy 1976, p. 86) of French socialism during the 1848 Revolution
(Nettl 1966, p. 840). The independence of small nations argued for by
such discussions was economically unfeasible, utopian and contradicted
all laws of history. In this latter respect she shared Engels's perception
of the 'non-historic' nation: those crushed by the process of history and
remaining only as 'national refuse'. Lowy (1976) argues that she failed
to separate the economic from the political sphere of society. He argues
that her adoption of an economistic approach prior to 1914 led her to
argue that political independence was inseparable from economic
independence; if the latter was impossible then so was the former.

The strongest point of her attack on nationalism is in her denial of the
existence of an entity which could be termed the nation:

> In a society based on classes, the nation as a uniform social politi-
> cal whole does not exist. Instead there exists within each nation
> classes with antagonistic interests and 'rights'. (Quoted in Nettl
> 1966, p. 849)

The analysis of nineteenth-century Wales supports the validity of this
statement. The complex network of opposed interests displayed between tenant farmers and landowners in the rural sector and between
ironmasters and workers in the industrial sector is evidence enough
against the existence of a homogeneous nation. It is very difficult to envisage Wales as an 'undifferentiated national whole' during this period
of highly visible class antagonism. Any image of a national unity or a
common national will must be recognized as an ideological construct of
nationalism itself.

However, despite this important conclusion, Luxemburg fails to
recognize that certain elements of the national struggle could constitute
an important contribution to the struggle of the proletariat, in that defeat
of national oppression is a blow to the economic, political and
ideological basis of the hegemony of the ruling class in both oppressor
and oppressed nations. Luxemburg's failure to recognize this is mainly
due to the development of her views on the national question out of the
specific conditions of Polish society (Lowy 1976, Nettl 1966). In
Poland, demands for national liberation originated from reactionary
groups and the allegiance of certain sections of the socialist movement

to those demands led them into questionable alliances with sections of the peasantry and petty bourgeoisie (Nettl 1966). Only later in the Junius Pamphlet of 1915 did she give any recognition to the principle of national self-determination, when she wrote:

> Socialism gives to every people the right of independence and the freedom of independent control of its own destinies. (From The Junius Pamphlet, quoted in Lowy 1976, p. 143).

The statement was, however, qualified by arguing that such independence could never be exercised in existing capitalist states, particularly in those engaged in imperialist activity. National independence could only be achieved through and in socialism. We see that even in her later writings the national question can only be solved through the victory of the proletariat in revolution. Luxemburg's perspective on the national question has created a paradigm in Marxist analysis which recognizes the internationalism of the proletariat and the threat to it from nationalist ideology. However, this particular paradigm is one of two which can be discerned in Marxist writings on the national question. The alternative one, found in the work of Lenin, provides the basis for a theory of nationalism.

Lenin

Lenin's work on the national question presents a fairly well-focused contrast with the basis of Luxemburg's views. In keeping with both Marx and Luxemburg the thrust of Lenin's argument is, of course, in support of the proletarian revolution; if Lenin is willing to engage with the national question it is only as an endeavour which strives to comprehend the complexities of revolutionary politics. Lenin is in no doubt as to the primacy of the proletarian revolution and that, for him, its success is dependent on the internationalism of the proletariat. To the nationalism of the bourgeoisie he opposes the internationalism of the proletariat:

> Bourgeois nationalism and proletarian internationalism — these are the two irreconcilably hostile slogans that correspond to the two great class camps throughout the capitalist world. (Lenin 1964, Vol. 20, p. 26)

In spite of this statement, we find in Lenin a willingness to equate the national struggle with that of the proletariat — whereas Luxemburg would only subsume one under the other.

Lenin's ability to equate the two political struggles derives from the distinction he makes between specific expressions of nationalism. He identifies two general types, best described as 'oppressed nation' and 'great power' nationalism. The former constitutes political movements struggling against economic, political and cultural oppression by an imperialist conquering or occupying nation, for example his contemporary Poland. The latter relates to nationalism of the imperialist nations which represent nationalism in its chauvinistic and reactionary clothing, exemplified by Great Russian nationalism. Lenin's ability to make such a distinction led him to perceive that nationalism could be a legitimate expression of the desires of the proletariat and represent a progressive element in political struggle (Lowy 1976). Lenin's opinion of nationalism is also shaped by his perception of the peasantry as a potentially revolutionary class. In contrast with Luxemburg he did not see an alliance between peasantry and proletariat as a betrayal of the revolutionary cause but as an important and crucial element of revolutionary strategy. Nationalism could provide a powerful rallying call in the creation of that alliance, bringing together two classes in a united struggle against the bourgeoisie. For Lenin the relationship between 'oppressed nation' nationalism and socialism was comp-lementary in that the gains and the achievements of one were also powerful blows on behalf of the other (Lowy 1966).

However, it must be stressed that for Lenin, as much as for Luxemburg, the prime struggle was that of the proletariat; the national struggle was allied only where it was a democratic movement seeking to end the oppression of a people by another nation.

> In advancing the slogan of the 'international culture of democracy and of the world working class movement' we take from *each* national culture *only* its democratic and socialist elements; we take *only* and *absolutely* in opposition to the bourgeois culture and the bourgeois nationalism of *each nation*. (Lenin 1964, Vol. 20, p. 24, author's emphasis)

For Lenin, as for Marx, where national oppression existed, national lib-eration was a pre-condition of the emancipation of the proletariat. The support of national struggles in such situations was implicitly the support of proletarian struggle. Such a view enabled Lenin to perceive the peasantry and petty bourgeoisie as potential allies of the revolution, despite their often conservative and reactionary ideologies. It was the role of the proletariat to defeat these tendencies within the class alliances through their leadership and domination of the national move-ment. Thus Lenin, by equating the national and socialist movements, and advancing the theory of national self-determination, developed a broader revolutionary strategy with obvious consequences for the Russian Revolution.

The advantage of Lenin's perspective is that, whilst it does not constitute a theory of nationalism itself, it includes the recognition of the role of class alliances in the analysis of national movements and raises the prospect of nationalism as an ideology capable of unifying diverse interests. Furthermore, in his distinction between the chauvinism of 'great power' nationalism and the democratic, progressive tendencies of 'oppressed nation' nationalism, he demonstrates that nationalism as an ideology is not the sole property of the bourgeoisie. It cannot be reduced to an ideological construct used only by the bourgeoisie in class struggle. National aspirations are not exclusive to the ruling class and cannot be analysed simply as a bourgeois counter-revolutionary ideology employed against the international proletariat engaged in socialist struggle. Rather, nationalism can provide an impetus for revolutionary activity within the proletarian movement itself.

The importance of both Lenin's and Luxemburg's writings is primarily the location of nationalism as an ideology within the context of class struggle. Luxemburg sees it as simply a reactionary and anti-revolutionary ideology which detracts from the socialist struggle. Lenin, perhaps closer to the view of Marx, regards nationalism as a potentially proletarian strategy. In this respect Lenin's is a less economistic conclusion than that of Luxemburg and allows a more flexible analysis, distanced from the economism of the Second International (Lowy 1976). Lenin's writings on the national question represent further refinement of the initial insight offered by Marx, discussed earlier in this chapter. Lenin has left no doubt as to the 'free-floating' quality of nationalist ideology.

Antonio Gramsci

Antonio Gramsci's work represents a continuity of this second paradigm I have identified in Marxist analysis and provides a resolution of some of the difficulties associated with Marxist attempts to engage with the national question.

Hobsbawm (1977) regards Gramsci as:

> . . . the only Marxist thinker to provide us with a basis for integrating the nation as a historical and social reality within Marxist theory. (Hobsbawm 1977, p. 19. Quoted in Mouffe 1979, p. 9)

This claim is generally indicative of the high value placed on Gramsci's writings on the national question. Gramsci addresses the national question in his discussion of the basis of hegemony. The national character of political struggle is central to Gramsci's analysis of the struggle for socialism in Italy. For Gramsci to have ignored the national question and its role in political praxis is inconceivable, given his Sardinian origins and his support for Sardinian nationalism during his early years at Turin. His sympathies for Salvemini's policies on the Southern Question are indicative of the importance Gramsci attaches to the solution of Italy's internal problems. The North/South dichotomy is recognized by Gramsci as the primary impediment to the achievement of socialism in Italy. It is these political contingencies which enable Gramsci to accommodate the national question in his work and integrate it more fully into revolutionary strategy. In particular the resolution of Italy's internal tensions is regarded by Gramsci as necessary for the creation of proletarian hegemony in Italy.

An understanding of the meaning of the term 'hegemony'[6] is essential to an appraisal of Gramsci's general political theory and particularly so to an analysis of the implications of his work for the national question. Gramsci's central task is to reintroduce the human subject into Marxist analysis and to deny the existence of immutable laws of historical development which led inevitably to the establishment of socialism. Whilst wishing to defeat economistic and positivistic tendencies in Marxist theory, Gramsci recognizes the role of the economic base in the determination of social formations but also wishes to reveal the causal effects of the superstructural elements (Boggs 1976). For Gramsci a dialectical mode of analysis is essential and requires the recognition of human actualization of the fundamental economic contradictions of the mode of production. Economistic Marxism saw class rule as a simple reflection of the economic power of the ruling class and its monopoly of the forces of coercion; domination of the working classes existed only at the economic level. Gramsci argues instead that it also exists at all other levels of society and in all social and cultural practices.

His construction of this argument depends on a distinction between 'coercion' and 'consent'[7] (Boggs 1976, Femia 1981). Whilst admitting the role of coercion, Gramsci argues that no ruling group can sustain its position permanently by coercive measures alone. Gramsci stresses the role of ideological maintenance of domination. Ruling classes are dependent on the consent of those they rule. This is achieved through the institutions of civil society, which he distinguishes from political society.

What we can do, for the moment, is to fix two major superstructural 'levels': the one that can be called 'civil society', that is the ensemble of organisms commonly called 'private', and that of 'political society' or 'the state'. These two levels correspond on the one hand to the function of 'hegemony' which the dominant group exercises throughout society and on the other hand to that of 'direct domination' or command exercised through the State and 'juridical' government. (Gramsci 1971, p. 12)

Hegemony represents the achievement of the consent of the subordinate classes for the continued domination by the ruling class. This entails the permeation of social and cultural life by a morality and belief system which reflects the general interests of the ruling group but conveys them as a general will. Gramsci argues that the vehicle through which this is achieved is the 'national popular collective will' (1971, p. 131).

For Gramsci, the earliest example of the creation of hegemony was the successes of the French Jacobin movement.[8] It constituted a 'historical bloc', through its synthesis of various class interests. Gramsci argued that the central Jacobin achievement had been the creation of a 'national popular' movement based on a synthesis of rural and urban interests. This synthesis had enabled diverse classes to become allied within an ideology founded on an emerging conceptualization of their common nationality and resultant shared interests.

In Italy, however, no national popular community had ever been established: the bourgeois liberal revolution had been undertaken on too narrow a base and remained an incomplete process. As a consequence, the nation state had not developed fully and no hegemonic force had emerged in Italian society. Instead, a northern bourgeoisie, in alliance with traditional élites, had maintained their rule through 'transformism'. Transformism[9] had been a process of co-optation and incorporation of the leadership of oppositional groups which threatened to undermine and overcome resistance to bourgeois rule. However, their domination had not been hegemonic. There had not been a bourgeois revolution as in France, Great Britain and America: there had been a 'passive revolution' (Gramsci 1971, p. 58) in which the ruling class had failed to establish its will as the will of the masses: their rule constituted 'dictatorship without hegemony' (Gramsci 1971, p. 106).[10]

Gramsci argued that the absence of a national popular basis for hegemony in Italy provided the opportunity for the proletariat to create just such a movement. Italian socialists did not need to wait for capitalist development to run its full course but could intervene and establish the necessary basis of socialist revolution: an alliance of various class interests but under the control and hegemonic leadership of the proletariat. Marxism could break down traditional barriers and social divisions in Italian society and amalgamate the interests of diverse classes. Particularly desirable was the synthesis of the narrow national beliefs of the intellectuals and the particularistic ideas of the southern peasantry. In formulating such a policy Gramsci did not deny the internationalism of the proletariat or the primacy of the revolutionary struggle, but argued that:

> In reality, the internal relations of any nation are the result of a combination which is 'original' and (in a certain sense) unique: these relations must be understood and conceived in their originality and uniqueness if one wishes to dominate and direct them. To be sure, the line of development is toward internationalism, but the point of departure is 'national' — and it is from this point of departure that one must begin. Yet the perspective is international and cannot be otherwise. (Gramsci 1971, p. 240)

Gramsci saw that sole reliance on internationalism led to 'passivity and inertia' (Gramsci 1971, p. 241), firstly, in that socialist movements believed that by initiating revolution their actions would be premature and they would become isolated. Instead socialists perpetuated the belief that the proletariat should make its move in a united world movement. Secondly, he argued that the belief in internationalism becomes a simple dogma which invalidates itself by simply not coming true. Although the proletariat may be international in character it must take the lead in the national context and 'knot' together the unique and specific national characteristics in the creation of hegemony and a national popular will.

Any assessment of Gramsci's contribution to the search for a theory of nationalism must involve an appraisal of the extent to which a body of prescriptive political writings can be applied as political analysis. Gramsci was primarily concerned with the specific setting of Italian society and, within that context, the specific aim of achieving socialism. His analysis and strategy weaves the national question into the 'unique' conditions of Italian society. Whilst we may accept his writings as informing socialist strategy generally, can they be employed as a theoretical basis for the explanation of nationalism?

There are specific aspects of Gramsci's work which further the development of a theory of nationalism. Firstly, the discussion of 'Jacobin' movements and 'Jacobin' states demonstrates Gramsci's understanding of the role of nationalism in the historical development of capitalism. He is not concerned merely with the period of industrialization but with the transformation of the social relations of production engendered by the development of capitalism. The subject of analysis is class conflict, in Gramsci's terms hegemonic struggle. The creation of a 'national popular will' is the ideological force behind the creation of the modern European nation state. It is the ideology of the nation which permits the synthesis of diverse class interests and the creation of 'historical blocs' — unified social and political movements which become the hegemonic force in society. The nation is created out of the conditions of class struggle. Thus, for Gramsci, the nation-building of nineteenth-century Europe was the culmination of the rise of the bourgeois class and the successful completion of the bourgeois revolution. Nationalism represented the ideological construct which permitted the alliances of classes and provided the basis of the 'moral, political and cultural' values which were essential to the establishment and maintenance of bourgeois hegemony. Nationalism was a powerful force in the creation of a national popular will. There is, therefore, in the work of Gramsci, effective explanation of the genesis of the nationalist doctrine within the development of the European nation states.

Gramsci's identification of nationalism as an ideological cement facilitating the bourgeois revolution does not mean that he identifies it with that class alone. A further contribution of Gramsci lies in his appreciation of the potential role for nationalism in the proletarian revolution. His recognition of the absence of a hegemonic class in Italian society points him to the value of the proletariat developing and utilizing a national perspective within their struggle. The ideology of nationalism could be developed by the proletariat to fill the hegemonic vacuum in Italian society. Nationalism could provide for the unification of proletarian interests with those of the intelligentsia, the peasantry and elements of the petty bourgeoisie. The overriding principle was, however, that to secure the path to socialism the proletariat must be the hegemonic class within the national movement; it must direct and control the movement in its ideas, policies and praxis.

This application of the concept of hegemony illustrates that it cannot be simply reduced to an analogous term for bourgeois ideology. Oppositional political movements themselves can be torn by hegemonic struggles in the same way as the social formation as a whole. In any alliance the differing classes and fractions of classes would attempt to establish their world view and its consequent political praxis as the hegemonic view. This perception offers explanation for the diversity of national movements which presents such difficulties for the development of a theory of nationalism.

It can be seen on the basis of Gramsci's ideas that the form and ideological content of a given movement will be determined by the interplay between the groups brought together in the class alliance. If one group is hegemonic within the movement, their world view and political praxis will prevail. However, the reality is likely to be a complex process of negotiation, compromise and internal hegemonic struggle within the movement itself. In this sense it can be explained why some nationalisms are conservative and others revolutionary, depending, for example, on the relative strengths of the peasantry and proletariat within the movement. Our conclusion must be that each movement will demonstrate a unique combination of classes in different positions of strength and weakness. This will result in a potentially infinite variety of ideological content and political actions by particular national movements. This conclusion points once again to the futility of the creation of ideal-types and taxonomies of nationalism as a methodology seeking its explanation.

Finally, Gramsci's formulations can help to explain the universality of nationalism. We can move forward in our explanation of the transmission of the doctrine from Kedourie's imitative intellectuals. We can transcend Gellner's process of modernization/industrialization which locates nationalism at a specific juncture in societal development. Instead, we locate nationalism, according to its central dynamic, as a feature of class conflict. Consequently, we are not dependent on establishing whether a society is at a particular stage of development but would recognize that hegemonic struggle is a constant process. We can recognize that the national popular will and its mobilization of nationalist ideology represents a particular class, or alliance of classes, within the hegemonic struggle. For Gramsci, hegemony existed in a society divided into classes determined by relations of production. The fundamental contradictions of the mode of production create the ground on which political struggles take place. Although in themselves abstract, the contradictions are 'seized upon' (Boggs 1976, p. 36) and 'actualized' by human actors. The source of unification in hegemonic formations is always class interests.[11] Nationalism mobilizes diverse groups within a national popular front and it is the nature of the groups and the terms of their combination which will determine the actual form of the nationalist ideology and its role in the creation of hegemony. If we recognize the 'unique' characteristics of the society and the ways in which they are knotted together in the nationalist movement we can begin to understand that specific articulation of nationalist ideology.

Clearly, within this formulation, the issues of culture, language and politics are of crucial significance; they are the 'unique' characteristics of our object of study. Whilst Gramsci's ideas provide the broad conceptual framework sought in the opening pages of this chapter, the specific characteristics of each nationalist movement also have to be understood. We form an initial approach to the study of a specific nationalism from knowledge of its origins and role in class struggle, but to understand the specificity of the movement we have to look away from the origins of class conflict in the economic base to the form of the class conflict in the superstructures. We have to discover how the ideology of nationalism is constructed and to what extent it is determined by the economic contradictions of the base and to what extent these are overlaid by political and cultural contradictions in the other levels of the social formation.

In order to achieve these objectives it is necessary to explore in greater depth the relationship between class relations, determined at the level of the mode of production, and their political and ideological effects within the social formation. The complexity of the relationship between base and superstructure has preoccupied Marxism in the post-war period. Some reference to the debates which have emerged is essential in order to assess whether the insights derived from Gramsci's political analysis of Italy and its unique characteristics can be applied more universally as a general theory of nationalism. It is necessary to develop more fully an awareness of the role of nationalism as an ideological element and its potential role in the political process, as well as its connection with class struggle.

CHAPTER 3

NATIONALISM AND IDEOLOGY

In Chapters 1 and 2 several theories were surveyed in terms of their capacity to explain expressions of nationalism. Moving from theories based on the idealist notions of nationalism as a 'spirit of an age' (Kedourie 1960), the survey progressed to the general Marxist framework which locates nationalism within the context of class conflict. Rejecting the rigid class reductionism of Rosa Luxemburg, this examination has argued for an alternative tradition of analysis evident in Marx, Lenin and Gramsci which regards nationalism as having a potentially pro-proletarian role to play in class struggle.

In particular, the work of Antonio Gramsci theorizes nationalism as an ideology which can be appropriated by various classes and class alliances in the struggle for hegemony. Nationalism cannot be identified as simply a bourgeois ideology but can be mobilized by the proletariat in its establishment of a 'national popular will', which for Gramsci was a crucial element of the 'wars of position' which the proletariat must adopt if its cause is to be successful.

Such a view of nationalism, however, necessarily presents it as an ideology removed in several ways from a strict determination by the economic base. For an ideology to have the capacity to be employed, not only by different classes, but by different fractions of classes formed into alliances, implies that Gramsci has a view of ideology far removed from the economism of the Second International. Gramsci's work indicates that ideologies are class neutral until appropriated by a given class in the context of hegemonic struggle. In fact, Gramsci credits ideology with a greater degree of autonomy and independence from the base than is normally associated with the Marxist perspective. In order to examine the role of ideology it is necessary to consider the nature of the relationship between base and superstructure and an overview of the attempts of recent writers to clarify that relationship.

The discussion of that relationship has preoccupied Marxism, and to some extent the recent development of Marxist theory can be seen as an attempt to rid itself of the inherent tendency toward economism identified by critics and Marxists alike.[1] Much of that debate has centred on the usage of the architectural metaphor of base and superstructure and the ways in which the usage of that metaphor has in itself suggested a 'mechanical' rather than dialectical relationship between base and superstructures. Consequently, much effort has been spent on elaborating, refining and transcending the metaphor. This has created a vocabulary and conceptual framework peculiar to Marxist literature which presents an almost impenetrable barrier to those outside the debates. Given that the discussion will be entered here, no claims are made as to the solution of the problems associated with the concept of ideology but the intention is only to clarify the usage and meaning adopted within this book. I believe that the concept of ideology, when applied to the analysis of nationalism, can provide major insights into the dynamic of national movements and their articulation with class politics. However, given the depth of the controversies which surround the concept, it is important initially to clarify the ambiguity of its role in contemporary political and social theory.

Ideology in the writings of Marx

The most obvious point of entry into the debate is the work of Marx himself and the easiest way to approach the explication of a theory of ideology in Marx is to examine the process of development of the concept in his writings. Marx's discussions of ideology are embodied within his development of the materialist conception of history. Initially, in a rejection of the idealism of German philosophy, Marx attempts to demonstrate the grounding of human consciousness in material reality, thereby inverting the relationship between consciousness and the material world put forward in the Hegelian body of philosophy.

It is in *The German Ideology* that Marx fully develops his critique of the Young Hegelians through a detailed statement of historical materialism. However the usage of the term ideology in this work is ambiguous and potentially a source of considerable confusion. This ambiguity arises from three different but connected uses the concept is put to in *The German Ideology*.

The first of these usages retains the pejorative association given to the term in the context of Napoleon's disagreement and break with De Stutt de Tracy and his 'science of ideas'. Marx labels the Young Hegelians as ideologists subsuming all categories of thought under religion and theology. Their claim to have created 'an unparalleled revolution' in thought in which they have broken with the past is merely an illusion, limited to the 'realm of pure thought' (Marx and Engels 1976, Vol. 5, p. 30). In reality they remain as conservative as the Old Hegelians in their emphasis on the supremacy of religion. Marx accuses them of being ideologists, trading only in ideas. He continues by challenging the Young Hegelians to examine the material reality of their Germany and enquire into the relation of their philosophy to their material surroundings. It is at this point that Marx introduces the 'materialist method' and in so doing establishes a more significant usage of the term 'ideology' than the one outlined above.

In the elaboration of the second application of the term, Marx claims that humans first distinguish themselves from animals when they begin to produce their means of subsistence as an active conscious process. The methods of that production are determined initially by the ecological factors of the human environment acting as conditions which influence the mode of production. However, he argues:

> This mode of production must not be considered simply as being a production of the physical existence of the individuals. Rather it is a definite form of activity of those individuals, a definite form of expressing their life, a definite *mode of life* on their part. As individuals express their life so they are. What they are, therefore, coincides with their production, both with *what* they produce and with *how* they produce. Hence what individuals are depends on the material conditions of their production. (Marx and Engels 1976, Vol. 5, p. 32. Author's emphasis)

This is the basic assumption of the materialist method, moving beyond the crude materialism of Feuerbach toward a more fundamental materialism which links human consciousness with the mode of economic production. Marx locates this production within the evolution of a division of labour arising out of population increase and the developing division and contradiction between town and country, between agricultural and industrial labour and between mental and manual labour. He defines this division of labour as expressing different forms of the pattern of ownership of the means of production in societies and he discusses various stages of development of the relations between classes in the history of society. In examining tribal, ancient communal and feudal forms of ownership, he describes how they influence social and political life through the relations of production implicit within each form of ownership. He writes:

Empirical observation must in each separate instance bring out empirically, and without any mystification and speculation, the connection of the social and political structure with production. The social structure and the state are continually evolving out of the life processes of definite individuals ... (Marx and Engels 1976, Vol. 5, p. 35)

To Marx, the social and political life of individuals and societies arises out of production. In short, consciousness is determined by the way production is organized and the relationships which exist in specific modes of production and forms of ownership. Conceiving and thinking — the complete process of mental production — are 'conditioned' by the productive forces.

Consciousness can never be anything else than conscious being and the being of men is their actual life processes. (Marx and Engels 1976, Vol. 5, p. 36)

Marx then proceeds to apply the term ideology to this consciousness, thereby developing even further the usage of the concept to encompass the various activities of mental production.

The phantoms formed in the brains of men are also, necessarily, sublimates of their material life process which is empirically verifiable and bound to a material premises. Morality, religion, metaphysics and all the rest of ideology as well as the forms of consciousness corresponding to these, thus no longer retain the semblance of independence. They have no history, no development; but men developing their material production and their material intercourse. (Marx and Engels 1976, Vol. 5, p. 36–7)

This represents the major exposition of the materialist conception of history.

It may be concluded at this stage in the reading of *The German Ideology* that Marx's writings are merely a form of economic determinism. The material activity of human production is ascribed the role of absolute determinacy of all levels of human consciousness and mental production. We could conclude that there exists a linear, causal relationship between the mode of production, the economic structure and the corresponding social and political levels of society. However, Marx continues by developing a further usage of the term which substantially removes the analysis from economic determinism by stressing the dialectical relationship between base and superstructure. In writing about the existence of a ruling class and a corresponding ruling system of ideas, Marx develops his usage of the term 'ideology' still further. He writes:

> The ideas of the ruling class are in every epoch the ruling ideas: i.e., the class which is the ruling *material* force of society, is at the same time its ruling intellectual force. The class which has the means of material production at its disposal, consequently also controls the means of mental production, so that thereby, generally speaking, the ideas of those who lack the means of mental production are on the whole subject to it. (Marx and Engels 1976, Vol. 5, p. 59)

Furthermore, the division of mental and material labour manifests itself within the ruling class, creating a body of thinkers, 'active, conceptive ideologists', who formulate the conceptions such a class has of itself. These conceptions become separated from the material conditions in which they develop and take on an apparently independent existence, free from connection with the interests of the class they represent. They become represented as a common interest or a universal will, necessary for the rational ordering of society.

Here is a usage of the concept of ideology which implies that the active ideologists of the ruling class consciously promote the value system and social conditions necessary for the reproduction of a particular set of relations of production, to which they owe their survival as a dominant class. It appears that this contradicts the earlier usage of the term ideology. Previously, Marx has claimed that consciousness is derived from the material conditions of productive activity; now it seems he is arguing that the consciousness or ideology of a particular class maintains and preserves a set of productive relations through the conscious mental reproduction of a specific set of values and beliefs. This is arguing for a degree of independence of the ideological sphere from the social formation and crediting it with efficacy in the determination of the relations of production.

Through the work of active ideologists in the dominant class, the class relations of production — which Marx has suggested previously are determined by the mode of production — are now seen as subject to influence by the actions and thought of the ruling class. That one class, through its domination of the mental means of production, is able to reify and establish as essential to the survival of the social formation practices and beliefs which reproduce its domination. The superstructure is seen to be bearing influence on the economic base.

Rather than this development representing a contradiction to the earlier usage of the term, it must be seen as demonstration of the dialectical relationship between base and superstructures. Marx is depicting a relationship which is more complicated than a simple one-way, causal relationship between base and superstructure. In describing the processes of class rule, Marx has demonstrated that individuals and classes have influence on the economic structure and actually transform it through their actions. We may also turn elsewhere in Marx's work to find support for the claim of a reciprocal relationship between base and superstructures. In *The Eighteenth Brumaire of Louis Napoleon*, Marx writes:

> Men make their own history, but they do not make it just as they please; they do not make it under circumstances chosen by themselves, but under circumstances directly encountered transmitted from the past. The tradition of all the dead generations weighs like a nightmare on the brain of the living. (Marx and Engels 1976, Vol. 11, p. 103)

Here Marx is describing the process by which ideologies derived from previous modes and their relations of production continue to bear influence on contemporary ideology. At any one time, although a particular mode of production will dominate, it will be articulated with others in a complex interplay of relations of production and of ideas arising from them.[2] Again this points away from a strict determination of the ideological superstructure by the economic base. Marx never intended to propose such a deterministic relationship and we have to look at the work of subsequent Marxists to discover the development of such a crude determinism in Marxist theory.[3] This discussion could be summarized by Denis Monière's assertion:

> So I shall insist again on the dialectical nature of relations between ideology and mode of production; although the former is indeed a mirror of material conditions, it exerts influence in turn on human actions that create these conditions, and reflects a dialectic that swings from the imagined to the real, the real to the imagined. (Monière 1981, p. 8)

In brief, in *The German Ideology* there is a discussion of ideology which applies three interrelated usages of the term. They are as follows:

1) The pejorative usage used critically against the philosophy of the Young Hegelians to attack the idealism of their apparent but not actual break with Hegel.

2) The use of the term ideology to denote the complete range of human consciousness and mental production arising out of the act of production. This usage argues that consciousness is derived from the social existence of human beings engaged in the practice of productive relations. [4]

3) The active formulation of ideas and values by the dominant class who by virtue of their possession of the material means of production also possess and control the mental means of production. The ideology arising out of this control attempts to maintain the conditions necessary for the continued reproduction of the existing relations of production.[5]

Much of the controversy surrounding the concept of ideology within subsequent Marxist theory has centred on the relative emphasis which should be given to the second and third of the above usages. The different implications of these two usages have led to significantly different interpretations of a Marxian theory of ideology. In the case of 2) above we can recognize that human consciousness derives from the experience of the life processes of production (Larrain 1979). Consequently different and discrete ideologies corresponding to the different parts played in the relations of production can be identified. In other words we would recognize specific class ideologies reducible to the experience of the relations of production.

In contrast, if more emphasis is placed on 3) above, we would expect the existence of a 'dominant ideology'[6] in which the consciousness of the subordinate class echoes the values and economic interests of the ruling class. These two forms of ideology can be identified respectively as 'particular ideologies' and 'ideology in general' (Althusser 1971, pp. 150-2). These alternative readings of *The German Ideology* produce an economism which, in the first instance, reduces consciousness to an experience of the economic relations of production and, in the second instance, reduces consciousness to an expression of the economic interests of the ruling class. For the working class such a consciousness would inevitably be 'false'. It is the attempt to overcome the limitations of these readings of Marx's work on ideology which has led to considerable discussion of the concept of ideology in recent years.

In spite of these limitations, there is in *The German Ideology* a theory of ideology which, whilst stressing the primary role of the relations of production in the determination of the social formation, also points to the role of the superstructures and the dialectical relationship between base and superstructure. Nevertheless, the ambiguity which exists in *The*

German Ideology has been the source of wide-ranging discussion in subsequent developments of the role of ideology in Marxist theory. Of particular importance within that discussion has been the extent to which the ideological and political superstructures are independent of the base. Before continuing with the attempt to resolve that debate within the context of this study it would be profitable to apply the insights developed so far to the analysis of nationalism. In the preceding chapter Gramsci's arguments that nationalism can represent an ideological element of hegemonic struggle and an attempt to establish a 'national popular will' under the hegemony of a specific class were accepted. There is justification for this view in the writings of Marx on ideology.

In the terms of the discussion in this chapter we can identify how nationalism and the appeal to nationhood can be presented as a general will which transcends narrow class interests. Nationalism draws on elements from the cultural, linguistic and religious spheres of social life which cohere and provide a legitimate basis for the creation of a general will. That general will illuminates a common cause, a single identity and a value system which is capable of transcending class barriers. However, if, as Gramsci argued, the concept of nationhood is employed by specific classes or class alliances within the context of class struggle, it can be recognized that nationalism is an illusory set of beliefs and values which obscures the objective economic relations of classes and holds them in suspension. Nationalism asks of its subscribers loyalty and obedience to a higher authority than their own class interests, that is, to the nation. The nationalism has been 'knotted' together by a specific class in the pursuit of hegemony. It is an appeal to those elements of identity which diverse classes share and which potentially can overcome antagonistic class interests. Nationalism can be employed, not necessarily consciously, by one such class as a unifying, ideological construct calling other classes to its assistance under a banner which obscures the economic relations between them. If nationalism appears to transcend specific class interests, it is because that is its very role.

This does not yet explain why it is nationalist ideology which sometimes becomes mobilized in pursuit of class interests. Why, in specific instances, does the ideology of nationalism become the most significant political factor in a social formation? Why should nationalism, above other ideologies, provide the framework for the synthesis of diverse class interests? It is necessary to explain why, within the context of specific social formations, it is nationalism which becomes the focus and ideological ground of hegemonic conflict.

Clearly nationalism is not the only available ideology which can achieve the unification of class interests. We can identify the role of socialism in uniting an urban proletariat, a conservative peasantry and a dissentient intelligentsia within class struggle, with considerable effect, for example in the Russian Revolution. Nationalism is not an inevitable outcome of the need to develop a unifying ideology within class struggle. The range of conditions which will call a nationalist ideology into existence have to be examined.

Here the existence of determining forces in the superstructures must be recognized if an analysis is to be complete. We have to look at those 'unique' characteristics identified by Gramsci (1971, p. 240). However, within the framework of analysis of ideology developed up to this point, despite recognition of the determining effects of the superstructures, a full understanding of the relationship between the superstructures and the base has not yet been reached. Nor have the conditions under which the superstructures become determinant, and to what extent, of the base itself been described. The analysis has not been extended into an examination of the way in which ideology gathers to itself elements which are not derived from the economic contradictions of the social formation.

As already stated, it is necessary to explain how cultural, ethnic, linguistic and religious differentiae become incorporated into ideology. Marx himself tells us little about this process: he points to its existence but not its detail. Gramsci informs us of its value in socialist strategy, to be adopted as a deliberate tactic in the amalgamation of classes in unity of opposition to the dominant class. He even points to the central role that nationalism should be given in that process; but he does not give any insights into how that process could exist as an inherent feature of ideological construction without the conscious intervention of a socialist movement. Gramsci's analysis is a political prescription to remedy the weakness of the socialist movement in the Italian context. It has provided knowledge of the potential origins of nationalism as a political ideology but it falls short of providing a theoretical framework capable of describing and analysing the process of incorporation of national characteristics into hegemonic struggle. The opening of a debate on ideology which contains the potential to resolve these problems can be found in the work of Althusser and subsequent elaborations and critiques (Boswell et al. 1986). Consequently, it is proposed to examine some of these contributions in order to arrive at an informed statement of the link between class, ideology and nationalism.

Althusser: the structuralist perspective

Within the argument developed in *For Marx* (1969) and *Reading Capital* (1970), several important concepts are raised by Althusser in the attempt to establish the relationship between the elements of the social formation. A number of these concepts have proved valuable in attempts to theorize the relationship between base and superstructure and have become widely accepted elements of Marxist theory, despite some of the problems associated with the work of Althusser.[7] Of particular importance have been the concepts of structural causality and relative autonomy.

To understand what is meant by these terms it is necessary to locate them in the development of Althusser's theory and to determine the ways in which they contribute to an understanding of the relationships which exist between base and superstructures. If base and superstructure are seen as two ends of a continuum, Althusser, like us, is concerned with 'what happens between them'. Althusser argues that the three forms of human action or practice, the economic, the political and the ideological, represent three separate but interrelated 'levels' or 'instances' of the social formation.[8]

His primary assertion is that the relationships between these levels is highly complex and cannot be described by the linear causality associated with economic determinism. Rather we have to recognize the structural or 'metonymic causality' (1970, p. 188) in which the three levels of the social formation exist. By structural causality is meant a relationship of reciprocity in which each structure is neither dependent on, nor independent of, the others. Each can be said to determine the structure of the others and in turn to be determined by them. Each level or instance of the social formation constitutes the conditions of existence of the others. For example, it is impossible to envisage a capitalist social formation without a politico-legal system which guarantees property rights (Abercrombie *et al.* 1980).

This structural causality is analysed in *For Marx* as 'over-determination' (McLennan *et al.* 1978). In orthodox Marxism it is the contradictions in the economic base which, in their causation of the recurrent crisis of overproduction, lead to a revolutionary conjuncture. Althusser argues instead that contradictions exist in all levels or instances of the social formation and that the economic contradictions alone cannot produce the revolutionary situation.[9] Althusser refers to the economic contradiction as the 'general contradiction' and argues that the contradictions in the other levels of society cannot be reduced to mere phenomena of the general contradiction but identifies them as:

> ... radically heterogeneous — of different origins, different
> sense, different *levels* and *points* of application — but which
> nevertheless 'merge' into a ruptural unity, we can no longer talk
> of the unique power of the general 'contradiction'. (Althusser
> 1969, p. 100)

These additional contradictions are derived from conditions within
the superstructures having their own 'consistency and effectivity'. For
the revolutionary conjuncture to occur these contradictions must come
together with the general contradiction. They must become a unity in a
process of 'condensation' in which the general contradiction is only part
of a structure and totality of contradictions:

> The 'contradiction' is inseparable from the total structure of the
> social body in which it is found, inseparable from its formal *con-
> ditions* of existence, and even from the *instances* it governs; it is
> radically *affected by them,* determining, but also determined in
> one and the same movement, and determined by the various *levels*
> and *instances* of the social formation it animates; it might be
> called *overdetermined in its principle.* (Althusser 1969, p. 101.
> Author's emphasis.)

Althusser gives to the superstructure a major role in determining the
form of the social formation. The superstructural instances do not arise
simply and directly from economic relations but exist also as the 'necessary conditions of existence' of the basic economic relations of the
mode of production. In the coming together of the general contradiction
and the superstructural contradictions the outcome of that specific combination is determined not by one of them, but by all of them acting in
complex unity. The economic level is not the sole determining level of
the social formation. The political and ideological superstructures are
seen by Althusser to be 'relatively autonomous' and cannot be read directly from the economic relations in the social formation.

Several important conclusions can be drawn from this discussion. The
first, and perhaps most important, is that politics and ideology are not
mere epiphenomena of class relations. The form of politics and the
content of ideology cannot be simply reduced to the objective interests
of the two great classes, opposed to each other by the terms of the
general contradiction. Secondly, given their relative autonomy, it is
possible for politics and ideology to contain elements of non-economic
or extra-economic relations. Finally, the political and ideological levels
of the social formation are themselves also important sites of class

struggle. We shall see below , however, that Althusser failed to develop fully these implications of his theoretical discussions (Boswell *et al.* 1986).

In the formulation of the concepts of structural causality and relative autonomy Althusser has done much to distance Marxism from cruder forms of economism. However, if he is to retain the central basis of historical materialism, then he must retain some degree of materialism. He must eventually recognize a greater role for the base than the superstructures. This he provides in the discussion of the 'last instance'. Within the structural causality or overdetermination discussed above, the levels or instances of the social formation are also arranged into a hierarchy of 'domination and subordination' (1969, p. 201). In a given social formation one level will have the dominant role. However, for Althusser it is the economic instance which determines this 'structure in dominance'. Which level of the social formation is dominant is determined by the economic instance.

This point can be illustrated by reference to the feudal mode of production in which the means of production are represented by land. In that it is owned by the non-producer but controlled by the direct producer there is no actual guarantee that sufficient surplus will be produced to be appropriated by the landowner (Craib 1984). The guarantee of surplus appropriation is secured in the ideological and political levels which establish the duties of the serf to his lord and legitimize them in religious and moral values backed by the legal use of force (Benton 1984). Thus it appears that it is the superstructures which dominate the feudal social formation but that capacity to determine is assigned to them by the economic level in 'the last instance'.

Within this formulation it is relatively easy to lose sight of the role of the base and credit the superstructures with autonomy especially when Althusser's qualifying phrase 'the lonely hour of the last instance never comes' is considered (1969, p. 113). This qualification is not a denial of the determining role of the economic level but is stating that it never exists in its pure form; it is always overdetermined:

> the economic dialectic is never active *in the pure state;* in History, these instances, the superstructures, etc., are never seen to step respectfully aside when their work is done or, when the Time comes, as his pure phenomena, to scatter before His Majesty the Economy as he strides along the royal road of the Dialectic. From the first moment to the last, the lonely hour of the 'last instance' never comes. (Althusser 1969, p. 113)

Althusser is not denying the determination by the economic in 'the last instance' but is reminding us that we have to consider the 'real causal efficacy' (McLennan 1978, p. 80) of the superstructures within the complex overdetermination of the social formation. This should not be taken as an attempt to autonomize the superstructures.

There is in the work of Althusser a systematic, if complex, analysis of the relationship between base and superstructures. If it is complex, it is because what he seeks to explain is complex. The simplistic and crude explanation offered by 'vulgar Marxism' is rejected in favour of an analysis of a structured whole, characterized by the principles of overdetermination and structure in dominance. These insights provide a significant advance in Marxist theory and effectively re-emphasize the dialectical relationship between base and superstructures, dismissing the economistic interpretations which dominated Marxism in the Stalinist era.

Ideology in Althusser's theory

Althusser's structuralist framework considered above underpins his writings on ideology. His earlier concern with ideology is in the context of a consideration of the role of philosophy and the development of epistemology. Specifically, he analyses the relationship between science and ideology (Benton 1984). These aspects of his work will not be reviewed here but instead, his theory of the constitution of subjects will be highlighted.[10] Of particular importance to an understanding of Althusser's theory of ideology is the essay *Ideology and Ideological State Apparatuses* (Althusser 1971b). The text is pivotal in that it develops some of the insights of *For Marx* (1969) and *Reading Capital* (1970), but additionally subjects those works to self-criticism (Benton 1984, McLennan *et al.* 1978).[11] As such it represents the clearest exposition of Althusser's concept of ideology.

In the *Ideology and Ideological State Apparatuses* (ISA) essay Althusser was concerned to redress some of the imbalances of his earlier writings. In particular it was an attempt to create a place for human agency in his theory. One of the principle faults of the structuralist perspective is its relegation of the human subject to a passivity determined by its role as the 'bearer of structures'. In the works considered so far there is little opportunity for the emergence of oppositional ideologies or for the class struggle itself. The ISA essay is an attempt to theorize ideology as the 'site' of class struggle.

The argument of the essay hinges on the concept of reproduction in that all modes of production have to reproduce the conditions of their existence. It is necessary to reproduce the 'productive forces' and the 'existing relations of production' (Althusser 1971, p. 124). Of the former it is the reproduction of labour power which is crucial and necessitates its reproduction on a day-to-day basis as well as a generational basis. More importantly it requires the reproduction of the skills and knowledge required in the production process. However, for Althusser the most important aspect of reproduction is that of the 'submission to the rules of the established order' (p. 127). The workforce is reproduced in a way which subjects it to the dominant or 'ruling ideology' (p. 128).

This element of reproduction is secured at the level of ideology. Althusser distinguishes between 'ideology in general' and 'particular ideologies' (1971, p. 150). The former, for Althusser, has no history in the sense that it is always present in history, ideology is universal or 'eternal'. In contrast, 'particular ideologies' can only be understood in context; they are always expressive of 'class positions' (p. 152). Yet he argues that an understanding of particular ideologies is dependent on a theory of ideology in general, that is, on the understanding of the process of reproduction of the relations of production.

His theory of ideology in general is developed via the exploration of the characteristics of ideology. A key departure from orthodox Marxism and notions of 'false consciousness' is that, for Althusser, ideology has a material existence (Hirst 1976). Its materiality derives from its existence in the practices and rituals of the various ideological apparatuses of the social formation. Rather than being a false representation of reality, consciously propagated by the ruling class, ideology is seen by Althusser as a 'representation of the imaginary relationship of individuals to their real conditions of existence' (p. 153). Applying a dualism of 'illusion/allusion' Althusser argues that individuals' world views are 'largely imaginary' — they are an 'illusion', yet they 'allude' to reality. They are an 'imaginary representation of the world' (p. 153). However, ideology is more than a simple false or imaginary representation of reality. Rather, ideology is an imaginary representation of an individual's *relationship* to the real world.

> What is represented in ideology is therefore not the system of the real relations which govern the existence of individuals, but the imaginary relation of those individuals to the real relations in which they live. (Althusser 1971, p. 155)

Central to this analysis of ideology is the process by which individuals acquire their 'imaginary relations to the real relations'. Althusser sees this as secured in the process of 'interpellation' or the constitution of subjects.

For Althusser, ideology interpellates or 'hails' individuals, constituting them as subjects in the process. Additionally, given that ideology has no history — it is omni-historical or 'eternal' (p. 152) — then 'individuals are always-already subjects' (p. 164). Individuals are born into an identity, a place in the structure, predetermined and 'pre-appointed' (p. 165). Additionally, this process contains a relationship of 'subjection' (p. 169). In the 'Subject/subject' pair[12] the subject is seen to be constituted in two senses, firstly, as 'free subjectivity' and secondly as 'subject being, who submits to a higher authority' (p. 169):

> the individual is interpellated as a (free) subject in order that he shall submit freely to the commandments of the Subject, i.e. in order that he (freely) accept his subjection. (1971, p. 69)

Ideology takes its 'concrete' form in the ideological state apparatuses. It is interpellation, expressed in the rituals and practices of the ideological state apparatuses, which constitutes individuals as subjects.

Such subjects suffer a dual recognition/misrecognition in that they recognize themselves in the hailing by the dominant ideology which addresses them as subjects. However, given that the hailing represents only 'an imaginary representation of the individual's relationship to the real', it also involves a misrecognition, a failure by the subject to see its subjection. Consequently, in ideology subjects believe themselves to be free whilst freely submitting themselves to the relations of production. In Althusser's words, the subjects 'work all by themselves' (p. 169). The few 'bad subjects' who rebel are dealt with by the repressive state apparatuses.[13]

Thus in Althusser's essay there is an analysis of ideology in general and the mechanisms of its reproduction. Althusser presents a sophisticated theory of ideology, particularly in his exposition of interpellation and the constitution of subjects. However, it is in the process of developing these ideas that we lose sight of the strengths initially identified with Althusser's framework.

It was suggested earlier that Althusser, in rejecting economism through the concepts of structural causality and relative autonomy, had opened a space for a disconnection of class, ideology and politics. It was also suggested that Althusser had enabled the recognition of the role of non-economic or extra-economic elements in politics and ideology and that, in addition, the political and ideological levels were important sites of class struggle. The implications of these conclusions for an analysis of nationalist ideology are self-evident. On the basis of these early insights it could be suggested that nationalism is an ideological construct with its origins in the relatively autonomous superstructures and bears no direct relationship to the class struggle of the general contradiction. It is, however, likely that its existence would be dependent on an articulation with the class struggle and, in keeping with the arguments derived from Gramsci in the previous chapter, we would expect the nationalist ideology to be a hegemonic strategy adopted by a class or class alliance.

Unfortunately, the insights which suggested that such conclusions were possible bear little fruit in the ISA essay. Here there is a strictly defined process of the reproduction of the dominant ideology. Despite the intentions of the essay and the assertions in the Postscript, we find no analysis of the mechanisms of class struggle and the processes by which oppositional ideologies can emerge (Thompson 1978). The 'always-already subject' differs little from the socialized individual of structural functionalism (Benton 1984). In this revision as much as in *For Marx* and *Reading Capital* the human subject has no role; the subject remains a 'bearer of structures'.

For Hirst (1976), this is a consequence of the inherent economism in Althusser's theory, which survives in spite of his intentions to analyse the role of the superstructures. For Hirst, if the ideogical superstructure is relatively autonomous it must 'effect a real determination' (1976, p. 395). This must mean that classes themselves are:

> formed and transformed by the conditions of the political repre-
> sentations and its effects, and by ideological social relations.
> (Hirst 1976, p. 395)

This criticism is echoed by Thompson (1978) in his discussion of the formation of classes in the process of struggle. For Thompson, classes are constituted by economic relations of production in conjunction with the actions of those classes as agents of change struggling over 'their antagonistic interests' (1978, p. 106–7). Instead, Althusser provides a formulation of ideology as a secondary level which merely fulfils the functions required by the reproduction of the relations of production. Althusser has stepped back from the concept of relative autonomy to a straightforward determination of the ideological level of the social formation by the functional requirements of the economic base.

To summarize, the functionalism inherent in Althusser's work reduces the potential of his framework adequately to present a theory of politics and ideology which recognizes sufficiently the relative autonomy of the superstructural levels. It has, however, given us the terms of the debate and the conceptual framework in which to theorize these problems more effectively (Callinicos 1976).[14] It is only through discussion of the problems raised by Althusser's analysis that progress can be made toward an adequate theory of ideology.

A partial resolution of the problematic absence of class struggle and agency in Althusser's theory is offered by the work of Nicos Poulantzas. Whilst ultimately restrained in the same way as Althusser by the structuralism of his writings, a number of his arguments provide useful elaborations of the discussion raised by Althusser (Boswell *et al.* 1986).

Poulantzas's theory of ideology

Poulantzas is more concerned with the analysis of ideology at the level of classes than with the issue of individual subjectivity (Boswell *et al.* 1986). More specifically, his theory brings political forces to the fore-front of the analysis to an extent which Althusser had failed to achieve, despite his intentions in the ISA essay (Meiksins Wood 1986). Poulantzas goes a long way towards providing a theory of class struggle and its relationship with ideology.

In *Political Power and Social Classes* (1973) Poulantzas departs from a simple distinction between ideology in general and particular ideologies, distinguishing instead two 'levels' of ideology. The one level can be seen as the dominant ideology which reproduces the social relations of production in much the same way as identified by Althusser. The other level is represented by the ideologies of specific classes and 'sub-ensembles' of ideologies relating to class fractions and minor classes. This latter form of ideology is derived from lived experiences of the social relations of production.[15] The picture Poulantzas paints is of a complex structure or 'ensemble' of ideologies in which the specific class ideologies exist in a sub-ensemble in which they dominate other ideologies but also take on some of their elements. In this way ideologies are never pure but are 'contaminated' by other class ideologies. Additionally, each of these class ideologies is dominated by and articulated with the dominant ideology, which coincides most closely with the interests of the dominant class. The relationship between dominant ideology and dominant class is not one in which the dominant class fabricates and propagates the dominant ideology but instead derives from the role of the dominant class in the reproduction of the relations of production. The structure of economic relations produces both a dominant ideology and a dominant class, the latter representing the effects of the structure 'in the field of class struggle' (1973, p. 209).

This formulation allows a separation of the dominant class from the dominant ideology. For Poulantzas, the dominant ideology never exists in a 'pure' form but is always contaminated by the ideologies of 'the various classes in struggle' (1973, p. 209). The dominant ideology, as well as containing the interests of the dominant class, will also contain elements of oppositional ideologies inserted by the outcome of class struggles. In this way the ideology of welfarism in contemporary capitalism can be seen as a consequence of struggle between the working class and capital in which the concessions gained are consolidated into the dominant ideology of advanced capitalism.

This conception of the dominant ideology moves us further from the economistic definition offered by Althusser and gives an active role to the class struggle in the determination of the ideological level of the social formation.[16] Rather than ideology simply reflecting the economic relations of the base, the concept of relative autonomy takes on some flesh in Poulantzas's work and the political and ideological levels can be seen to bear real influence in the social formation. This increased autonomization of the ideological and political instance is also demonstrated in the way in which Poulantzas discusses the process in which one of the ideological 'regions' comes to dominate the ensemble of ideologies.

The concept of hegemony plays a central role in Poulantzas's discussion of the reproduction of the social formation. For Poulantzas, the dominant ideology obscures the relations of production by limiting the 'horizon' (1973, p. 207) of subjects, preventing them from penetrating their misrecognition of exploitative class relations. Instead, they see the world as a 'lived experience' which is 'obvious but false'. Social cohesion is the result (Clarke et al. 1978). Ideology reflects rather than creates the social unity of the social formation. In this sense Poulantzas retains a distance between himself and the 'humanism' of Gramsci in that, for him, the concept of hegemony in Gramsci's work overstates the role of ideology (Boswell et al. 1976). For Gramsci hegemony can be seen to create a world view which dominates the social formation by reproducing its unity. Hegemony secures reproduction of the relations of production through its leadership of the people and by securing 'consent'. In such a formulation there is little space for the emergence of oppositional ideologies. By contrast, Poulantzas argues for the recognition of one particular ideological region as dominant over all others. That region carries the role of obscuring class relations from individuals. In the capitalist mode of production it is the 'juridico-political region' which has this role and achieves it by representing the interests of the dominant class as universal interests shared by all 'individuals/agents of production'. The state in capitalism thus presents itself as class neutral and takes the form of a 'popular-national-class state' (p. 133). Individuals see themselves as free agents rather than as class subjects.

This then is a more complex relationship between class and ideology than can be found in the work of Althusser. Building on Althusser's conclusions, Poulantzas presents a less economistic theory of ideology which allows for the contamination of ideologies by other ideologies. Ideologies do not exist in a pure state, derived genetically from class positions. More importantly, his work points to the role of class struggle in the determination of ideologies; these cannot be read directly from the economic relations of the base but arise from the outcome of struggle between fractions within the primary classes and between the classes themselves. Furthermore, the subject is no longer inserted into the social structure as an 'always-already constituted subject' restrained by the dominant ideology and unable to derive any oppositional ideas. Instead the lived experience of the subject creates a localized, ideological region which corresponds to the individual's class location. In this latter sense, the work remains economistic in that the ideological regions always represent a class or class fractional location in social relations. Poulantzas has not extended the autonomization of the superstructures to the point where non-class world views are recognized as part of the ideological regions. Poulantzas has, however, moved the theory of ideology much closer to that point.

The ability to introduce non-class ideologies into the analysis has formed the basis of the work of Ernesto Laclau which has culminated in recent years in his theories of post-Marxism. For Meiksins Wood (1986) the process of autonomization of the superstructures begun in the work of Althusser and Poulantzas is completed in the post-Marxism of Laclau and Mouffe and in the writings of Hindess and Hirst. Meiksins Wood (1986), Bocock (1986) and Geras (1987) see Laclau's work as a rejection of Marxism and the basic premises of historical materialism.[17]

Laclau and a theory of class-neutral ideology

Laclau attempts to move further along the Althusserian road of relative autonomy and explore more fully the relationship between ideology and class. His concern, like Poulantzas, is more with the particular ideologies of classes than with ideology in general (Boswell *et al.* 1976).

Whilst recognizing the significance of Poulantzas's work to the discussion of politics and ideology (Laclau 1977a) he also identifies remnants of economism in Poulantzas's theory of ideology. In particular he is concerned with the identification by Poulantzas of ideologies as class ideologies, without exception. In Poulantzas's framework the various 'sub-ensembles' of ideologies reflect class positions and are determined by the lived experiences of structural positions. Ideologies always have a class character in the work of Poulantzas.

Laclau develops this criticism of Poulantzas in an analysis of the latter's *Fascism and Dictatorship* (Poulantzas 1974). He is particularly concerned to criticize Poulantzas's identification of nationalism as an inherently bourgeois ideology. In his essay *Fascism and Ideology* (1977b), Laclau supports the anti-fascist strategies of the German Communist Party (KPD) and their mobilization of nationalist sentiments as a basis of a popular alliance against fascism in the 1930s. Poulantzas (1974) rejects these policies as producing, after 1928, debilitating concessions to social democracy, parliamentarianism, and the bourgeoisie. For Poulantzas, such strategies resulted from a 'completely mistaken conception of the steps and turns of the struggle' (1974, p. 157) as well as theoretically misguided policies.

In contrast, Laclau accepts the validity of alliance strategies in a clear attempt to theorize the policy of alliances identified with the developing Eurocommunism of the early 1970s (Meiksins Wood 1986). The justification of these policies requires a further dislocation of class and ideology from that encountered in the work of Poulantzas. Laclau offers an alternative perspective which finally resolves the presence of class reductionism in Marxist theory of ideology. Whilst retaining the Althusserian notion of interpellation, Laclau argues that all ideologies interpellate, not just the dominant ideology. Consequently, oppositional ideologies exist which resolve their antagonism with the dominant ideology in the class struggle.[18] In this sense the ideological domain becomes the major site of class struggle. However, most importantly, as well as class ideologies there also exist non-class interpellations, for example 'popular-democratic' ideology. Non-class interpellations 'have no meaning in themselves' (p. 102) until they are inserted into the dominant discourse. Thus the elements of ideology are class-neutral but are always articulated with class ideologies; the class ideology represents an organizing principle articulating and assigning effects to the various components or 'elements' of a discourse.

Laclau counterposes his argument with a traditional reductionist view which claims that

> all ideological content has a clear class connotation and any contradiction can be reduced — through a more or less complicated system of mediation — to a class contradiction. (Laclau 1977b, p. 105)

To illustrate his views he points to the difference between an analysis which only recognizes the contradictions between bourgeoisie and proletariat, determined by the mode of production, and the complexity of a social formation with a plurality of classes derived from the articulation of more than one mode of production. In the latter instance, the most important determinant of struggle is the alliance of a number of dominated classes — 'the people' — against the dominant class — 'the power bloc' (p. 107). Laclau replaces the primacy of the class struggle in Marxist theory with 'popular-democratic struggle'. He has autonomized the superstructures, moving the analysis from the relations of production to the 'ensemble of political and ideological relations of domination' (p. 108).

This clearly represents a major departure from orthodox Marxist analysis and has caused controversy in its more developed form found in Laclau's most recent work (Laclau and Mouffe 1985). Laclau and Mouffe's ideas have been identified as a 'new revisionism' (Meiksins Wood 1986) and 'anti-Marxist' (Geras 1987). The central argument of Laclau and Mouffe is a refutation of what they regard as essentialism in Marxist theory, that is, the reduction of all explanation to the economic relations of the mode of production. They expose Marxist theorists, one by one, to a critique which identifies the economism of their theories. Only Gramsci is credited with almost breaking with economism in his theory of hegemony, which unfortunately reveals 'an inner essentialist core' (Laclau and Mouffe 1985, p. 69) when subjected to the searchlight of anti-essentialism.

For Laclau and Mouffe, Gramsci's work represents a watershed in the development of the concept of hegemony in Marxist theory. It moves beyond the association of the term with mere 'class alliances' identified with Lenin and representing forms of political affiliation between classes. Instead, Gramsci's usage of hegemony brings the ideological implications to the fore by seeing hegemony as a 'collective will' which cements together the 'historical bloc'. This transcends the limited, political implications of Lenin's usage of hegemony and creates a concept of hegemony as 'intellectual and moral leadership'. Ideology rather than politics becomes the 'terrain' of hegemony (Laclau and Mouffe 1985, p. 69). More importantly for Laclau and Mouffe, Gramsci sees political agency as the product of 'collective wills' rather than classes. However, Gramsci ultimately fails to develop a full theory of hegemony by his insistence on a relationship between class and hegemony.

> Nonetheless, the entire construction rests upon an ultimately inco-herent conception, which is unable fully to overcome the dualism of classical Marxism. For Gramsci, even though the diverse social elements have a merely relational identity — achieved through ar-ticulatory practices — there must always be a *single* unifying principle in every hegemonic formation, and this can only be a fundamental class. (Laclau and Mouffe 1985, p. 69)

Their project is to rescue the concept of hegemony from this essen-tialism.

If Gramsci maintains a recognition of an organizing principle in the social formation, they reject its existence. For them, the social formation is open, as opposed to 'sutured', in that there are no underlying, universal laws of economic or other origins which determine the nature of the social formation. The social formation is the consequence of permanent negotiation, conflict and struggle between groups which are not reducible to classes. In a final dissociation with the base/ superstructure metaphor, ideology as a level of the social formation is discarded in favour of the 'symbolic' constitution of the social formation in discursive practices.[19] The final break from Marxism has occurred and a new conception of hegemony is presented. Hegemony becomes an articulating ensemble permitting the coming together of diverse and unrelated elements of discourse and consequent 'subject positions'. Hegemony serves to articulate these diverse elements, modifying and combining them in the process. Hegemony becomes the vehicle of historical change rather than classes.

In common with many critics of this position it must be said that Laclau and Mouffe's Post-Marxist tendency to render the world as a chaos of unlinked and contradictory discursive practices which have no organizing principle with which to make sense of them, offers no opportunity to advance either social theory or socialism. The criticisms of their position are too numerous to deal with here and have been presented effectively and convincingly by other commentators.[20] It is sufficient here to identify those elements of Laclau's work which contribute to a theory of ideology but do not necessarily contain the logic of development found in his most recent work with Mouffe.

Of particular relevance to our discussion of nationalism is the debate with Poulantzas in which Laclau argues for the recognition of the class neutrality of nationalist ideology. This is an important insight which goes a long way to giving theoretical rigour to the political prescriptions identified in the work of Gramsci in the preceding chapter. Laclau offers a distancing of Marxist theory from the remnants of class reductionism in Poulantzas's work whilst at the same time retaining the basic premises of Marxism, that is, determination in the last instance by the economic. In *Fascism and Ideology* Laclau achieves a theoretical complexity which reflects the actual complexity of the social formation. It is indeed important to identify the class-neutrality of elements of ideological sub-ensembles as long as their articulation within, and by, class ideologies and practices are fully recognized. At this stage of his theoretical journey he avoids the extreme conclusions of his later work. Further autonomization of the ideological instance would not be supported.

Theories of ideology and the analysis of nationalism

The purpose of examining theories of ideology in detail was to attempt to define the link between ideology and class and to fit the analysis of nationalist ideology into that relationship. Here is a summary of the basic claims regarded as essential to a theory of ideology:

1) The social formation is a complex structure best represented by the recognition of three instances or levels: the economic, the political and the ideological.
2) The relationship between these levels is one of structural causality or overdetermination.
3) The economic is determinant 'in the last instance' in that it assigns places to the three levels in a hierarchy of domination of the social formation.
4) There is a distinction between the dominant ideology and the ideology of the dominant class. The former is a product of class struggle and never exists in pure form.
5) There is a distinction between class ideologies and non-class ideologies but that the latter are always articulated with the former.

These claims are seen as necessary for the creation of an effective theory of ideology which gives full credence to the relative autonomy of the superstructures and the full recognition of the role of class struggle.

Tracing the development of theories of ideology has identified a number of arguments which can inform an analysis of nationalism. The conclusions drawn above have clear implications for a deeper understanding of nationalist ideology and its role in social formations. The primary conclusion based on the above discussion is that nationalism can be recognized as a class-neutral or non-class interpellation centred on issues of language, culture, religion and ethnicity or race. Nationalist ideology will combine these factors in the creation of a national identity which is mobilized politically by social classes. Given its class neutrality, nationalism cannot be identified as an inherently bourgeois ideology, a status frequently assigned to it in Marxist theory.[21]

Rather, nationalism is a 'free floating' ideological element which can be appropriated by classes and class alliances which are both hegemonic and counter-hegemonic. Nationalism will always be articulated with class struggle; it has no independent class connotation. In the case of its articulation with a dominant ideology it will constitute one element of the ideological reproduction of the social formation and its relations of production. In such instances it will reinforce or substantiate a representation of the nation as a homogeneous whole, undivided by class. Nationalism creates a national will, constituting individuals as national subjects rather than class subjects and consequently represents a crucial underpinning of the hegemony of the dominant class. In this sense nationalism has constituted a fundamental element of bourgeois ideology. However, this should not lead to its identification as a necessarily bourgeois ideology.

The alternative role for nationalism is as an ideological element of a counter-hegemony, that is a movement of opposition to the dominant class and its moral and political leadership. Nationalism in this context is an important cement of class alliances providing an ideological basis for the neutralization or suspension of class antagonism, permitting classes to ally themselves to a common objective. However, such alliances go beyond political combination and nationalism can provide a hegemonizing influence by which one class dominates the alliance and establishes its moral and intellectual leadership. In this can be seen the reasons for the diversity of the nationalist doctrine and its articulation with conservative and revolutionary movements. The form a nationalism takes will depend on which class is hegemonic in the structuring of an alliance. Nor is the hegemonic role static within class alliances but is a process of constant, internal struggle within the counter-hegemonic movement itself.

The image of nationalism arrived at here is of an ideological element articulated with class ideologies as part of the class struggle within social formations. Nationalism will represent the 'original' and 'unique' (Gramsci 1971, p. 240) characteristics of the social formation. In this sense we have come full circle in ratifying and confirming the ideas of Gramsci in relation to the national question. Gramsci's arguments developed from his analysis of Italian politics and his prescriptions for socialist strategy have been inserted in a more rigorous, theoretical discussion but remain largely unchanged. The adoption of his concept of hegemony in the work of Poulantzas and Laclau has allowed Marxism to reduce its dependency on more economistic theories of ideology and politics. Gramsci's work has had a significant role in the development of Marxism in recent years, building towards a more sophisticated analysis of the social formation and the relations between its levels or instances. It is ironic that the concept of hegemony should form such an important element of 'Post-Marxist' theory with its denial of many of the central assumptions of Marxist analysis, which are fundamental to the work of Gramsci.

To summarize, it is here claimed that nationalism represents a class-neutral ideological element which, when articulated with class ideologies, derives a class connotation and is inserted in the class struggle. As such, nationalism is not outside the class struggle but is part of it, but cannot be reduced to a specific class ideology. A full understanding of nationalism is therefore dependent on the recognition of its class-neutrality in conjunction with its articulation with class ideology. This suggests that there can be no universal theory of nationalism but rather a broad analytical framework which constitutes a method of enquiry. This method recognizes the 'uniqueness' of each nationalist ideology and its approach depends on an analysis of the complex class relations in a social formation. The analysis must lay bare the bases of class struggle and the role that nationalist ideology has to perform in that process. The site of investigation encompasses the economic, political and ideological levels of the social formation, yet at the same time recognizing that economic relations of classes constitute the organizing principle within the social formation. The remainder of this book applies this method to the analysis of a specific nationalism, in order to assess its validity and ability effectively to explain the emergence and persistence of Welsh nationalism in the nineteenth and twentieth centuries.

CHAPTER 4

THE MODE OF PRODUCTION, CLASS AND ETHNICITY IN NINETEENTH-CENTURY RURAL WALES

It was suggested in the previous chapter that nationalism is best seen as a class-neutral ideology which acquires class connotations when inserted into the class struggle within a social formation. In this sense nationalism cannot be identified as a specific class ideology but an ideological element which can be mobilized by varied classes and alliances of classes within the context of hegemonic struggle. Nationalism plays an important role as an ideological cement in the formation of class alliances whereby classes and fractions of classes can combine in political alliance but, more importantly, can achieve a synthesis of their ideological values and political objectives establishing a political and ideological force which is not directly reducible to the economic interests of a specific class. It is these claims which will be tested in the remainder of this study. The first testing ground will be the emergence of a Welsh ethnicity and political nationalism in the nineteenth century. This first expression of Welsh nationality is of crucial significance in understanding contemporary Welsh nationalism, both as a point of origin and as a point of comparison. Contemporary expressions of ethnicity in Wales retain much of this earlier expression and yet differ significantly in a number of ways.

The nineteenth century in Welsh history is characterized by the resolution of the tensions between feudalism and the increasingly dominant capitalist mode of production. The process of transition from feudalism to capitalism reaches fruition as the social relations of the feudal mode of production are gradually dominated and eventually transcended by capitalist relations of production in both the rural and industrial sectors of the economy. It will be suggested that the nineteenth-century expression of national sentiment arises out of the conditions of this transformation in Welsh society. At a superficial level this appears as the effects on the social formation of the industrialization process. However, the real site of analysis is a Welsh social formation undergoing the more significant process of change involved in the development of the capitalist mode of production.

A superficial investigation might lead to the identification of two discrete arenas of class struggle. The first, in the rural economy, represents a struggle between a landed élite and peasant direct producers engaged in political struggle centred on the control of land. The second arena is confined within the boundaries of the emergent industrial economy, a struggle between developing bourgeois and proletarian classes. Such a view is, however, far too simplistic and relies on a dualism which divorces rural social change from urban social change and more significantly separates the feudal mode of production from the capitalist mode of production at a time when in reality they are intimately linked. There existed in nineteenth-century Wales a complex unity which tied the developments in the industrial, manufacturing economy to changes in the social relations of agricultural production. The contradictions identified in the Welsh feudal economy are only resolved through the intervention of social forces which have their origin in the capitalist sector. In short, in this period of transition the various elements of feudalism and capitalism are not in a state of irreconcilability but conjoin to form a complex social formation which contains the contradictions of two modes of production.

In order to sustain these claims it is necessary to present the theoretical framework within which the analysis takes place. This exercise represents a continuation of the debates engaged in Chapter 3 by the development of one particular concept of the Althusserian body of literature, namely that of mode of production, and the related concept of articulation.

Modes of production and their articulation

One of the most systematic attempts to define the term 'mode of production' and the related concept of articulation is to be found in the contribution of Étienne Balibar to *Reading Capital* (Althusser and Balibar 1970). In his essay 'Basic concepts of historical materialism' Balibar is concerned to give substance to the 'abstract concepts' of Althusser's earlier analysis. He begins by presenting a picture of the centrality of the concept of the mode of production within Marx's historical materialist method. The concept represents the starting-point from which the complexity of the social formation can be clarified. He identifies two related applications of the concept in Marx's writings; what Balibar terms as 'diachronic' and 'synchronic principles' or:

... the principle of *periodization* and the principle of the *articulation of the different practices* in the social structure. (Althusser and Balibar 1970, p. 204. Author's emphasis)

The diachronic principle of periodization segments history into a series of 'epochs' consisting of identifiable economic structures in which the fundamental components of economic organization are related in differing ways. If all social structures contain 'an economic base, legal and political forms and ideological forms' (p. 204) as invariate elements, then different modes of production bring them together in varying relationships with each other. History can be identified as a series of different modes of production separated by periods of revolutionary transition.

The 'synchronic principle' looks inside this conception of the mode of production to describe the articulation of links between the invariate elements.

> The principle of the articulation of the practices refers to the construction (Bau) or mechanism of 'correspondence' in which the social formation is presented as constituted out of different levels (we shall also speak of them as instances and practices). Marx lists three: the economic base, the legal and political superstructures and the forms of social consciousness. (Althusser and Balibar 1970, p. 204)

Balibar maintains that Marx's application of the concept of mode of production never achieves more than mere description. Marx's limitation lies in his inability to address anything other than the classicist problematic of periodization. Marx simply approaches the problem of periodizing history from the novel criterion of economic organization — merely substituting a new criterion for periodizing, rather than realizing the potential of transcending the need to periodize.

Similarly, the 'synchronic principle' contained in the mode of production concept remains 'remarkably vague' in its evaluation of the relations between the various levels or instances of the social formation serving only to separate the economic structure from the other instances and to identify it as Marx's specific target for more detailed analysis. In contrast, Balibar sees the task of contemporary Marxism as the analysis of the 'plurality of instances' in the social formation:

> ... the problem of the science of society must be precisely the problem of *the forms of variation of their articulation*. (Althusser and Balibar 1970, p. 207. Author's emphasis)

At this point in the discussion Balibar introduces the possibility of the co-existence of several modes of production within a single social formation.[1] Consequently, analysis of 'concrete social formations' necessitates analysis not only of the articulation of its various levels, but also of the hierarchy and structuring of the levels of the other modes of production which are identified within it. In other words, a social formation is a unity which arises from the complex interplay between the economic, politico-legal and ideological instances of several modes of production articulated within the same social formation. It is the totality of this complex process of overdetermination which must be grasped if effective analysis of social formations is to be achieved. For Balibar, Marxism has engaged in analysis of social formations as expressions of single modes of production and has failed to recognize the consequences of the articulation of several modes of production within the social formation. This crucial insight will be developed more fully below, but for now we wish to consider Balibar's discussion of the characteristics of modes of production to enable full recognition of the salient features of the nineteenth-century Welsh social formation we are about to analyse.

Balibar is interested in 'the determination of the criteria for the identification of a mode of production' (p. 209). Firstly, he extracts from Marx's writings what he calls the 'elements' of a mode of production which can be seen as universal. These are identified as, firstly, the 'labourer or labour power', secondly, the 'means of production' and thirdly, 'the non-worker, appropriating surplus-labour' (p. 212). These elements can be found in all modes of production but with different relations to each other. For Balibar, it is the form that these relations or 'connexions' take which designates the mode of production. He identifies two 'connexions'.

The first 'connexion' is termed 'separation/property' and signifies that there is a relationship between the labourers, their labour and the non-producer. In capitalism labour does not belong to the labourer but to the capitalist, as it is the capitalist who sets the labourer to work. In this sense we can speak of a social relation of production in which workers are separated from their labour which becomes a commodity owned by the capitalist. The second 'connexion' identified by Balibar is termed the 'real material appropriation'. To use capitalism as an example once again, the product of labour does not belong to the labourer but to the non-producer, and is appropriated in the form of surplus value appropriation. It is the nature of this appropriation, its mechanisms, which further defines the mode of production. It can be pictured as the extent to which the direct producers are autonomous in relation to the non-producers, or whether or not they can set their own labour in motion. Thus Balibar presents a conceptualization of the mode of production as a complex duality of relations between its constituent elements.

In the capitalist mode of production we can identify a coincidence of the property 'connexion' and the material appropriation 'connexion'. In capitalism, labour power is the property of the non-producer and the labourer is incapable of setting his or her own labour in motion without the non-producer. By contrast, in feudalism the direct producer occupies the land and sets his or her labour in motion. The possession of the means of production by the direct producer necessitates the practice of extra-economic coercion to maintain the appropriation of surplus labour. In feudalism this coercion exists in the political sphere which takes on the appearance of the determinate level of the social formation. However, that apparent capacity to determine has been assigned to the political instance by the connections between the various elements in the economic level of the social formation. It is the nature of the 'separation/property' and the 'real material appropriation' connections which makes the political level determinant. In short, for Balibar it is the economic mode of production which is always determinant 'in the last instance'.

The elements and their relations within the mode of production which will inform the analysis of nineteenth-century Wales have been identified. However, before moving on it is necessary to open a little further the insight mentioned earlier into the process of articulation of a plurality of modes of production within the single social formation. What begins as a footnote (p. 207) in Balibar's opening pages has become a central feature of contemporary Marxist theory.

The mode of production debate was initially developed in the context of what has been described as 'economic anthropology' (Clammer 1978) and in particular with reference to the writings of Claude Meillasoux and the subsequent discussion of his work by Pierre Phillipe Rey and, in Britain, Hindess and Hirst (Benton 1984). This initial debate centred primarily on the discussion of pre-capitalist societies and the validity of applying Marxist concepts in analysis of lineage- and kin-based societies. Whilst this general discussion is not of direct relevance here, one specific aspect of that debate is essential to an analysis of social change in nineteenth-century Wales. Earlier, brief reference was made to Balibar's discussion of the articulation of several modes of production within a single social formation. For Balibar, the complexity of the relationship between the economic base and the corresponding superstructures is rendered more complex by the potential existence of parallel base and superstructure relations which derive from the existence of other modes of production within the same social formation. For Balibar, the articulation of two or more modes of production is essential to the analysis of the process of transition between modes of production.

Orthodox Marxism conveys a teleological process of social change whereby each mode of production contains within it the 'seeds of destruction' which result in the transformation of one mode into another.[2] Thus, for example, feudalism is replaced by capitalism when its own conditions of existence are said also to bring about the conditions of its dissolution. Each mode of production contains a contradiction which is irresolvable and culminates in a rupture of the social formation. More recently, the implicit teleology of this simplistic view of transition has been rejected and more sophisticated theories of transition have emerged.[3] Two basic positions can be identified.

The first, most clearly stated by Hindess and Hirst (1975), argues that transition can only be achieved by the destruction of one mode of production and its replacement by another. They claim that there exists an irreconcilable clash between the conditions of existence of separate modes of production which prevents their co-existence within the same social formation.

> Thus a social formation in which the conditions of existence of the feudal mode of production are present and continue to be re-produced cannot, at the same time, be responsible for producing the conditions of existence of the capitalist mode of production. (Hindess and Hirst 1975, p. 263)

Only the more limited 'elements' of one mode of production can co-exist with another in the same social formation. However, they deny that this implies that transition can only be achieved during an 'irrational hiatus' (p. 263) — a social formation without structure where the basic elements of economic activity have been suspended (Benton 1984).

> Social production as a whole is not suspended while we wait for transition to take place. (Hindess and Hirst 1975, p. 264)

They also reject the concept of a transitional mode of production which they identify in Balibar's writings. They claim a transitional mode would begin its existence with its termination already temporally defined. For them the idea of a transitional mode contradicts the concept of the mode of production itself in that modes of production, in their existence, also reproduce themselves and have no natural or universal tendency toward dissolution. For Hindess and Hirst a transitional mode is by definition one which contains the conditions of its dissolution; such a view is historicist and teleological. Similarly, they reject Balibar's formulation of the non-correspondence between relations and forces of production in transitional modes of production. Acceptance of the existence of a correspondence between the two precludes the existence and analysis of variations in the forces of production.

> If there is to be a unitary correspondence of the form of organization of the labour process (the productive forces) with the mode of appropriation of surplus-labour (the relations of production), then the variable features of the labour process cannot be pertinent to the concept of the mode of production. Thus the variations will appear as *real*, empirically given, variations from an *ideal*, or theoretical model: the mode of production is then seen as an ideal type. (Hindess and Hirst 1975, p. 267)

So again, for these authors, Balibar's formulations are reduced to teleological correspondence, a product ultimately of his application of structural causality. The concept of structural causality in Althusser and Balibar creates 'Spinozistic eternities' (Benton 1984) which preclude transition. For Hindess and Hirst, Balibar is attempting to theorize something which cannot exist within his general theoretical framework. Therein lies the source of his errors. They conclude there can be no general theory of transition.

Benton (1984), however, defends Balibar against these charges on several grounds; firstly in that his approach does not employ a concept of transitional modes of production as identified by Hindess and Hirst. Particularly, his discussion of the 'articulation of two or more modes of production within a single social formation' (Benton, p. 132) provides a means of theorizing transition which avoids the teleology identified by Hindess and Hirst (Benton 1984, p. 130). This brings us to the second general position on transition within contemporary theory. This is a rejection of the notion of irreconcilability between modes of production and an argument instead for their articulation. Benton makes several claims for the validity of this position. Firstly it allows analysis of transition without resort to a general theory of transition.

> Secondly, the concept of articulation of modes allows for the possibility that economic and social reproduction may be continued throughout more or less extended historical periods of transition. (Benton 1984, p. 130)

This, for Benton, avoids the trap of having to choose between the 'chaotic hiatus' rejected by Hindess and Hirst or a 'momentary spasmodic dissolution and restructuring' (p. 130) which Benton believes Hindess and Hirst are committed to by their insistence on the irreconcilability of modes of production.

Thus Benton defends a theory of transition which sees it as a result of a complex process of articulation of modes of production in which the existence of one mode and its reproduction of itself also has effect on the other modes in the social formation, either reproducing them or bringing about their dissolution. For Benton:

> The central theoretical point is this: there is absolutely no theoretical necessity that practices which reproduce one mode may not also have effects which contribute to the reproduction of another. Co-existing modes may contribute to one another's preservation or dissolution, depending on the specific features of the articulation and its dynamics. (Benton 1984, p. 132)

Transition now becomes the result of a complex interplay of different modes of production and their corresponding ideological and political instances. Transition takes place, not as a teleological assertion or an evolutionary process but as the open result of the particular patterning of overdetermination within this, now even more complex, social formation.

Generally, the outcome can be seen as a relationship of changing subordination and domination of one mode of production by another. An emergent mode is initially reproduced by an existing mode but gradually becomes self-reproducing and in the act of self-reproduction eventually brings about the necessary conditions for the dissolution of the original mode of production. Foster-Carter (1978) identifies this position in the writings of Pierre Phillipe Rey who, he claims, sees three stages in the penetration of capitalism into the pre-capitalist social formation.

> (i) an initial link in the sphere of exchange, where interaction with capitalism *reinforces* the pre-capitalist mode; (ii) capitalism 'takes root', subordinating the pre-capitalist mode but still making use of it: (iii) — not yet reached in the Third World — the total disappearance of the pre-capitalist mode, even in agriculture. (Foster-Carter 1978, p. 218)

This debate gives us a theoretical point of entry into the concrete analysis of nineteenth-century Wales. However, much of the literature on articulation has emphasized the economic dimensions of the process, especially in the area of development theory. Here in keeping with Rey's purposes (Foster-Carter 1978, p. 217–18) we have expounded this line of thought to illustrate political and ideological processes. The following analysis of nineteenth-century Wales as a period of transition will attempt to draw out the political and ideological linkages between feudalism and capitalism which emerged in the articulation of the two modes of production. Of particular interest will be the implications of such a complex pattern of overdetermination for the formation of class alliances between the feudal, agrarian sector and the capitalist, industrializing sector.

Social class and ethnicity in rural Wales

In keeping with the theoretical framework developed, the analysis of ethnicity in nineteenth-century rural Wales starts with a consideration of the class structure of the rural economy. Unfortunately, such an analysis is severely hampered by the paucity of material on the rural, Welsh class structure. The traditional concern has been with the material conditions of rural life with particular emphasis on the study of housing, diet and social life. Until recently few Welsh historians adopted a perspective which seeks explanation of such aspects of rural life in the economic relations of production.[4] Consequently, it has been difficult to engage in a well-informed analysis of class in the nineteenth-century rural economy. What follows is a tentative mapping of the primary social classes visible.

The most significant factor in the determination of rural class formations is the pattern of ownership and usage of land (Barrington-Moore 1967, Paige 1975). In the agrarian economy, land represents the means of production, and its ownership — and the consequent relations of production — largely determines the boundaries and divisions of the class structure. In a pure model of feudalism two classes present themselves for analysis, a landed class and a class of peasant direct producers. However, recognition must be given to the complexity of the social formation, particularly in the ways in which class elements and economic relations survive from previous modes of production. In the Welsh context much has been made of the effect of the tribal system of tenure on the ownership and control of land in the nineteenth century. Without denying the influence of this historical legacy, it is necessary to place the level of influence in perspective and analyse its role carefully to filter out the inherent symbolism that the tribal heritage conveys in nationalist imagery.[5]

The first point to stress is the early incorporation of much of what is now recognized as Wales into the English legal and economic system. Although the conquest of Gwynedd in 1282 and the Act of Union of 1536 have major symbolic value as signalling the death of Wales, the process of subjugation and incorporation began with the Norman Conquest. Then, large areas of the border counties were taken into the Norman Settlement. In such areas the manorial system was quickly imposed, endowing the new masters with virtual sovereign rights, for all intents and purposes independent of the Crown (Williams 1919). Within these Marcher areas both the traditional practices of inheritance by gavelkind and the developing practice of primogeniture coexisted, causing some confusion (Williams 1919). Under the tribal system, gavelkind theoretically divided land equally between sons upon the death of the father. However, the constant fragmentation of holdings created considerable pressure to adopt the 'English' custom of primogeniture. The result was a duality of practices.

> Naturally as there were one hundred and forty three Lords Marcher exercising semi-regal authority in various parts of Wales great diversity of law and practise prevailed. Primogeniture pre-vailed in some lordships while in others the old Welsh system of gavelkind survived. In some lordships the two systems remained side by side, the eldest son inheriting in the English portions of the March, while among the Welsh subjects of the land the old Welsh custom still lingered. (Williams 1919, p. 30)

Following the conquest of Gwynedd by Edward I in 1282 the whole of Wales experienced a similar situation of dual practices. In the newly conquered areas the defeated tribal chiefs became Crown tenants with rentals fixed at that time, commuted and remaining unchanged for cen-turies. With the gradual devaluation of the silver currency these payments became nominal and, where a continuity of tenure survived, created a class of effective landowners. Rhys and Brynmor Jones argue:

> the descendants of the old tenants had remained in occupation during the three centuries following the conquest, they would have practically grown, as did English copyholders under the same circumstances, into absolute owners, charged with a merely nominal and trivial quitrent of a few pence at most per acre. (Rhys and Brynmor Jones 1900, p. 406)

Gavelkind was formally abolished in certain areas by charters issued by Henry VII from 1505 onwards as a reward for the 'loyalty of the Welsh lords' (Williams 1955, p. 27). Henry VII was also responsible for the emancipation of tribal bondsmen in the north Wales counties in 1504 and their holdings were either purchased by the bondsmen themselves or passed into the hands of the freemen and larger landowners who were better placed to afford the payments of the fines accompanying the Charters of Liberties which granted the emancipation (Williams 1955). In this gradual way the tribal system had virtually died out in advance of the Act of Union of 1536. The actual legal union of Wales with England thus represented a consolidation of changes already well established by the beginning of the sixteenth century. Primogeniture had been established in the Marches long before and the persistence of gavelkind was limited to the Welshries. Despite the perception of the Act by nationalist writers as the end of the free Welsh nation (for example, Evans 1973), it must be seen rather as a formalization and rationalization of a process of incorporation which had been under way for several centuries.[6]

This brief account has argued that the decline of the traditional tribal system was a gradual and inexorable process and cannot be attributed to the Edwardian Conquest or the Act of Union, as it is perceived in nationalist ideology. In common with similar social forms throughout Europe, feudalism had brought an end to such traditional social formations. That Wales should have been an exception to this process is an argument which is difficult to sustain. The declining significance of tribal society had begun before the Norman Conquest and the subsequent creation of the Marches greatly accelerated the process by placing large areas of Wales under external control (Williams 1955).

The major impact of this gradual process of change was that it laid down the conditions which made possible the accumulation of vast estates by the landed gentry which was to have significant effect in the class relations of eighteenth- and nineteenth-century Wales. In summary, an assessment of the impact of traditional tribal patterns of inheritance must conclude that they were of less significance to nineteenth-century rural conditions than were the results of the settlement and conquest and ultimate incorporation into the English legal system.

The legacy of gavelkind is often offered as explanation of the small size of holdings in Welsh agriculture.

> One reason for the small average size of Welsh farms lay in the system of gavelkind in the Welsh areas until Tudor times, whereby a holding was equally divided among the sons upon the death of the father. For this reason farms were generally larger in the

English speaking areas than in the Welsh districts. (Howell 1977, p. 70)

However, the early decline of gavelkind and the integration into English custom and practice calls for some qualification of this view. Howell (1977) indicates that the nature of agricultural production in Wales is not conducive to the development of large farming units. Limitations on size are imposed by the geographical conditions and the consequent emphasis on husbandry rather than tillage. This is most notable in the upland areas which coincide generally with the 'Welsh areas' identified by Howell above. It will be argued later in this chapter that the small size of holdings was a feature of the power structure in the rural economy and served to buttress the political control of the gentry by strengthening the dependency of the tenant class on the landlords.

The predominance of small, rented holdings is significant in the formation of social class in Wales in the nineteenth century, but must be placed in context if that significance is to be understood fully. Although accurate figures are not available until the Census of 1851, the findings of that Census can be taken as evidence of holding size for the first half of the century, in that changes in size would have tended toward consolidation rather than fragmentation. David Howell cites the following findings (1977, p. 21):

SOUTH WALES: 68% under 100 acres.
                      22% 100 to 200 acres.
                      10% over 200 acres

NORTH WALES: 75% under 100 acres.
                      16% 100 to 200 acres.
                      10% over 200 acres

Figures for 1875 show the mean size of Welsh holdings to be 47 acres, a figure which remains stable until 1905 (Howell 1977). Given that in Wales the dominant form of agricultural production is pasture rather than arable farming, the viability of such small holdings is highly questionable (Howell 1977). The primary agricultural activity of the nineteenth century was the raising of store cattle and sheep for the English market; consequently it was considered that a minimum of 40 acres was necessary for a holding to be viable in its own right (Royal Commission on Land in Wales and Monmouthshire, 1896, pp. 340–1). Below this size it was necessary for the tenant to engage in other activities to supplement the income from the holding. Howell (1977) cites evidence of occupants of holdings between three and twenty acres in Caernarfon and Merioneth being dependent on wage labour in the slate quarries. Alternative sources of income were found as day labourers on the larger holdings or working as skilled artisans in the wider community.

Growing out of these rural conditions was the social structure which contained the contradictions manifest in the major antagonisms between landlord and tenant in nineteenth-century rural Wales. To summarize, there was an accumulation of large estates on the part of a landlord class. This process begins with the defeated tribal chiefs acquiring Crown tenant status and slowly evolving as effective landowners. These estates are consolidated and enlarged particularly under the patronage of the Tudors, through the assimilation of monastic land after the dissolution of the monasteries, and by the Enclosure Acts of the nineteenth century. In contrast to this pattern of land ownership, the system of tenure is characterized by the distribution of the great landed estates into the hands of many tenants, each operating a small holding and suffering a standard of living little above that of subsistence farming. It is this division which provides the major contradictions and class antagonisms of nineteenth-century rural Wales and will provide the focus of the analysis below.

Class and class relations in the rural economy

If, as suggested earlier, it is land which constitutes the means of production in the rural economy, then the relations of production and the class formations will be largely determined by the pattern of ownership and control of the land. Any group which emerges in possession of the land will occupy a significant position of control and domination of rural society. This is certainly evident in Wales in the nineteenth century with the rural economy demonstrating extreme concentration of land ownership in the hands of a relatively small, landowning class which controlled vast estates throughout the Principality.

> Estates of over 1000 acres occupied 60% of the total area of the principality. This concentration of land was even more marked than in England where estates of over 1000 acres covered 53.5% of the total area. Welsh estates exceeding 1000 acres were in the hands of 571 owners which constituted a mere 1% of the total number. Within this category the squires' estates of between 1000

and 3000 acres covered 16% of the total area and those of the great landowners of over 3000 acres, 44%. (Howell 1977, p. 21)

This concentration of landownership promoted the emergence of a cohesive landed élite by the turn of the nineteenth century. A significant characteristic of this group was its close identification with the English landed classes (Morgan 1963). During the years of the Civil War the landowners in Wales had remained staunchly Royalist, largely a result of the patronage they had enjoyed under the Tudors. There was frequent intermarriage with English families and the education of their sons was primarily in the English schools and universities (Morgan 1963). Yet at the same time the landed class celebrated their Welshness, their direct lineage from the Welsh princes and their sponsorship of the Welsh arts. These landlords were frequently absent, leaving their estates in the control of agents.

> Moreover they [the landowners] were often non-resident and employed English or Scottish land agents for the precise reason that these were alien to their tenants and therefore unlikely to be favourably disposed towards them. The 'agent' remained the most detested character in the popular literature of Wales throughout the nineteenth century. (Williams 1950, p. 199)

Thus the landed class remained a very separate and visible element in the rural social formation, characterized not only by their wealth but by their Anglicization.

If the possession of land gave this class its existence then the actual use of land created the second most significant grouping in the rural economy, the tenantry. The vast majority of landlords farmed only a small proportion of their land, the greatest part of their estates being rented out as smallholdings to a tenantry. The small size of holdings occupied by these tenants has already been noted. Whilst this group was not engaged in purely subsistence agriculture, market activities were limited to the production of store cattle and sheep for the English markets together with local dairy production usually under the control of the farm wife. These market activities financed their participation in the local cash nexus, providing for the payment of rents, tithes, and the wages of labourers. Little opportunity existed for the accumulation of capital and their standard of living is believed to have been little better than that of their hired labourers.[7] The small size of holdings and the geographical conditions, particularly in the upland regions, militated against large surplus production and created limited opportunities for improvement of farming techniques. Agricultural technology in Wales was generally considered to have been a full century behind developments in England during the nineteenth century (John 1950). The poor returns from holdings often forced tenants to subsidize their incomes with economic activity as labourers in mines and quarries and on the holdings of their better-off colleagues and landlords (Howell 1977). The consequence is a blurring of the class boundaries particularly between the smaller tenants and the landless labourers.

So far the primary class boundaries between landlord and tenant have here been delineated as the most significant feature of the rural class formation. However, elsewhere considerable importance has been attached to the emergence of landless agricultural labourers as a significant and crucial element of rural class conflict. The emergence of such a grouping in the English context is well documented (Thompson 1968) and is crucial to the understanding of English rural society. In Wales the situation was somewhat different and calls for special consideration. A cloak of invisiblity appears to be drawn around the farm labourer in Welsh rural life for much of the nineteenth century.[8] Evidence of agitation and combination on the part of the farm labourers in Wales is patchy and does not convey any impression of a conscious class actively asserting its interests. When active, it was frequently in conjunction with their employer in common effort against the landlord (Jones 1973). If there was a 'rural proletariat' it could be found in the 'radical triangle' identified by Williams (1980, p. 18). For Williams, this area, with its points in Montgomeryshire, Carmarthenshire and the Valleys, was populated by 'worker-peasants' employed primarily in the early wool, cloth and textile industries which characterized the eighteenth century in the rural areas, and the industrial iron workers of the eastern valleys. Various explanations have been offered for the apparent absence of the landless labourer in Welsh rural class conflict in the nineteenth century.

Firstly, it has traditionally been argued (Rhys and Jones 1900) that the common cultural basis of life shared by tenant and farmer, demonstrated in their shared language and religion, gave to them a uniformity of purpose and opposition to the landlord class (Morgan 1963). In addition to these close cultural ties it is suggested that the predominance of indoor labour created close social ties whereby the labourer enjoyed virtual member status in the families that employed them. They lived on the premises, shared food and kitchen and a standard of living which differed little in its daily reality between employer and employee. Additionally, they may frequently have been the sons of neighbouring farmers with a not unrealistic expectation of one day possessing their own holding (Williams 1950). Whilst this explanation may be convenient for nationalist mythology and its imagery of a classless nation, it is necessary to look further for explanation of the low levels of independent political activity on the part of the landless labourer in Wales. Initially, it is necessary to consider the actual numerical presence and distribution of landless labour in the Welsh rural economy. It is clear that the small-scale nature of tenant farming provided less opportunity for the employment of labour than did the larger holdings of the English rural economy. Figures from the 1861 Census reveal that the average number of labourers on Welsh farms was 1.5 to 2 compared with 10 in the eastern counties of England and 5 in Middle England (Rhys and Brynmor Jones 1900, p. 434). There were 35,775 outdoor labourers and 82,291 indoor and household labourers in Wales: this represents a low density of agricultural labour compared with English agricultural production.

Contrary to the idealized claims that the labourers shared a common life-style with their employer and a virtual family status, the evidence of contemporary statements to various commissions of inquiry suggests that employment conditions were often harsh and tenant employers unsympathetic to the conditions suffered by the labourers (Howell 1977). Evidence of long hours and poor wages were pushed into the background by the descriptions of living conditions. Generally the sleeping quarters were in the lofts above the livestock where overcrowding and insanitary conditions were the norm. Additionally, the housing for outdoor workers was considered to be the poorest available in the country and was entirely dependent on maintaining employment. Pretty (1989) substantiates the view that labourers existed as a separate class with different economic interests from those of the tenant farmers. For Pretty, exploitative relations to the means of production, minimal rewards for labour and the lowest social standing in the rural community created a pattern of life substantially more emiserated than that of the poor tenant farmer. Yet, despite these deprivations, agitation specifically on the part of the labourers does not feature in the historiography of this period.

Despite their considerable numerical presence, many labourers were isolated from their counterparts by the geographical conditions and the distances between farms, especially in the upland regions. The small numbers employed in any one location would have effectively limited their ability to develop a consciousness of their position and organize accordingly. If we add to this physical isolation the inherent social

control of their linguistic and religious affinity with their employers and
the similarity of their lifestyles, we paint a picture of a rural labouring
class in an inherently weak position economically and with virtually no
opportunity to organize politically in its own interests. Finally, we can
add to this framework of explanation the fact that the rural economy was
by this time articulated in a complex interplay with developing centres
of industrial production. This provided an alternative source of
employment at times of acute rural hardship. In Wales it is clear that the
resettlement of rural labour began from the turn of the century onwards,
frequently at this stage on a seasonal basis, but becoming increasingly
permanent as the century progressed (Williams 1980). This relocation of
the population was to become the most significant demographic change
of the nineteenth century in Wales, with its consequent effect of rural
depopulation. This movement of people provided a potential safety
valve and aided the social control mechanism in the rural social
formation and defused potential labour unrest.

The combination of the above factors explains how the very real
contradictions between tenant farmer and landless labourer failed to
emerge in the form of a conflict of class interests between them until late
in the nineteenth century. There existed an implicit, if unconscious,
alliance between the tenants and their hired labour in which the
labourers were tied to a dependency on their employers just as they in
turn were dependent on the landowners. The depressed conditions of the
tenantry ensured the depressed conditions of the labourers.
Consequently, co-ordinated action against the landlord class was a
visible outcome. For example, in the Rebecca riots, what was initially a
tenant resistance to raised costs was frequently participated in by
labourers (Williams 1955, p. 65). Pretty (1989) suggests that such
participation allowed farm labourers to give voice to their own demands
but that their activities were 'nipped in the bud' (p. 4) by the tenant
farmers. No coherent labourers' organizations appeared until the end of
the century and the labourers remained uncoordinated and disorganized.
At least for the first half of the century, rather than thinking in terms of a
tripartite class structure of landlord, tenant and labourer, each attempting
to secure their interests as separate and active classes, it must be
considered that the labourers remained economically and politically
dependent on their tenant employers. Unable to develop a consciousness
of their objective position in the rural relations of production, the
labourers perceived their interests as being best served by the
improvement of the position of their employers. It was not until the
tenant farmers themselves overcame the power of the landlords that the

class antagonisms between farm labourers and their employers surfaced to become a central feature of rural conflict.

There were other groups with different relationships to the land from those already discussed. Although such groups had little impact on the outcome of rural class conflict in nineteenth-century Wales, some mention must be made of them. The first of these marginal groups is best described as the yeomanry, a lesser class of landowners possessing relatively small parcels of land with freehold rights. Their life-styles were very unlike those of the large landowners, and their poverty usually on a par with the poorest tenants (Howell 1977). As a group they suffered particularly during the recession which followed the Napoleonic Wars, many being forced to sell their holdings in the inflationary climate which lasted into the 1820s. Adversely affected by enclosures and unable to finance land improvements required by Acts of Enclosure, many of them sold their holdings to the larger landowners. By the 1870s, private ownership of holdings between 1 and 100 acres constituted only 10% of total land (Howell 1977, p. 21). In terms of general life-style there would have been little or no difference between this group and the tenant farmers discussed earlier.

A further social grouping which existed in nineteenth-century Wales but which had little influence on the outcome of the rural class struggle was the squatters who had generally established some use of the land in the eighteenth century. The neglected status of much Crown property had allowed the practice of *tai un nos* to flourish in some parts. According to custom, a dwelling erected overnight and possessing a lighted fire by the next day could lay claim to any land marked by an axe or other implement thrown to the compass points (Dodd 1951). Although having no legal status the practice had been approved in many parishes, as it generally relieved the burden on the system of poor relief. However, with the increasing usage of Enclosure Acts, the squatters frequently lost the entitlement to their holdings. Unable to afford legal representation and ignorant of the few legal rights they possessed, the squatters generally lost both home and land. Little can be said of what happened to such people, some becoming dependent on poor law relief, others joining the many beggars that wandered the countryside at this time (Thompson 1968). Many would have followed the same path as peasants displaced by enclosure in England and identified by Lazonick (1974): having lost their traditional means of subsistence, they were forced into the ranks of the labouring classes, either remaining as participants in the rural economy or migrating to the growing centres of industrialization. Finally, two relatively small social groups must be addressed to conclude this provisional description of the rural social classes.

Firstly, there were the servants employed by the large-scale landowners. In *Social Life in Mid Eighteenth Century Anglesey* (1936), Nesta Evans gives abundant evidence of the conditions of employment of this section of the rural occupational structure. Her studies of estate records and household diaries reveal servant employment conditions which included board, lodge and clothing, as well as cash wages. However, the latter were frequently withheld for several years at a time. Generally, this group enjoyed better conditions than their counterparts employed by the small tenant farmers. The final social group that can be identified consists of the skilled labourers and artisans of the rural community. Usually they worked on a piece-rate basis for tenants and landlords alike. They do not appear to have commanded high wages and were frequently small tenant farmers subsidizing the meagre income obtained from their holdings (Howell 1977).

Much of the literature on the primary social classes of the rural Welsh economy in this period (Rhys and Jones 1900, Dodd 1961, Morgan 1963) identifies a blurring of differences in the lower levels of the social structure with tenants, labourers and yeomanry sharing a common life-style characterized by poverty. This gives substance to the myth of a classless rural Wales identified earlier. However, we are concerned with class relations determined primarily by patterns of land ownership and control. When the economic, political and ideological relationships between these groups are analysed, their relationships to one another as classes within the context of a rural struggle for hegemony can be identified.

An analysis of the relations of production between the classes entails examination of the pattern of land ownership, control and use in order to determine to what extent these factors are responsible for the shaping of the ideological and political relations evident in the social formation.

Rural relations of production

The preceding description of the primary rural social groupings has shown the central characteristic of land distribution to be its concentration in the hands of a small landed élite. Such a pattern of land ownership creates a structure of domination and dependence between landlord and tenant familiar in many agrarian economies (Foweraker 1978) and is usually associated with a rigid political control of rural society by the landed élite (Paige 1975). These features have also been identified as characteristic of nineteenth-century rural Wales.

> In a variety of guises, as lords-lieutenants, commanders of the county militia and above all as justices of the peace they dominated the life of the countryside. They constituted in fact a ruling caste. (Morgan 1963, p. 4)

Such a totality of control is not peculiar to Wales, and similar structures of power and privilege can be identified in many agrarian economies where concentration of land ownership is maintained through rigid mechanisms of political control of the distribution of land (Paige 1975, Shanin 1971, Migdal 1974). Correspondingly, in such a social structure, the tenants are entirely dependent on the goodwill of the landlords for their economic survival. Their security of tenure is entirely linked to the satisfactory maintenance of duties, obligations and payments to the landlord class. This effectively restricts their ability to resist landlord power and reinforces the overall structure of domination and dependence.

> It is apparent from our construct that the poorest of the peasantry, and especially the great majority who are poor tenants, are the least likely to mobilize. The poor tenant and his family are totally dependent on the landlord (that is he is most completely 'immobilized') . . . (Foweraker 1978, p. 151)

Paige (1975) places this general claim in a more precise model of analysis. He develops a series of hypotheses which seek to encompass the various combinations of land ownership and use which can occur in agrarian economies. Specifically, he argues that it is the relations of production within specific patterns of land ownership and control which determine the nature and likely outcome of the conflict between the primary classes brought into existence by that pattern. Two of Paige's hypotheses deal directly with the relationship between landowner and tenant or 'non-cultivator' and 'cultivator' in his terminology.

> A non-cultivating class deriving its income from the land tends to be economically weak and must therefore rely on political restrictions on land ownership. These restrictions tend to focus conflict on the control and distribution of landed property. (Paige 1975, p. 18)

In an agrarian economy where land is the sole source of income of the non-cultivating class, increases in wealth are only achieved by increases in the quantity of land owned. If a free market for land exists the landed class suffers open competition for the acquisition of land. Competition is therefore prevented by rigid political control of the distribution of land. Furthermore, Paige argues that land tends to be appropriated from the cultivating class by practices which are legitimatized by the legal structure, which in turn is controlled by the non-cultivating class. This analysis has some bearing on the examination of nineteenth-century Wales and can inform an explanation of the conflict between landlord and tenant which, it will be argued below, is the primary source of Welsh ethnicity in that century.

Firstly, the pattern of land ownership and use appears to fit the conditions prescribed by Paige. The concentration of land discussed earlier and the consequent political control by the landlords appear to fulfil his predictions accurately. Through their control of the local political and legal institutions the landlords effectively reproduced a pattern of land ownership which gave them wealth and status. Additionally, their effective control of the state institutions of coercion, such as the local militia, placed them in positions from which they could quickly crush any organized resistance to their authority. That the landowning class was entirely dependent on land as their source of income is confirmed by Howell (1977):

> The landowners therefore lived as a class of 'rentiers' most of them deriving their main source of income from their estates in the form of agricultural rents. (1977, p. 34)

Finally, as Paige suggests, land was appropriated from the tenantry and yeomanry through the legal practice of enclosure. The enclosure of land by private act had been possible from the late seventeenth century onwards, but enclosures in Wales had been few until the nineteenth century. In the opening years of that century there was a sudden increase in the number of enclosure acts (Dodd 1951). The landowners themselves were under pressure from Crown enclosure orders and began to direct their attention to the upland areas which had traditionally been given the status of common land, used primarily by the tenant farmers as summer pasture for sheep. The use of such land had customarily been regarded as an unalienable right of the tenantry, although such rights had no legal status and were easily eliminated in the legal process of enclosure (Dodd 1951).[9] Consequently, it was the tenantry which suffered from the enclosure of common land, with rents becoming due on the sheep walks, and in many instances they suffered a total loss of grazing rights. The practice of enclosure is indicative of an emerging capitalist ethos on the part of the landowners who were beginning to recognize the higher returns that could be gained from the land. Thompson (1968) argues that enclosure

> consisted precisely in the drastic, total imposition upon the village of capitalist property-definitions . . . Enclosure, indeed, was the culmination of a long secular process by which men's customary relations to the agrarian means of production were undermined. (pp. 238–9)

This breaking down of traditional relations of production was to have crucial significance to the genesis of tenant dissent.

Thus the conditions and predictions of Paige's first hypothesis appear to fit closely the features of nineteenth-century rural Wales. An economically weak but politically dominant landlord class maintained the pattern of land distribution and usage through various mechanisms of political and legal coercion. Their survival depended on their political control of land distribution and the prevention of competition in the acquisition of land.

In this context the small size of rented holdings takes on new significance. Rather than being a vestige of the tribal system of land tenure or even a geographically imposed limitation on land usage, it can now be seen as a central feature of a land tenure system which seeks to prevent accumulation of land and capital. Small peasant holding sizes are a frequent characteristic of the political structure of many agrarian economies, reinforcing the political servitude of the peasantry and their dependence on the landowning class. In such a context, Paige argues that conflict is expressed as conflict over the distribution of land; conflict is manifest as political competition for the control of those institutions which determine the pattern of land distribution and the conditions of land tenure. However the genesis of that competition poses a central problem for the cultivating class; their total dependency on the landed élite effectively limits their ability to organize politically. Paige's second hypothesis echoes the claims of Foweraker quoted earlier:

> The greater the importance of land as a source of income for culti-vators the greater the structural isolation or dependence on non-cultivators and the weaker the pressures for political solidarity. (Paige 1975, p. 30)

Despite the overwhelming political weakness of peasant classes and impoverished tenantries, such groups do become politically active and organized, and are sometimes successful in their objective of destroying the hegemony of the landed élite (Barrington-Moore 1967). Various explanations have been offered as to how such structurally weak social groups are able to organize themselves as a class 'for itself' and organ–ize effectively in pursuit of freedom from their exploitation. Landsberger (1974) argues that to search for a 'single universally present ultimate cause' is mistaken in that far too many factors are involved. However, if there is one most frequently underlying cause, for Landsberger, it lies in

> the integration of the society under consideration into a larger, possibly international market; the consequent drive to commercialize agriculture, and the subsequent encroachment on peasant land and peasant rights and status in general. (Landsberger 1974, p. 29)

Wolf (1969) makes similar claims but goes further in his explanation of the emergence of peasant unrest which frequently ends centuries of servitude. He argues that peasant movements arise out of the impact of three great crises in rural society. Firstly, the effect of rapid demographic growth places great strain on traditional patterns of social and economic organization. Secondly, the period of population growth has historically tended to coincide with the commoditization of land and the consequent seizure of peasant lands and the capitalization of rents. These changes destroy the peasant ability to allocate resources according to traditional practices. Finally, for Wolf, these two crises converge in a crisis of the legitimacy of the landed class. What Landberger and Wolf are describing are forms of social change which challenge and break what Paige (1975) describes as the 'traditional links' which bind cultivator and non-cultivator together in a state of equilibrium.

These frameworks of explanation of rural resistance to landed interests are of considerable value in explaining the conflicts of nineteenth-century rural Wales. Many of the conditions identified in the above discussions of peasant political movements can be identified in this context. It is in the nineteenth century that many of the traditional links between landlord and tenant are finally broken, thereby weakening the political dependency of the tenantry and leading to a strong political rejection of the landlord class as legitimate authorities in the rural social formation. The conflict that arose as a consequence of these changes in rural society provided the basis for the formation of a nationalist political movement in Wales.

Until the early years of the nineteenth century, agricultural tenants in Wales had enjoyed considerable security of tenure. Leases of tenant holdings had traditionally been long-term, frequently for a period of up to three lifetimes. Thus there had existed a continuity in rural relations whereby a family developed a connection with a particular holding and its owner. The disadvantage of this from the owners' position was that rents remained fixed for long periods and were devalued over time. Increasingly leases were fixed for shorter periods with twenty-one years appearing as the norm by the beginning of the century, with rent reviews at seven-year intervals (David Williams 1955). However, the inflationary economy at the time of the Napoleonic Wars created a need for even greater flexibility in the setting of rent levels. In consequence, the practice emerged of allocating leases annually, frequently by auction. The inflationary effect of these changed leasing practices was considerable, forcing many tenants off the land. The holdings thus vacated were usually amalgamated into larger units or added to the lord's demesne. These practices created a further land shortage and fuelled the 'inflationary' spiral (Dodd 1951, p. 45). This change in leasehold practice can also be connected with the emergence of new attitudes to land and land use held by the landlord class in the opening years of the century.

Dodd (1951) identifies a 'passion for improvement' emerging, with an increasing dissemination of improved agricultural techniques. The vehicles for that dissemination were the numerous Agricultural Societies which were being formed throughout Wales at that time which

> organized ploughing matches and sheep shearing competitions, introduced new types of agricultural implements, distributed seeds, imported skilled workers. (Dodd 1951, p. 40)

This was very much a response to the high price levels commanded by agricultural produce during the Napoleonic Wars (Jones 1973), which gave rise to an increasing perception of the land as a source of potential income, additional and separate from its rent value. The high prices provided ample incentive for the landowners to improve the efficiency of land use on their estates. Jones (1973) identifies the appearance of 'spirited entrepreneurs' in the rural sector who perceived the land increasingly as a source of direct profit and wealth:

> Gold medals were awarded to 'spirited entrepreneurs' who made significant improvements on their farms. In some cases changes were made as a matter of necessity as well as inclination. Still the result was the same, there was a passion for raising rents, shortening leases, consolidating farms and enclosing land hitherto little used. (David Jones 1973, p. 7)

Thus the entrepreneurial activities of the landlords worsened the plight of the tenantry. Whilst the landlords were in a position to capitalize on the inflation of the period, the same conditions had an adverse effect on the tenantry. In particular the smallholders were unable to change to wheat production where the greatest sources of profit were to be found.

> The small tenant farmer was not so fortunate. He had been accustomed to grow mainly for the subsistence of his own household and he was not equipped with the capital for competing in distant markets. To him war meant only higher prices for farming and household necessities, higher burdens in taxation and local rates and often bigger rents. (Dodd 1951, p. 45)

In summary, the changing leasehold practice, 'the passion for improvement', the raising of rents and the increasing application of enclosure acts can be seen as symptomatic of the 'commoditization of land' identified by Wolf (1965). The conditions for the genesis of rural unrest identified above were evident in nineteenth-century Wales as it entered the final stages of its transition from feudalism to capitalism. The changing attitude to the land, outlined above, is symptomatic of the growth of a capitalistic ethos on the part of the landed élite. No longer was land seen as a source of income merely in the rent it could command, but additional sources of revenue were identified in the actual direct usage of land by the landowner.

If rural conditions such as these are identifiable as the prerequisites for peasant dissent (Wolf 1965, Paige 1975) rural Wales is not exceptional. However, in addition to these almost universal conditions, in the analysis of Wales we must be aware of the specific and unique elements of the Welsh social formation which gave the inevitable conflict its actual form and structure. Whilst these changes in the rural society broke the traditional links which bound the tenantry in a relationship of dependence on the landlords, they were not the only factor responsible for the politicization of the tenantry. These economic factors determined a fundamental and irreconcilable clash of interests between tenant and landlord, but they provided no political basis for the development of a collective consciousness of that conflict on the part of the tenantry. The economic exploitation of the opening years of that century was an exaggerated form of what had prevailed for centuries. Whilst the quickening of the pace of exploitation provided the basis for tenant resistance and particularly created such an insecurity of tenure that tenants had little to lose by declaring their opposition, the potential resistance lacked focus and there still existed no basis for a common consciousness of the tenants' position. To adopt the terminology of the theoretical framework developed in the preceding chapters, the economic clash between landlord and tenant can be referred to as the 'general contradiction' (Althusser 1969, p. 101). It is the fundamental economic contradiction between a class of exploiters and an exploited class.

However, in the context of the 'overdetermined' (Althusser 1969, p. 101) social formation, other factors in the ideological and political instances of this social formation will have a role in determining the outcome of the general contradiction. The various contradictions in the different 'levels' of the social formation must come together as a unity if a rupture in the social formation is to occur (Althusser 1969). No level on its own is the absolute determinant of the outcome of the potential conflict, which will be impeded or exaggerated by contradictions in the other levels of nineteenth-century Welsh society. However, 'in the last instance' the conflict is between classes which have their existence in the economic base of the social formation. The potential for conflict is created in the relations of production, although its form and expression may be determined elsewhere. Consequently, to understand completely the rural conflict in case, we must refer to the political, ideological and cultural levels of the social formation and examine the superstructural contradictions which exist in a relationship of overdetermination with the general contradiction.

The political and cultural relationship between landlord and peasant

Political relations

If the century begins with a hegemony enjoyed by the landed class, it closes with its complete negation. In between is a complex process in which the political structure of Wales is transformed and the vestiges of landed power are almost destroyed. It is a period in which the representation of the Welsh people in the process of government moves almost entirely from the Tories to the Liberals, and this process represents the final transcendence of feudal political structures by the popular, liberal, democratic institutions of capitalism. Of necessity, part of the analysis of this process will take place in the following chapter where the industrial regions of nineteenth-century Wales are discussed. What is charted here is the role played in this process by the implicit struggle between landlord and tenant and the conditions of that struggle which gave rise to specifically national expression of tenant political activity. The economic conditions giving rise to rural conflict have already been identified: it is now time to turn to the political conditions which gave it many of its characteristics.

The central feature of rural politics in the early years of the nineteenth century is its total domination by landed interests represented by Toryism. The larger landlords were frequently Members of Parliament for their areas and effectively controlled the local political institutions and legal structure (Morgan 1963). Theirs was a hegemony founded on the economic servitude of their tenants but also legitimized in patterns of paternalism and claims to a Welsh lineage dating back to the tribal princes. The reality of absentee landlordism and Anglicization of the landowners has already been discussed; despite this reality the legitimation remained effective in the early years of the century.

Thus there existed an overwhelming political servitude and allegiance of tenant to landowner. Despite this political servitude in the formal arena of political praxis, opposition to the landlords had been growing since the late eighteenth century. The increasing incidence of food riots particularly in the first three years of the nineteenth century was symptomatic of a growing rural crisis of legitimacy (Jones 1973). Additionally, as the difficult economic conditions worsened in the first two decades of the century, there developed increasing antagonisms between magistrates, their bailiffs and the tenantry. Increasing levels of rent debt and consequent evictions were the results of the changing conditions of tenure discussed earlier (Dodd 1951). The building of toll-gates provided an an added source of discontent which found expression in rural rioting (Williams 1955, Jones 1973):

> Many of the riots were no more than attempts to enforce a kind of natural justice. The houses and fences of landlords who coveted peoples' property were destroyed ... Obedience to the people's code was maintained by threatening letters, nightly meetings, firing of guns and visits by mobs disguised as women. (David Jones 1973, p. 61)

These rioters were predominantly small farmers, closely followed in number by agricultural labourers (David Jones 1973, p. 65). Within this general climate of unrest and disaffection more specific issues arose to weaken the political affiliations between landlord and tenant.

The most significant of these was the issue of Corn Law repeal. Most tenants were compelled to purchase corn for their own consumption and the high prices artificially maintained by the Corn Laws were a particular source of hardship experienced by an already hard-pressed tenantry. Their support for repeal was therefore in contrast to their landlords' opposition.

> The repeal agitation was in fact of great importance in the political development of the nation, for through it, Welsh nonconformism became politically articulate for the first time. Besides, the farmers were shown that their economic interests did not coincide with those of the great Tory landowners who opposed repeal and the peasantry were weaned thereby from their traditional political allegiance to the ruling families. (Morgan 1963, p. 11)

To this clash of interests can be added a fundamental resentment felt by the tenantry with regard to the payment of Church tithes.[10] This had long been a source of discontent but was exacerbated by the passing of an act of Parliament in 1836 which commuted the payments, thereby imposing an additional cash burden on the poverty-stricken tenantry. The net effect of the change was a real increase of 7 per cent in the value of the tithes paid (Howell 1977). The opposition to tithe payment is more clearly understood if it is considered that the majority of the tenantry were Nonconformist and resented paying to maintain what was described as 'Yr Eglwys Lloegr' or the 'alien Church' in Wales (Morgan 1963). Tithe riots were numerous and tithe payment remained a contentious political issue until, after a period of considerable unrest in the 1880s, the 1891 Tithe Act placed the burden for payment on the landlord rather than the tenant (Morgan 1973). However, the charge quickly found its way into rent increases although the issue lost its political significance as it was now an invisible cost to the tenant. Clearly, the tithe agitation contributed much to the disestablishment movement which was to form a central platform of Welsh political radicalism in later years.

This considerable degree of informal political opposition to the landlord hegemony eventually found its way into the formal sphere of electoral politics. In 1868 the Liberal share of the vote in the rural constituencies increased in the general election and the first Liberal Nonconformist MP, Henry Richard, was elected at Merthyr Tydfil. This event is of key significance in nationalist ideology, being regarded as the re-awakening of the Welsh nation (Morgan 1981). In reality, it represented the accumulation of social and economic change in both the rural and industrial sectors of the Welsh economy; of particular importance to this analysis, it marked the beginning of serious opposition to the landlord hegemony in the rural economy. In retaliation for their support of Liberal candidates, many tenants were evicted.

> The unwise retaliation by some Tory landlords as the reprisal for the defection at the polls greatly added to the tension of the countryside. In many parts of Wales and especially Caernarvonshire, Carmarthenshire and Cardiganshire, farmers were evicted for having thus challenged the structure of local authority. (Morgan 1963, p. 25)

Allegations of 200 evictions in Cardiganshire alone were made and the subsequent furore was largely instrumental in the establishment of a Commons Select Committee of Inquiry into election procedures (Morgan 1963). Other farmers had endured less direct reprisals, the majority suffering punitive rent increases. Thus there entered into popular culture an experience of direct physical repression. The politicization of the tenantry was in progress and the way was paved for subsequent increases in Liberal support. By the 1874 general election the balance of power in Welsh parliamentary representation was in Liberal hands with their 19 seats to 14 Tory seats. These Liberals were, however, primarily Whigs and the most significant feature was the election of three Nonconformist MPs with a further two added in by-elections in the same year. The trend continued in the election of 1880 with the Liberals capturing 29 of the 33 Welsh seats, 8 of them Nonconformists. By 1885 the Tories retained only 4 seats and only 9 MPs were identifiable with landed interests (Morgan 1963). Twenty MPs were Welsh-born, ten Welsh-speaking and fourteen were Nonconformist. This new generation of Welsh representatives are described by Morgan as 'sober, moderate bourgeois whose politics were dictated by their religion' (1963, p. 67). The existence of a distinctly Welsh group of MPs in Parliament lent itself to a unity of action in the House of Commons, and the successes of land reform and disestablishment in Ireland fuelled demands for similar legislation for Wales. The MPs identified increasingly with specifically Welsh issues, particularly the disestablishment of the Church, which was to constitute the central concern of Welsh Liberalism throughout the century. One significant event in the development of this Welsh political perspective had been the success of the Welsh Sunday Closing Act of 1881 which set the important precedent by which Parliament created law peculiar to Wales (Morgan 1963). This growing political awareness and increasing demand for Welsh legislation was to culminate in the *Cymru Fydd* movement of the 1890s, the first overtly nationalist organization in Welsh politics. *Cymru Fydd* will be discussed in more detaii in Chapter 6 when the analysis can be extended with details from the industrial sphere and its political connection with rural Wales.

Thus in the political level of the rural social formation there was an increasing politicization of the tenantry as successive links with the landed élite were broken. Gradually the domination of the landed class was weakened and the structural limitations on peasant political organization identified earlier were overcome. By the turn of the century landlordism was defeated and the political representatives of the tenant class were part of a new hegemonic alliance in Welsh politics. As predicted by Paige (1975), the struggle took place on political grounds in that the fundamental economic contradiction between these two primary rural classes had been resolved at the political level, by the eventual elimination of the power base of the landed élite. The ascendancy of Welsh radicalism in the form of the Liberal Party led to the political defeat of the landed class and thereby destroyed the mechanisms which had reproduced the system of land tenure which gave the landed class its power and status. By the end of the nineteenth century a significant redistribution of land had taken place and many of the great estates had been dissolved, usually sold to the tenants of the various holdings (Morgan 1963). Thus the economic contradiction was overlaid and reinforced by the contradictions in the political level, giving a unity of effect which heightened the process of social change in rural Wales. We now need to consider the ideological and cultural instances of the social formation in order to complete the picture and arrive at an understanding of the genesis of Welsh ethnicity and political nationalism in nineteenth-century rural society.

Ideological and cultural bases of conflict

> Superimposed on this simple economic division between the landowning and occupying classes was a growing divergence in social attitudes; the owners remained Church, Tory and English-speaking while their tenants to an ever-increasing degree were becoming Nonconformists, and radical, as well as Welsh. (Morgan 1963, p. 11)

The Anglicization of the landlords (Morgan 1963), their frequent absenteeism, their appointment of land agents (Williams 1950) and their close identification with their English counterparts (Morgan 1963) led to an ever widening social chasm between landlord and tenant. The most visible dimensions of this chasm were the differences of language and religion. The clear identification of the landed class with the Church of England and the increasing Nonconformism of the tenantry was most forcefully expressed in the resistance to tithe payments discussed earlier. Here the economic dimensions and the cultural aspects of tenant-landlord relations came together as a single source of dissent. A fundamentally economic issue of a taxation burden on an impoverished tenantry coincided with a religious divide between the two classes. The economic contradiction is overdetermined by a cultural contradiction and each reinforces the other, giving rise to political resistance in a unity of all three levels of the social formation. The issue of tithes provided a focus for the dissent in the community and provided a means of identifying the landlord class as alien and exploitative. The vehicle of resistance to landlordism was consequently Nonconformism. The political opposition was to be an opposition to an imposed religious structure, the English Church in Wales. The Nonconformist faith became the ideological basis of resistance to landlord hegemony and successfully challenged the legitimacy of the landlords' power in rural Wales.

Conventional interpretations of the conflict evident in nineteenth-century Wales have centred on the cultural and religious divisions between landlord and tenant.[11] Instead, it is suggested here that the primary division between the two groups is that of class, in that both groups occupy different positions in the relations of production within the rural economy. The basic antagonism is a clash of economic interests, or, in our borrowed terminology, the 'general contradiction' (Althusser 1969). Landlord and tenant are opposed as classes with irreconcilable economic needs. The superstructural dimension of religion becomes the ideological clothing of that economic division. The ideological dimensions of the conflict are articulated with the economic relations between the two classes and the structure in dominance of the social formation is characterized by determination by the ideological and political levels. The conflict appears to be between cultural opponents rather than class enemies. Religion becomes the site of resistance and creates a unifying and mobilizing ideology which calls a politically weak and subservient tenant class to political activity.

The growth of Nonconformism in rural Wales has traditionally been represented as autonomous and dependent only on the symbiotic relationship between the Welsh language and Nonconformism. Here it is maintained that the growth of the faith was a direct result of its ability to offer resistance to landlord hegemony. Nonconformism grew so dramatically precisely because it offered the means and the strength to oppose the landlords. It created an ideological space enabling the tenantry to step outside their dependence and subservience and to perceive the landlords as exploitative. Thus the resistance to landlordism is expressed through the vehicle of Nonconformism and the Welsh language. The imagery of resistance is of a Welsh tenantry oppressed and exploited by an English landed class. That class imposes a foreign religion in an alien language on a culturally and religiously homogeneous people, the Welsh. The discourse of tenant politics is national in character. Such was the mobilizing capacity of this ideology that the land issue was to be the election platform of Henry Richard in the industrialized constituency of Merthyr Tydfil in the general election of 1868. In his pre-election address he left no doubt of the national character of his appeal:

> The people who speak this language, who read this literature, who own this history, who inherit these traditions, who venerate these names, who created and sustain these marvellous religious organizations, the people forming three fourths of the people of Wales, have they not the right to say to this small propertied class . . . We are the Welsh people and not you. This country is ours and not yours and therefore we claim to have our principles and sentiments and feelings represented in the Commons' House of Parliament. (In Morgan 1963, p. v)

Little wonder that Richard's victory is seen by nationalists as the re-awakening of the Welsh people. Growing out of the rural conditions of the nineteenth century was a powerful force leading to the development of a nationalist political perspective. A politically weak and economically dependent class rejected the legitimacy of its oppressors and mobilized religion, language and nationhood in its struggle against landlord hegemony and political control. The resistance was enacted in the political level with a rallying call based in religion. To this analysis we have to add an explanation of the actual physical organization of tenant resistance. From where did the organizational basis for a political movement appear? The answer lies in the growth of the Liberal Party and its close identification with Nonconformism.

The mechanisms and organizational structures were provided by a Liberal Party machine the origins of which were in the industrializing sector of Welsh society and its connections with wider British political movements. The new indigenous bourgeoisie had itself an interest in ending the political supremacy of the landed élite. This emergent capitalist class was in pursuit of its own hegemony; and the feudal landed class were the primary impediment to that process. In addition to the conflict between landlord and tenant, that is, classes belonging to the feudal social formation, we find conflict between a landed class and a capitalist class, the latter being an element of the transition from feudalism to capitalism. The defeat of the landed class is a prerequisite for the establishment of a new economic, political and social hierarchy determined by the relations of production in the capitalist industrial sector of the economy. Once again this situation can be identified in the study of developing nations where the impetus for rural change and land reform derives more from the political organizations of the modern sector than it does from the participants in the rural economy (Shanin 1966). The pressure for change is frequently derived from bourgeois class groupings emerging in the modernizing sector, who have powerful motives for destroying the existing power structure and its control by traditional landed élites. For Shanin (1966), Migdal (1974) and Wolf (1965) the role of movements from outside the rural community is crucial in the development of rural protest. For Shanin (1966) 'guided political action' provides the mechanism and organization which overcomes the structural limitations on peasant mobilization. Wolf (1965) sees the emergence of new élites as an essential element of the challenge to traditional landed classes. The following chapter deals with developments in the industrializing regions of nineteenth-century Wales. It analyses the complex articulation of separate class struggle within the two identifiable modes of production which produced a temporary alliance between a Nonconformist tenantry and a Nonconformist bourgeoisie.

CHAPTER 5

CLASS AND NATIONALISM IN NINETEENTH-CENTURY INDUSTRIAL WALES: THE BASIS OF AN ALLIANCE

The previous chapter suggested that the conflict in the rural sector of nineteenth-century Wales was articulated with class struggles in the industrializing sector of the economy. Additionally, it was argued that there were dimensions of the class struggle in the rural sector which promoted the emergence of a nationalist political perspective on the part of the tenantry. It is now proposed to illustrate additional pressures in the industrial sector which predisposed the emerging bourgeoisie toward a similar political stance. These conditions created a temporary alliance between tenant farmer and the new indigenous bourgeoisie and petty bourgeoisie. In order to understand the genesis of ethnicity and the eventual emergence of a political nationalism in Wales, the totality of the process of change from a feudal, agrarian society to a capitalist, industrial economy must be analysed.

Class in early capitalist society

Theories of class in a capitalist society are discussed fully in Chapter 8. It is sufficient here to state briefly the views which inform the discussion of class in nineteenth-century industrial Wales.[1] The earlier discussion of the mode of production identified labourers producing surplus value and non-labourers appropriating that surplus value. In the capitalist mode of production we can identify, at the abstract level, two classes resulting from this relation of production.[2] The identification of two antagonistic classes, bourgeois and proletarian, founded on the relations of production, establishes the nature of the primary contradiction in capitalist society.

However, when the analysis moves from an abstract level to a consideration of a specific capitalist social formation the picture is complicated by additional classes. In keeping with the earlier discussion of the articulation of modes of production in nineteenth-century Wales, we expect to find classes with their origins in the declining feudal economy as well as classes originating in the emerging capitalist economy, whether in the agricultural or industrial sectors. The surviving feudal classes engaged in increasingly capitalist agricultural production in nineteenth-century rural Wales have been discussed, and the analysis now proceeds with a discussion of the emerging classes of the industrial sector.

Class in nineteenth-century industrial Wales

The seat of industrialization in Wales has been located in Merthyr Tydfil with the enormous growth of metal manufacture in the early years of the nineteenth century (Williams 1980). Smith (1980) describes entering Merthyr from the north at that time as a journey 'in time as well as space' (p. 216) as the traveller left the rural environment and entered the confusion of what was little more than a shanty town, thrown up around the ironworks. However, this was not necessarily a journey between feudalism and capitalism. Williams (1980) paints a picture of the proletarianization of large sectors of the rural work-force, identifying a 'radical triangle' (p. 18), encompassing Montgomeryshire, the south Wales valleys and Carmarthenshire and Pembrokeshire in the west. He also identifies the complex articulation of different modes of production:

> A plurality of modes of production co-existed within a country measuring scarcely 200 miles from end to end, to generate a bewildering response. Each mode of production produced its own working population; each working population had to live with others and with a rural population of peasants and worker peasants in complicated interaction. (1980, p. 23)

Despite his broad application of the term 'mode of production', Williams correctly identifies the complexity of the Welsh social formation at this time.

At the opening of the nineteenth century, although wage workers could be identified in both agriculture and industry it was too early to identify a unified Welsh working class (Williams 1980). Where political unrest materialized it was sometimes a combination of industrial and agricultural workers. Jones (1973) describes the Corn Riots of 1793–

1801 as 'a movement of industrial wage-earners, artisans, village craftsmen and small rural property owners' (p. 92). Nor was the conflict easily reducible to one between wage-earners and capitalists. Rather, the targets for protest were the corn merchants and petty bourgeois traders. However, Jones (1973) points to the active and militant role played by colliers in the riots. The first decade of the nineteenth century is in fact too early to attempt a distinction between agricultural and industrial workers. Jones identifies the recent origins of those colliers in the rural economy:

> When the agricultural labourer migrated to the mining villages and factory towns his character was said to have undergone a transformation . . . it must have been a swift change for it was the colliers recently recruited from the Welsh farms who were responsible for much of the violence of this period. (Jones 1973, p. 202)

Similarly, many workers belonged to both the agricultural and the industrial spheres of production, working seasonally on farms and in mines and iron works (Williams 1980).[3]

The conditions which brought a Welsh working class into existence developed in the first two decades of the nineteenth century, which were years of rapid social, economic and political change as Wales responded to the emergence of manufacturing capitalism. The major social change was demographic — an increase and relocation of the Welsh population. A flood of immigrants from the rural to the industrializing areas transformed the population distribution. From the predominance of the rural market towns in the seventeenth century, the focus of Welsh life shifted to the rapidly growing centres of population at the heads of the valleys and on the southern coastal plain. The greatest centre of growth was at Merthyr Tydfil which developed from a small village in 1750 to the 'metropolis of south Wales' (Jones 1973, p. 152) with a population of 22,000 by 1831.

It is at Merthyr Tydfil that Gwyn Williams (1978, 1980) identifies the first serious political consequences of these changes in Welsh life with the emergence of a 'visible and audible' (1980, p. 24) Welsh working class.[4] For Williams, the 1816 miners' strike, the Scotch Cattle skirmishes of the 1820s and the workers' adoption of parliamentary reform demands were all embryonic forms of working-class consciousness which coalesced in the Merthyr Rising of 1832. It is in Merthyr Tydfil that the emerging class structure of manufacturing capitalism first appears. In contrast with the increasingly conscious and organized working class were the ironmasters living their very separate and different lives in their fortress-like mansions. Much of the investment of the period had been of external origin. Minchinton (1969) claims the expansion of the iron industry had been made possible by '. . . the skills of Midland iron masters and the finance of London merchants like Anthony Bacon and Benjamin Hammet and Bristol merchants like the Harfords and Reynolds, Getley and Company' (p. xvii). The resident ironmasters represented the pinnacle of the local class structure, often imitating the life-styles of the Welsh gentry. Jones (1973) writes of their provision of finance for the building of 'halls, markets, chapels and schools and entertaining men on special occasions in the manner of country squires' (pp. 88–9). Between the masters and the men were the administrators and overseers of the iron production. Plant managers and their foremen were powerful figures in the community representing a 'small middle class' (Jones 1973, p. 89). Frequently English or Scottish immigrants, they remained distinct from the general community in terms of language and religion as well as occupational status. Whilst they might objectively be identified as part of the working class, they were identified subjectively by themselves and those they commanded as of a very different social standing.

Constituting the middle classes with these ironworks managers were a range of local shopkeepers and petty bourgeoisie, who were, however, distinct from them politically and culturally. Frequently of local origin, these shopkeepers occupied a central place in the articulation of demands for electoral reform. In the 1830s these were the radicals of the Merthyr Tydfil community; for Gwyn Williams (1980) they were Unitarian and Jacobin. They articulated the demands for Reform and in these early years were allied to the working class and instrumental in the fomentation of unrest leading to the Merthyr Rising of 1832 (Jones 1973). Their relationship with the working class was however ambiguous and short-lived and will be discussed in detail below.

So a class structure can be identified, determined, to the greatest extent, by the developing relations of capitalist, manufacturing production. However, it is possible to underestimate the differentiation in even this early capitalist social formation. Williams (1980) identifies sixteen categories of skilled and unskilled occupations in iron manufacturing alone, with the skilled workers articulating the demands of the emerging working class. Similarly, coal extraction had its own hierarchy of skills, creating a complex division of labour in the industrialized areas (L. J. Williams 1980).[5]

Overlaid on this pattern of class relations were superstructural elements of language and religion as changing patterns of immigration into the industrial districts began to change the linguistic, ethnic and religious mix of the community. In this period of rapid change, developments in the class structure were inevitable. Minchinton (1969) identifies a second stage in the industrial development of south Wales: the opening of the Rhondda coalfields. Whilst the capital for the expansion of iron production had been of external origin, the coalfield was financed by local capital. The petty bourgeoisie emerging out of the first phase of development had now accumulated sufficient capital to become members of a Welsh bourgeoisie (Morgan 1963). Still largely Welsh-speaking and Dissenting in religion, their promotion to the capitalist class easily fractured the fragile alliance that this class once had with the nascent working class. It is out of these conditions that the basis for an alliance between the Welsh bourgeoisie and the rural tenantry emerges.

Bourgeois/proletarian relations

The relations that existed between the bourgeoisie in Wales and the working class changed considerably during the course of the nineteenth century. It opened with a temporary and fragile alliance between the two nascent classes and ended with them irreconcilably divided. In between lay the birth of both nationalist and radical working-class political practices.

As stated previously, the initial capital for investment in, and expansion of, iron production, was of external origin (Minchinton 1969). Inevitably, opportunity for capital accumulation grew in the vicinity of the ironworks in parallel with the growth of the iron industry itself (L. J. Williams 1980). Local traders, artisans and shopkeepers benefited from the rapid population increase and the trade it brought them. Williams (1980) identifies them as petty bourgeois and radical. Dissenters by religion, many of them were Unitarians, rejecting the Anglicanism of the ironmasters and the landed gentry. Williams celebrates the radicalism of this group and their support for working-class demands as well as the parliamentary reform demands which were of more direct benefit to them. It is the issue of religious Dissent which provides the key for understanding the relationships between this class and the proletariat as well as their link with the rural tenantry.

The role of Nonconformity

Nonconformity provided at various times ideological cement for alliances between objectively antagonistic classes. This was true, initially at least, of the relationship between the nascent working and bourgeois classes. The role it played was dynamic, changing as the structure of the class system developed toward that associated with the domination of the social formation by capitalist relations of production. Nonconformity was distinctly rural in its origins, travelling to the industrial areas with the wave of immigrants at the opening of the nineteenth century (Davies 1965). Williams (1980) suggests that the adherence to the familiar religious practices of the rural communities might have provided continuity of experience in times of considerable change. Initially, in the emerging industrial communities, Nonconformist beliefs were spread by itinerant preachers travelling a circuit between rural and industrial society. However, settled ministries were appearing in these areas by the turn of the century and the period is characterized by the rapid growth of Nonconformism in the industrializing south.

Assessment of the actual levels of support for Nonconformity at this time is very difficult. There is a general lack of statistical evidence and what little exists is frequently coloured by the exaggerated claims of rival denominations. Wilkins (1867) describes in some detail the substantial increases of chapel-building during this period but unfortunately gives little indication of membership levels. The numbers of places of worship do not give a very useful surrogate measure as the proliferation of chapels in these early years of Nonconformity owed as much to minor disagreements between the chapel hierarchies as it did to the search for spiritual enlightment by the population. Wilkins (1867) provides details of denominational schisms developing over the appointment of ministers, the settling of chapel debts and the respectability of places as seats of worship. More theological arguments also created fragmentation, especially the issue of Sunday labour in the ironworks. Some of the chapels resulting from this fragmentary development had as few as three members (Wilkins 1867), indicating the exaggerated impression it is possible to derive of the level of popular commitment to religious Dissent.

More reliable data is available from 1840 onwards. A report of the Committee of the Council on Education cited by Davies (1965) records that, in 1840, in the parishes of Bedwellty, Aberystruth, Mynyddislwyn, Trevethin and Merthyr Tydfil there were 11 Established churches compared with 93 Nonconformist places of worship. Furthermore, 80 Nonconformist Sunday schools were in operation alongside only 6 provided by the Established Church. It can be surmised that Nonconformity had a substantial following in these communities.

That impression is confirmed by the results of the Census Sunday of 30 March 1851. In his analysis of the findings of this survey, Davies (1965) presents an image of Wales as significantly influenced by Nonconformity but not to the extent the findings initially suggest. The findings suggested that some two-thirds of the population of Wales belonged to Nonconformist denominations. Davies, however, expresses qualifications to those claims which can be summarized as follows:

1) The census enumerated attendances not membership. Nonconformist denominations held two Sunday services in comparison with the one held by the Established Church.
2) The census did not distinguish between members and adherents. The latter were usually referred to as 'hearers' (*y gwrandawyr*). Davies claims they were often infrequent attenders and just as likely to belong to clubs and benefit societies which often met in public houses and swore secret oaths condemned by the ministers of Nonconformism.

Thus, the Census Sunday findings are unreliable. Illustration of this can be gained by considering that the figure for attendances at Calvinistic Methodist chapels that day in Monmouthshire was 8,867, yet their self-disclosed membership in the same area one year later was only 2,067. Similarly the Independents recorded 17,660 attendances on Census Sunday yet disclosed a membership of only 7,459 ten years later, following a period of population growth (Davies 1965, p. 38). These figures hint at the most significant feature of Nonconformity, that is, the sporadic nature of popular adherence. Nonconformity is identified by Davies as primarily revivalist in nature. He writes:

> Throughout the nineteenth century, and into the first decade of the present century, Welsh Nonconformity in these industrial districts generated a revivalistic atmosphere. Religious revivals were endemic in these parts. (1965, p. 55)

He claims many of these revivals were linked to cholera epidemics, outbreaks of the disease promoting higher chapel attendances in the affected areas. He also notes that the Census Sunday followed closely on the cholera epidemics of 1849. Finally, he quotes the Revd Evan Price, writing before the revival of 1859:

> The meetings in the week were largely forsaken and on Sundays the empty pews were more suggestive of a timber yard than a congregation. (Davies 1965, p. 59)

That Nonconformity represented the most significant form of worship for the emergent working class is undeniable. However, that claim must be qualified to the extent that we recognize the alternative institutions and social practices that existed and drew support from the working population. The working class of this period were not a homogeneous Nonconformist congregation; nevertheless Nonconformity was of considerable influence culturally and politically in this period. Substantial numbers of the working class would have been in contact with the cultural practices and ideology of Nonconformity in one of its denominational forms.

To analyse the relationship between Nonconformism and the working class necessitates the recognition of its dynamic nature. Not only does it vary between denominations, but it also alters through time as the class positions of Nonconformist leadership and membership become polarized. In the early years of industrialization the emergent nature of the class structure renders such an analysis difficult. In the 1820s and 1830s an element of Nonconformist support for the Merthyr Rising and subsequent Chartist demands can be identified. This support was, however, limited to the Unitarian movement and needs some qualification.

The radicalism of the Merthyr Unitarians was a significant contributory factor to the 1832 rising at Merthyr Tydfil. Jones (1973) claims:

> The Merthyr workmen had shown a lively interest in politics in the previous weeks. Perhaps the Nonconformist ministers . . . had influenced the workmen . . . The most radically minded section of the Merthyr population was indeed the Unitarians of Heolgerrig and Georgetown on the West side of town. (p. 154)

Williams (1980) supports this view and clarifies the commanding position leading Unitarians occupied in the local political hierarchy. As shopkeepers, artisans and small property owners they supported the reform demands of the period. It was they who would benefit from the extension of the franchise. Additionally they articulated free trade demands, placing them firmly in the radical tradition which would crystallize as radical Liberal Nonconformism. Williams (1966) writes:

> They played the same role here as they did in Birmingham and Manchester, they were the mainspring of Reform . . . They embraced the most dynamic sector of the new middle class of the town. (p. 14)

However, despite their radicalism and their apparent role in the fomentation of unrest prior to the 1832 rising, their actual participation in the events was non-existent, although Williams (1966) argues that their general support is indicated by their disappearance when it became likely they would be enlisted as Special Constables to control the rioting.[6] However, subsequent Unitarian support for Chartism points to a continued radicalism within this denomination in the period of working-class organization following the Merthyr Rising.

Unitarianism represented the closest links between a petty bourgeoisie and a nascent working class. Their common antagonism with the ironmasters of the Merthyr community necessitated close co-operation in the class conflicts of this period. More generally, Nonconformists did not ally themselves with working-class demands, demonstrating indifference if not direct antagonism.

> It is well known that Welsh Nonconformity was antagonistic to the early workers' unions and benefit societies which played an important part in industrial life in the last century. (Davies 1965, p. 76)

Apart from predictable attacks, including those from ministers related or connected to the ironmasters, [7] many speeches, articles and sermons condemned the activities of the labour organizations. Much of the initial antagonism derived from the oaths of secrecy demanded by the early unions and benefit societies.[8] The antagonisms heightened when worker organizations became a threat to the stability of the local communities and to the chapels themselves. For many Nonconformist leaders, Chartism was too extreme a movement to command their support.[9]

> Chartism shook many congregations in industrial Monmouthshire to their foundations. The democratic spirit, characteristic of independency, was carried to excess, to the detriment of law and order. The movement brought to the fore a type of leader who disturbed the peace of congregations and in some places strained the relationship between pastors and their flocks. (Davies 1965, p. 78)

More generally, the relationship between Nonconformism and working-class organization was one of indifference. As a movement, Nonconformism was preoccupied by its temperance campaigns and the more fundamental objective of the disestablishment of the Church of England in Wales. These were the twin concerns of Nonconformism by the second half of the nineteenth century.

In this first phase of industrial development we find a new middle class rising in Welsh society to occupy the prime social and cultural positions in the Nonconformist churches and society generally. Their radicalism encompassed support of freedom of worship, association, electoral reform and free trade but, with the exception of the Unitarians, did not extend support to the working-class demands of Chartism. It is in the second phase (Minchinton 1969) of industrial development that the hegemony of this Nonconformist élite becomes established as its class position develops into that of an indigenous bourgeoisie.

It has already been suggested that a large proportion of the capital for the opening of the Rhondda coalfields originated from the petty bourgeoisie which had accumulated capital from its provision of services and supplies to the ironworks and their workers.[10] It was local entrepreneurs who dominated this second phase of industrialization (Minchinton 1969). The Nonconformist petty bourgeoisie now became fully bourgeois, owners of capital and direct exploiters in their own right. The new positions of civil authority in the developing local and central state system were theirs for the taking (L. J. Williams 1980). They emerged as Welsh-speaking, Nonconformist Liberals, leading Welsh radicalism into its most successful years.

This rise of an indigenous bourgeoisie was also matched by a lessening in the radicalism of the Welsh working class.[11] With the demise of Chartism, working-class politics became intimately connected with Nonconformity and its leadership, despite the objective class antagonisms that relationship obscured. In effect, the new Welsh bourgeoisie had achieved a relatively unchallenged hegemony with Nonconformism operating as its ideological cement. Williams (1980) points to the cultural nationalism of this hegemony. Nonconformism celebrated its Welshness, the language of worship was Welsh and the cultural practices of an imagined past were cultivated and extended, creating what Williams calls 'Dissenting populism' (1980, p. 41). The culmination of this 'awakening' was the election of the first Nonconformist Liberal MP at Merthyr Tydfil in 1868. Despite the industrial character of his electorate, Henry Richard's campaign had been based on the plight of the rural tenantry and had articulated opposition to the Anglicized characteristics of the landed gentry.[12]

There were additional pressures in south Wales toward the emergence of a nationalist perspective. After 1860 the characteristics of immigration into south Wales changed considerably. The rural hinterland could no longer satisfy the increasing demand for labour and immigrants from further afield began to arrive in vast numbers. Between 1881 and 1891 63 per cent of the new arrivals in Glamorgan were

English-speaking (Davies 1965, p. 153). The symbiotic relationship between the Welsh language and Nonconformist worship was inevitably weakened by this influx. The decline of the Welsh language began to erode the social basis of Nonconformity. Attempts were made to stem the decline in Nonconformism by adopting the English language as the medium of worship. As early as 1807 the Baptist denomination had implemented an Anglicization programme with bilingual Sunday schools and English-language preaching instruction at its Abergavenny Theological College (Davies 1965). However, Davies argues that as the identification between the Welsh language and Nonconformism weakened, much of the attraction of the faith evaporated; it was no longer so distinct from other religious movements.

Similarly, as the century progressed, the hegemony of the Non-conformist bourgeoisie was additionally weakened by the growing radicalism of the work-force. By the 1880s socialism was attracting the Welsh working class (Morgan 1981) and increasingly the legitimacy of the Liberal coalowners as the representatives of the mine-workers was being challenged (Stead 1980). Such organizations as those then emerging had always been regarded as, in some way, 'unWelsh'. Of earlier stirrings of working-class consciousness Wilkins (1867) had written:

> About the stirring time of 1831 the Trades Unions principle was introduced amongst the workmen. It is to Englishmen we are in-debted for most innovations and to this in particular. (p. 305)

Despite the clearly localized nature of the Merthyr Rising and the indigenous character of the participants, the myth of English agitation contributed to the explanation of events.[13] Later, in 1839, the pastor of the Baptist Tabernacle at Pontypool claimed that Chartist activities in the area were the consequence of the work of English agitators, 'of whom he said it were better if they drowned in the Severn than come to Wales' (Davies 1965, p. 80). Additionally, R. W. Lingen, one of the Commissioners of the 'Blue Books' inquiry into education in Wales, identified coalfield unrest as originating from English agitators (Davies 1965).

Thus, workers' expressions of discontent with their lot were seen as the results of outside agitation, a foreign import, alien to the culture and values of Welsh society.[14] Increasingly, as the century progressed, these tensions heightened, as the Nonconformist bourgeoisie identified increasing working-class radicalism with Anglicization and the erosion of Nonconformity. Growing labour organization in the 1890s, the coal strike of 1898 and the victory of Keir Hardie in 1900 were symptomatic of the culmination of these tensions in the separation of the political praxis of Nonconformism, Liberalism, and the working class. In the last two decades of the nineteenth century the working class increasingly looked to socialism for its salvation instead of a Nonconformism which remained aloof and preoccupied with disestablishment.

The antagonisms between Nonconformism and working-class interests, first revealed in the Nonconformist commentaries on the Merthyr Rising and Chartism, reached their culmination at the end of the century.[15] The challenges to the hegemony of the bourgeoisie could no longer be contained within the framework of Nonconformism and Liberalism. The response to those challenges on the part of the Nonconformist bourgeoisie was to stress increasingly the value and role of the Nonconformist basis of its hegemony. Nonconformism had performed the role of an ideological cement in establishing a Welsh bourgeoisie as a Jacobin class in the Gramscian sense. It had synthesized bourgeois interests with those of the rural tenantry and the urban proletariat, establishing a Welsh bourgeoisie as the intellectual and moral leaders of the social formation. They had created a 'national popular will' which they attempted to buttress as challenges to it increased as the century progressed. The Nonconformist, Liberal leadership emphasized the need for stability and appealed for support of the existing order. Their language was national in character, articulating language and religion in an appeal to the other fractions in the class alliance they had forged. But particularly, in their appeal to the proletariat they stressed the dependence of the Welsh industrial economy on the stability of the existing social order.

> What the business and political leadership did in conjunction with
> their press was to stress those characteristics which underlay the
> culture and also firmly relate the economic well-being of the com-
> munity to the existing social order and political norms. In South
> Wales there was the emphasis on Welshness and Nonconformity
> . . . (Stead 1980, p. 153)

The Nonconformist bourgeoisie had succeeded in establishing a social, cultural, political, moral and religious leadership which had its economic origins in the development of the capitalist relations of production in south Wales. From the earliest expressions of a capitalist division of labour, it had moved from a petty bourgeois class position toward the role of bourgeoisie in the second phase of industrialization. Its early links with the nascent working class could not survive this transition without a hegemonizing ideological element. In place of a simple class alliance, there emerged a ruling-class ideology based on Welsh Nonconformist radicalism. In that sense, the Welsh bourgeoisie were a progressive class, sweeping aside the landed gentry and its political domination and establishing a capitalist class society. The vehicle for the development of Nonconformism as the ideological obscurant of the exploitation of the working class had been the Welsh language and a concomitant celebration of Welsh culture and history. The social activities and cultural practices of Nonconformism had been completely Welsh in character, reviving and, where necessary, inventing tradition, custom and folklore. The well-being of Nonconformism and the hegemony of the ruling class were dependent on the continued ascendancy of this cultural and political conjuncture. Faced with the twin pressures of Anglicization and secularization, together with the growing class pressures of working-class organization, the bourgeoisie stressed the basis of its hegemony and became increasingly nationalist. In this way, the nationalism of the period reflected class interests in the industrial sector as much as it did in the rural sector.

The articulation of feudal and capitalist classes

At the end of Chapter 5 it was suggested that the ability of the rural tenantry to organize against their domination by the landed gentry had been partially dependent on events in the industrializing sector of Welsh society. The need for outside intervention in the resolution of peasant struggles is well recognized (Shanin 1966, Migdal 1974 and Wolf 1965). Shanin argues that 'guided political action' provides the most effective means of overcoming the strategic and structural limitations on peasant political mobilization. Wolf's claim that new élites emerge in an industrializing sector to challenge landlord hegemony is also of clear relevance here.

The intervention of classes with their origins in the capitalist industrial sector is crucial to the resolution of tensions between the feudal classes experiencing the transition to capitalist agricultural production in the rural sector. The result is a complex alliance of capitalist bourgeoisie and feudal peasantry, with, however, the bourgeoisie as the leading force in that alliance. In the process of liberating the tenantry from the landed class, the bourgeoisie secured their own position and created a rural petty bourgeoisie as the tenantry gradually become smallholders.

Welsh Liberal Nonconformism was the ideological cement of this relationship in the same way as it bound the working class to the bourgeoisie in the industrial sector. Following the initial electoral victories of this political movement in both rural and industrial constituencies, the basis for an overtly political nationalism emerged. By the 1890s Welsh Liberals occupied a pivotal place in British politics and were in a favourable position to articulate specifically Welsh demands in Parliament (Morgan 1963). Chapter 5 outlined the gradual replacement of Tory MPs by representatives who were Welsh-speaking, Liberal and Nonconformist. These behaved as a coherent group propagating specifically Welsh legislation. This parliamentary grouping eventually resulted in an attempt to establish a specifically Welsh political movement focusing on these Members for Wales and giving voice to a Home Rule policy which mirrored similar demands from Ireland (Morgan 1981). Prominent in the articulation of such demands were the voices of the Nonconformist intelligentsia and exiled Welsh in London.

In 1886, T. E. Ellis, an Oxford-educated Nonconformist, met with others at Westminster and drew up a political programme giving voice to nationalist political demands and providing the basis for his election as MP for Merioneth later that year (Morgan 1963). In April 1887 the London *Cymru Fydd* society was formed with Welsh Home Rule as its major political objective. At this stage the movement had little public support and few members in Wales. Its membership was primarily drawn from Welsh intellectuals resident in London. The printed organ of the movement, entitled *Cymru Fydd*, first appeared in January 1888. Its first page left little doubt that the cultural nationalism of the previous decades had now become political.

> State Churchism, educational monopoly and jobbery, a landed system which has degenerated into rude despotism:- these and other baleful evils have oppressed beyond the bounds of further endurance the life of the people of Wales. (*Cymru Fydd* 1888, p. 1)

The first Welsh branch was established at Barry in 1891, followed by rapid growth throughout Wales (Morgan 1963).

The reason for the sudden interest appears to be the successes of Welsh Liberalism in a Parliament where the Liberal Party was dependent on the support of Welsh Liberals for its continuation in office. Key *Cymru Fydd* members entered the centre stage of British politics with Lloyd George as their spokesman and T. E. Ellis as government Whip. In 1894 a national *Cymru Fydd* League was established in an attempt to unify Welsh Liberalism behind the Home Rule banner. In 1894 *Cymru Fydd* and the North Wales Liberal Federation merged (Morgan 1963). However, problems were encountered in forging such close links with the Liberal Party in south Wales, and despite successful recruitment in parts of the coalfield, the South Wales Liberal Federation refused to merge with *Cymru Fydd*.

Lloyd George toured the area in late 1895, but his campaign collapsed following a hostile meeting in Newport (Morgan 1963). The *Cymru Fydd* movement lost momentum and it was confirmed as an ineffective vehicle for the expression of Home Rule demands. The *Cymru Fydd* editorial comment on W. J. Parry's Home Rule for Wales Bill in 1890 was clearly lacking in any real commitment to the achievement of independence.

> We want Home Rule in Wales, but let us make sure first of all what it is we want. Just now our hands are full with the working of the County Councils, the launching of the Intermediate Schools and the Disestablishment of the Church. (*Cymru Fydd,* February 1890, p. 11)

In his account of these events, from which much of the the above is drawn, Morgan (1963) stresses the inherent distrust of commercial south Wales for the rural north and the impossibility of reconciling the opposed views of Welsh society which each held. Morgan, however, places undue emphasis on the clash of personalities between D. A. Thomas of the South Wales Liberal Federation and Lloyd George. Instead, the failure of *Cymru Fydd* successfully to unite north and south in an appeal for nationhood can be seen as the result of the erosion of the basis of the alliance between the urban bourgeoisie and the rural peasantry. In addition, the conditions which had created a nationalist perspective, in both the rural and industrial sectors, were now dissolving, leaving no social basis for a national movement in Wales after 1890.

In the rural sector the contradictions between landlord and tenant had been largely resolved. The tenantry were now politically represented by the Liberal Party and its Members of Parliament and the control of rural life by the landlords had disintegrated. By the 1890s many of the great estates were being dismantled and bought by the tenants (Howell 1977). The basis of rural conflict had disappeared and the capitalization of agricultural production completed.

The primary class conflicts were those emerging in the industrial sector as the hegemony of the Nonconformist bourgeoisie began to break down in the face of increasing labour organization. If there was a secure future for the indigenous bourgeoisie it was increasingly under the umbrella of the British state. The Nonconformist élite in the south could not support the Home Rule demands of *Cymru Fydd*, given their total dependence on the economic relations between Wales and England. Nationalism as ideological strategy in the cementing of a class alliance between the rural tenantry and the industrial bourgeoisie had become redundant. Furthermore, it failed to remain effective as the ideological instrument of bourgeois hegemony. By the turn of the century, nationalist demands had practically disappeared from Liberal politics, surviving only as the preoccupation of Welsh intellectuals (Butt Philip 1975). Despite its appearance in the rhetoric of the early Labour movement, the question of Welsh independence failed to achieve any serious political attention until the foundation of *Plaid Cymru* in 1925.

In this way, nationalism, which had been a crucial dimension of the class struggles of the second half of the nineteenth century, was superseded by a more direct ideological and political clash between capital and labour. With the disappearance of the feudal class formation in the rural economy the social basis of nationalism in rural politics also ended. In the industrial sector the heightening crisis of the economy and the increasing organization of labour set Welsh politics on a path which was to establish a different radicalism in the inter-war years in which Nonconformism and Liberalism were to play little part. Nationalism as an ideological cement between an indigenous bourgeoisie and working class was redundant: nationalism was no longer articulated with class struggle.

CHAPTER 6

THE NATIONALIST RESURGENCE IN
TWENTIETH-CENTURY WALES

A nationalist dimension reappeared with some force in Welsh politics in the early 1960s. As we have seen, following the collapse of *Cymru Fydd* at the turn of the century, nationalism retreated in Wales, playing no part in mass democratic politics. The political stage in Wales was occupied by labourism, and nationalism existed as a fringe interest of Welsh intellectuals and literati.[1] Popular politics after the First World War were characterized by struggles between labour and capital in a society facing severe economic crisis. Periodic recession and eventual collapse of Welsh economic activity engendered socialist responses from a population experiencing mass unemployment and serious deprivation. The embryonic labour organizations present in the days of *Cymru Fydd* coalesced to form the Labour Party and became the ascendant force in Welsh politics. The national question was no longer central in the programmes of change sought by the new representatives of the Welsh working class.

Yet the legacy of the powerful representations of earlier forms of Welsh radicalism survived in vestigial form as a token attachment to Home Rule for Wales in both the Labour and Liberal manifestos until after the Second World War (Butt Philip 1975). Ironically, it is during this period that *Plaid Cymru*, the Welsh national party, was established in 1925, emerging from an amalgamation of several nationalist societies prominent in Welsh student and academic life (Davies 1983). However, for Davies, *Plaid Cymru* did not take on the objectives and strategies of a political party until after the Second World War. Rather, the movement existed primarily as a vehicle for the protection and promotion of the Welsh language and culture. Social and economic policy, despite some limited internal discussion, remained subordinate to the primary goal of cultural and linguistic survival. Economic planning was of secondary importance and after 1934 was based on Saunders Lewis's *Ten Points of Policy*. It remained a celebration of pre-industrial, rural Wales emphasizing de-industrialization as the central solution for the crisis of the Welsh economy. At its heart lay a conservative and reactionary philosophy derived from the attachment of the leadership to the ideas of *Action Française*, the radical French right movement (Davies 1983). The emphasis was always on language and culture and the need to protect both from centralism and socialism. Davies concludes:

> In reality, the Welsh Nationalist Party was a social and educational movement which created a dedicated core of cultural nationalists rather than a political group campaigning vigorously to gain popular support for the objective of Welsh self-government. (1983, p. 262)

During the inter-war years *Plaid Cymru* failed to affect the course of Welsh politics or to stem the decline of the Welsh culture it sought to protect; it is to the post-war period that we must look to identify the entry of nationalism into popular politics in Wales.

During this period, in the wider context of British politics, the primary political concerns were with securing economic recovery and social justice, establishing in that process a central role for the state in the planning and administration of social and economic life. The centralist tendencies of British reform socialism, tempered by compromise and its accommodation of professional and business interests, permeated Welsh economic and political life. Through regional economic policy and the role of nationalized industries in Wales, the state took on the central role in the Welsh economy as major employer, as well as the major agent of investment and relocation of industry. The state represented the main platform of Welsh economic recovery (Rees and Lambert 1981).

In Welsh political life it was the British Labour party which dominated. In the 1950 general election Labour took 27 of the 36 parliamentary seats with 58.1 per cent of votes cast (Balsom and Burch 1980). Similarly, in local government, control of the majority of councils, especially in the north and south-east rested in the hands of the Labour Party. The party's ascendancy in Wales appeared unassailable (Morgan 1981). The consequences of this situation in British terms were that Wales represented one of the foundations of Labour's validity as a second party. It could not take office without its mass base of support in the Celtic fringes of Scotland and Wales. This then was the political scenario in which nationalism began to reassert itself as a political force from the early 1960s onwards.

Welsh nationalism failed to make any impact on the Welsh political scene in the first half of the century. The nationalist party had existed only on the fringes of Welsh politics and had been torn by internal struggles (Davies 1983). However, these years of political isolation experienced by nationalist leaders were compensated for by the force with which nationalism re-entered Welsh and British politics. By the late 1960s the issues of language and culture were beginning to occupy a central place in Welsh affairs and to press their attention on the machinery of the British state. Gradually, the recognition of specifically Welsh dimensions to wider economic issues changed and broadened the nationalist appeal and threatened the ascendancy of the Labour Party in Wales, and, for some commentators, the unity of the British political system (Nairn 1977, Birch 1977).[2]

The resurgence of ethnicity and nationalism

The nature and form of this resurgence has been well documented (e.g. Butt Philip 1975, John Osmond 1979 and 1985).[3] Consequently what follows is not an attempt to write its history but to give sufficient detail to make meaningful to the reader the application of our theoretical framework to this crucial period in the history of Welsh nationalism and ethnicity. Some attention will be given to the downward turn of the resurgence as these events have not been widely recorded at this time.

The nature of the reassertion of Welsh identity can best be described as having two parts. Firstly the political and protest activities of *Plaid Cymru* and *Cymdeithas Yr Iaith Gymraeg* and secondly the more cultural activities of organizations such as *Urdd Gobaith Cymru* and *Merched Y Wawr*. Whilst no clear line can be drawn between cultural and political activities and particularly between memberships of organizations which, in reality, tended to overlap considerably, nationalist activity can usefully be divided between the cultural manifestations of Welsh ethnicity and the more overtly political activities of organized nationalism. We will deal here primarily with the political activities.

Plaid Cymru clearly represents the formal political wing of Welsh nationalism, participating in the general framework of British political orthodoxy and following what has been, almost without exception, a constitutional road to Welsh independence (Butt Philip 1975). The lack of focus and political naïvety of the pre-war years was partially corrected by the party's participation in the Parliament For Wales Campaign in the late 1950s. However, it was the issue of the flooding of Tryweryn which was to provide the symbolic focus for the genesis of a more popular programme of nationalist action. Public opinion in Wales opposed the proposals to flood Tryweryn to form a reservoir for the Merseyside local authorities and Welsh MPs were unanimous in their condemnation of the scheme (Butt Philip 1975). The eventual failure to prevent the flooding demonstrated the intrinsic weakness of the local state in Wales to resist central pressures and highlighted the way in which the collective resistance of the Welsh MPs had been side-stepped by Parliament. The forms of direct action and protest which resulted included mass demonstrations and sabotage and formed the model for the subsequent activities of *Cymdeithas Yr Iaith Gymraeg* (the Welsh Language Society) which was founded as much in response to Tryweryn as to the exhortations of Saunders Lewis.[4]

At this time, *Plaid Cymru* had moved more clearly to an identification with a parliamentary road to Welsh independence, thereby precluding overt support for civil disobedience which would have damaged the image of electoral respectability it was attempting to build for itself. Despite the precedent set by *Plaid Cymru*'s founders by their burning of the Penyberth bombing school in 1936, in the 1950s and 1960s civil disobedience was seen as damaging to the party's electoral aspirations (Butt Philip 1975). This dichotomy between *Plaid Cymru*'s quest for electoral respectability and the direct action of other nationalist organizations characterized nationalist politics in Wales throughout the post-war period. It has been argued that the civil disobedience campaigns of *Cymdeithas Yr Iaith Gymraeg* have been seen by *Plaid Cymru* as a major source of damage to its electoral image and as partially responsible for its failure to gain a more widely dispersed and varied base of public support (Betts 1976).[5] *Plaid Cymru* has frequently been in ambiguous situations where support for a nationalist objective has had to be qualified by denunciation of the tactics of the organizations *Plaid* shares the objective with. This has posed particular problems when the overlapping membership of *Plaid* and other nationalist societies is considered. *Plaid Cymru* has occasionally found itself in the position of condemning the actions of elements of its membership.

This has been especially difficult in relation to the language issue where the party's dependence on support from the Welsh-speaking heartlands has had to be balanced by the necessity of extending the social base of support into the English-speaking, industrial areas of south Wales. As a result of these conflicting demands *Plaid Cymru* has, on occasions, had to distance itself from the more radical language campaigns of groups such as the Welsh Language Society. This has had the effect of weakening the party's identification with the language issue and bilingualism has been the established language policy since the late sixties. This drift away from a purely cultural base has been particularly true in the 1970s and early 1980s when the party has moved continually to a more economically orientated body of policy. Thus the political action of nationalist organizations has generally adopted one of two strategies. The first adopted by *Plaid Cymru* has emphasized participation in the democratic framework of the British state. The party has attempted, with varying degrees of success, to gain representation at both local and national political levels. The alternative strategy has been the civil disobedience and direct action campaigns adopted by *Cymdeithas Yr Iaith Gymraeg*. These strategies have primarily involved confrontation with the state and the use of court appearances to publicize and draw attention to the specific claims of the defendants (Bankowski and Mungham 1980). These methods usually centre on a single-issue campaign, for example, Welsh road signs, Welsh-language broadcasting and, more recently, a central Welsh-language education authority. These campaigns have been largely successful and, following what has become ritualistic resistance from the state, major concessions have been won.[6]

In contrast with the tangible results of direct action the successes of *Plaid Cymru* are more difficult to assess. Despite a permanent presence in the British Parliament since 1966, the influence on central state policy is impossible to quantify. Since that time extensive measures of administrative devolution and regional aid have occurred, but it is difficult to assess the role of *Plaid Cymru's* representatives in that process. In fact, the party itself has found it difficult to determine the value of parliamentary representation to the furtherance of the national question and repeated debate has taken place as to the extent to which the party should rely on this as its primary strategy in winning the support of the Welsh people.[7] Despite the difficulties in measuring effects in concrete political results such as legislation, it is possible to argue that the benefits of representation at Parliament have been the increased credibility of the party in Wales as well as the increased awareness of Welsh issues forced on the British political system by the constant questions and activities of the party's representatives in Parliament.

To summarize, the political activities of both *Plaid Cymru* and *Cymdeithas Yr Iaith Gymraeg* have been collectively successful in winning from central government key concessions in the administration of Wales and its economy. Substantial devolution of administrative functions in most major government departments has been overshadowed by the establishment and growth of the Welsh Office. In broadcasting, Welsh-medium education and important areas of social administration, the Welsh language and its usage has developed a far more acceptable status than was previously thought possible. More importantly, the state has been forced to recognize the existence of a separate identity and territorial integrity of the geographical region of Wales. In many ways it is the British state which has created a contemporary Wales by its establishment of a complex network of institutions dealing specifically with the administration of Wales. This represents a transformation in state ideology in terms of its partial recognition and acceptance of the nationalist definition of Wales as a separate cultural and social unity, distinct in many ways from England. Rees and Lambert (1981) argue that there exists a 'regionalist consensus' which permeates attitudes to the region at all levels of the social formation, producing accord between 'organised labour and capital and the major political parties'. . . (p. 125). However, for Rees and Lambert this 'regionalist consensus' differs from the nationalism of *Plaid Cymru* and has had the effect, even if unintended, of legitimizing the actions of the state in Wales and of preserving and maintaining the existing social formation.

The image of Wales contained in the 'regional consensus' only extends to the level of tackling what is seen as the 'regional problem'; in reality this means securing the reproduction of capital in Wales and avoiding major economic imbalances and high levels of unemployment (Rees and Lambert 1981). This conceptualization of Welsh identity does not extend to the perception of Wales as a viable political, social and economic unit in its own right in keeping with nationalist images of Wales. We have to be wary of judging as 'success' in nationalist terms the political responses by the state to nationalist activity. That nationalism has been able to elicit these, usually positive, responses from the central state machinery does not necessarily signify anything other than the accommodation and incorporation of limited reform into the mainstream political processes. Much of state concession to nationalist demands represents the attempt of the major political parties, especially the British Labour Party, to defuse the challenge to its support that nationalism came to constitute in both Wales and Scotland. Many of the concessions granted in terms of recognition of the language can be seen as attempts to appease one of the most radical and vociferous sections of the Welsh electorate (Adamson 1986). Additionally the devolution proposals of the Wales Act of 1978 must be seen as an attempt to stem the nationalist advance by a beleaguered Labour administration facing serious opposition from *Plaid Cymru*, even in the Labour heartlands of industrial south Wales.

The Labour Government's proposals for devolution

> as contained in the Wales Act were prompted, in large measure, by the electoral threat posed by the nationalists, notably in Scotland. In that context it is possible to link the proposals to the nationalist advance made in by-elections during the late sixties and particularly to Gwynfor Evans' victory in Carmarthen in July 1966. (Jones 1983, p. 20)

To summarize, the overtly political forms of nationalist activity represented by *Plaid Cymru* and *Cymdeithas Yr Iaith Gymraeg* have achieved results which have furthered the nationalist cause in cultural terms, if not in the achievement of economic objectives. However, the successes achieved by nationalist organizations in the cultural sphere may have had the unintended consequences of appeasing and incorporating potentially radical elements of the Welsh-speaking middle classes. This has done little to improve the poor quality of economic, social and cultural life of the majority of Welsh people. Furthermore, the actions of those organizations may have alienated potential support in the Anglo-Welsh section of the population, considerably weakening the long-term prospects of a higher status being ascribed to the region by the British state.[8]

The second form of nationalist activity identified earlier is represented by the less overtly political organizations which have attempted to assert Welsh identity through more cultural vehicles. However, it must be stressed that at times the lines between these and the political organizations have been very blurred. During the sixties a number of quite diverse organizations came to the fore and paralleled the political activities of *Plaid Cymru* and *Cymdeithas Yr Iaith Gymraeg*. Of particular importance here was *Urdd Gobaith Gymru*, the Welsh-language youth movement which had been founded in 1922 to 'foster Welsh awareness, Welsh culture and the Welsh language' (Butt Philip 1975). Despite its non-political outlook and attempts to remain cultural, the movement was inevitably drawn into the political milieu by its overlapping membership with *Plaid Cymru* and *Cymdeithas Yr Iaith Gymraeg*. Butt Philip (1975) paints a complex picture of the attempts of the movement to remain non-political whilst at the same time fulfilling the objectives of Welsh cultural promotion it had been established to secure. The result was that the *Urdd* was constantly criticized from one side for being too political, and from the other side for not being political enough, in its intervention in cultural maintenance. Other 'non-political' institutions which emerge during this period and are listed by Butt Philip include *Ysgolion Cymraeg* (the Welsh Schools Movement), *Undeb Cenedlaethol Athrawon Cymru* (the National Association of Teachers of Wales), *Merched Y Wawr* (Women's Institute equivalent) and *Undeb Amaethwyr Cymru* (the Farmers' Union of Wales). To these must be added the later developments of a Welsh Trade Union Congress and *Undeb Myfyrwyr Cymru* (Welsh Students' Union). Some of these organizations have derived from initiatives by *Plaid* members unhappy at the sole emphasis on electoral strategy taken by the party (Butt Philip 1975).

The formation of these organizations is indicative of the impact, from the early sixties onwards, of nationalism and ethnicity in Welsh society. A pervasive atmosphere of nationalist sentiment extended into social, economic and political institutions in Wales, previously unaffected by the limited nationalist concerns of the inter-war years. The foundations were being laid for a popular nationalist movement which was to become, albeit for a brief period, a considerable force in both Welsh and British politics.

Whilst this force has to be measured in terms wider than the simple electoral results of *Plaid Cymru*, it must be recognized that the successes and failures of the party have largely been the barometer by which nationalists themselves have judged their actions. Success and failure at both local and national elections, and particularly in the Devolution Referendum of 1979, have instigated, at times, major changes of direction in nationalist thinking and strategy. These changes are of particular interest within the context of this volume, concerned as it is with the ideological elements of nationalism and their relationship with wider political and economic processes. Consequently, in the following pages the key turning-points in the construction of *Plaid Cymru*'s ideological formulations and their consequences for nationalist strategy generally will be briefly delineated.

Butt Philip (1975) paints a picture of varied fortunes for *Plaid Cymru* in the early post-war years. Although steady gains were made during the 1950s and 1960s, the party's electoral fortunes were not consistent and frequent doubt was called upon the relevance of a strategy entirely devoted to electoral endeavour. *Plaid*'s ability to field candidates increased steadily despite temporary set-backs when frequent elections strained the party's limited finances. Across Wales the highest share of the national vote gained, prior to the 1970s, was in 1959 when the party polled 5.2 per cent of the votes cast (Balsom and Burch 1980). However, the party had more encouraging results at constituency level, particularly at by-elections, gaining creditable results in Ogmore in 1946 with 29 per cent of the vote and Aberdare with 20 per cent of votes cast (Butt Philip 1975). However, the period is characterized by the party's inability to capitalize on its successes or to respond to its failures. By the early 1960s the party was once again losing ground in local and national elections.

The importance of this period lies more in the discussions which emerged in the party rather than in terms of the actual election results. The terms of the debate which was prompted by these varied electoral performances signalled the beginning of a period of reflection and theorizing within the party about the nature of the movement and the nature of the Welsh society and culture the party was attempting to preserve. Many of the gains of the period had been in the industrial south and increasingly economic arguments and policies had been at the forefront of the campaigns in these areas. South-east Wales had provided a major injection of new blood into the party in the form of young and radical members from the industrial south Wales valleys (Butt Philip 1975). The constitutionalism of the leadership increasingly contrasted with the direct action of the party's rank and file and increasingly the initiative was being taken by young, radical members from south-east Wales.

Although the policies remained within the traditions of the party's concerns with language and culture, this change constituted, in embryo form, a shift in emphasis within the party from the rural north to the industrial south, a shift which was to have major consequences in the seventies and eighties. Davies (1985) discusses the role of this influx of new blood in the by-election victory of 1966:

> . . . that following the influx of new members (largely from the south-east . . .), Plaid Cymru became more rigorously political in its approach, more palpable in its concern for issues of interest to the ordinary voter, and more effective in its administrative structure. The Carmarthen by-election, Phil Williams argued, 'was not a turning point; it was instead the first real product of a turning point that had already occurred'. (p. 137)

Davies argues that it was this electoral success that created the urgent need for relevant and realistic policies that were distanced from the narrow cultural conservatism of *Plaid*'s earlier philosophy. The terms of debate within the party moved increasingly to encompass economic issues as the basis of political action in Wales. In 1966 the party established its Research Group to aid formulation of policies that could be seen as relevant to the Wales of the 1960s rather than to the 1930s, when many of the party's policies had first emerged (Butt Philips 1975). The consequences of the deliberation of the Research Group was the gradual development by 1969 of a rational and credible economic policy which identified the problem of economic decline which Labour appeared incapable of reversing. It raised, in opposition to the Welsh Office's *Wales: The Way Ahead* (1967) its alternative series of measures which were eventually accepted as party policy at the 1969 Annual Conference. *Plaid Cymru's Economic Plan for Wales* (1969) was a closely argued document stating a firm commitment to the radical reconstruction of the Welsh economy. Although it shared many dominant mainstream assumptions about economic planning it presented a well-researched appraisal of the needs of the Welsh economy, even if the funding proposals were a little naïve. The three stated aims of the plan were:

1) *To remove excess unemployment*, whether direct or hidden;
2) *To halt the net migration* of young people out of Wales;
3) *To replace employment in declining industries* by introducing new industries before the old industries disappear. (*Plaid Cymru* 1969, p. 6)

For the first time *Plaid Cymru* had, as its central platform, a policy which was almost entirely economically orientated. More significantly, it was directly relevant to the economic needs and terms of political debate in industrial south Wales rather than the areas of support in the north on which *Plaid Cymru* had historically depended.

It was on the basis of these policies that *Plaid* entered its most successful period of electoral achievement which reached its peak in the February and October elections of 1974 and presented the Labour Party with a serious challenge to its ascendancy in the traditional Labour heartlands. The extent of that challenge, although less than Labour experienced from the Scottish National Party, was sufficient to shake the Labour establishment in several previously secure constituencies, including Merthyr Tydfil, Aberdare, Rhondda East and West (amalgamated 1971) and Caerphilly (Balsom and Burch 1980). A Welsh Labour Party which had stagnated and taken its support for granted was faced with effective political opposition for the first time in post-war elections. During the 1974-9 Labour administration *Plaid Cymru* MPs were able to exploit the minority basis of the government and secure limited concessions.[9] *Plaid Cymru* supported the Labour Government to the last when their Scottish counterparts voted against the government on a vote of confidence.

This period was to close, however, with a devastating humiliation for nationalist politics with the result of the Devolution Referendum of March 1979. With a turnout of 58.3 per cent only 11.8 per cent voted for the proposals of the 1978 Wales Act. An overwhelming 46.5 per cent voted 'No' in the referendum, leaving nationalist aspirations in tatters (Foulkes *et al.* 1983). Although *Plaid Cymru* had voiced considerable dissatisfaction with the proposals for devolved powers set out in the Wales Act, they had committed themselves to support of this Labour Party initiative. The defeat in reality was a defeat for *Plaid Cymru* (Davies 1985). The identification of the Labour Party with the 'Yes' campaign had been very weak, with some of the most prominent Welsh Labour MPs highly active at the head of the 'gang of six'[10] which waged a very effective campaign against the devolution proposals. Foulkes *et al.* (1983) demonstrate that it was largely Labour voters who decided the result of the referendum which was immediately interpreted by the opponents of the proposals as a defeat for nationalist sentiment in Wales. A considerable majority of the electorate were seen as voting against the principle of administrative devolution, demonstrating their total opposition to anything which put Wales on the 'slippery slope' to independence.

Nationalist leaders attempted to save face with the counter-argument that the people of Wales had rejected the proposals because they had not gone far enough toward a real devolution of power. However, such claims sounded hollow and empty in the face of the extent of the opposition in Wales, especially in contrast with the clear, if small, majority for devolution which had been registered in Scotland. The referendum result was followed rapidly by a serious erosion of *Plaid*'s support in the general and local elections of 1979 and the party began an immediate post-mortem in a mood of complete despair.

The period of self-criticism and introspection which followed led to the most significant ideological shift by the party since its formation in 1925. The initial organizational response was the establishment of a five-man committee of inquiry[11] charged with investigating the party's failure and the steps necessary to reverse the decline in nationalist support. The inquiry reported in January 1981, producing a majority and a minority report, the latter written by Dr Phil Williams. However, there were no major differences in the conclusions drawn and the policies advocated (Davies 1985).

In the majority report the authors identified the 'English middle-of-the-road constitutional image' (p. 5) that the parliamentary path had imposed on *Plaid Cymru* and argued that whilst not 'rejecting consensus politics . . . the party no longer has to be bound by it' (p. 8). The report identified certain non-nationalist issues as of concern to *Plaid Cymru*, including an argument for the centrality of anti-nuclear weapons policies. Additionally, it argued for the validity of Anglo-Welsh culture. More fundamentally, however, it advocated the adoption of a 'decentralist socialist' (p. 13) ideology by *Plaid Cymru* based in 'organic communities' (p. 13) which were natural defences against the bureaucratic centralization of left and right British political parties. These arguments were presented more forcefully and within a more historical perspective in the minority report of Dr Phil Williams. The general arguments of the report were accepted at the party's annual conference in 1981, with only limited resistance emerging in the formation of a right-wing faction which called itself the Hydro Group.

The break with the past was completed by the publication of Hywel Davies' *The Welsh Nationalist Party. 1925–45: A Call To Nationhood*. Davies examined closely the fascist sympathies of *Plaid Cymru*'s founders, Saunders Lewis and Ambrose Bebb. He concluded that whilst some of the contemporary claims had been exaggerated there was considerable support for fascist ideas and movements in the thinking of both men. In a review of the book, Dafydd Elis Thomas (1983) argued that these two nationalist figureheads had appropriated the 'Liberal and Labour nationalism' of the nineteenth century, shaping it into 'right-wing Conservative nationalism' (p. 18). Elis Thomas concluded:

> . . . I will never let anyone get away with calling me a 'nationalist', and I will never call myself that, if I ever did. (1983, p. 18)

Symbolically at least, the party had emptied its cupboard of skeletons and moved fully to a socialist ideology.

Despite this apparent acceptance of objectives which would have been anathema to *Plaid Cymru*'s founders, it is not apparent that there was a major shift in emphasis in grass-roots beliefs amongst party activists.[12] At local level policy became confused and the actual operationalization of the term 'decentralist socialism' was uncertain and lacked rigour and understanding of general socialist principles.[13] The thoughts of the left-wing elements of the leadership were slow to percolate through to activists who, throughout their political careers, had identified socialism with the Labour Party and its antagonistic stance against nationalism in Wales, especially after the Second World War.

The leading advocate of the socialist path, Dafydd Elis Thomas, advocated the strategies of 'popular front' politics which were at that time gaining ground in the political actions of Labour Party organizations in the metropolitan authorities. New definitions of socialism were being explored which eschewed the mono-cultural centralism of the British Labour Party and offered policies which could be applied as much in Wales as in London. The effect was to

> encourage a close committed study of Welsh problems and to create bridges between Welsh nationalism and a wide range of movements including those of the trade unionists, the feminists, the anti-nuclear campaigners, the liberation theologists, the ecologists, the anti-racists and the advocates of the validity of an English-language Welsh culture. (Davies 1985, p. 150)

These policies were most forcibly argued for by a grouping which called itself the National Left and which became increasingly identified with *Plaid Cymru*'s new quarterly English-language journal, *Radical Wales*, launched in 1983. The first issue advocated decentralist socialism and argued for the need to 'build links' with English-speaking Wales. It saw the industrial south as the new site of nationalist struggle. The first editorial argued:

> . . . Plaid Cymru has for too long failed to build strong links with the English speaking majority particularly in the South. The scope for further advances in the north and west is limited. If the party is to make significant headway in truly national terms, it must concentrate on the south east and particularly the Valleys . . . (*Plaid Cymru* 1983, p. 3)

These major ideological and strategical shifts were insufficient however for a number of socialist thinkers who had left to form the Welsh Socialist Republican Movement in January 1980. Dominated intellectually by Gareth Miles and Robert Griffiths, this movement sought to establish a more orthodox Marxist-Leninist debate over Welsh politics. Highly critical of the dominant political institutions of Wales, especially the Welsh Office, it also targetted the policies of *Plaid Cymru* as objects of scathing criticism. In its English-language publication, *Y Faner Goch* ('The Red Banner') *Plaid Cymru* leaders were berated for what was regarded as an insincere and opportunist commitment to socialism. Following a vigorous, if unsuccessful, intervention in Welsh politics, the movement finally broke up after a controversial conspiracy trial in 1982[14] and elements of its membership joined the Communist Party.

A more extreme development at this time was the commencement of an arson campaign directed against holiday homes in Wales and more recently against the growing levels of English migration into the Welsh heartlands. In the late eighties an organization calling itself '*Meibion Glyndŵr*' claimed responsibility. Despite concerted police efforts the only convictions which have resulted have been for offences which have appeared to be isolated rather than the consequences of an orchestrated campaign. No link has been established between those convicted and their offences have been seen as copy-cat or opportunistic acts. Such conclusions by commentators do not rule out the existence of an organization which has completely rejected more orthodox political actions and forms of protest.

To summarize, in the aftermath of the devolution defeat *Plaid Cymru* completed the process of transforming itself from a primarily culturally motivated party to one dedicated, in principle and title at least, to the achievement of socialism in Wales. Nor were these changes limited to the national party itself: *Cymdeithas Yr Iaith Gymraeg* quickly declared itself a socialist organization. The ascendancy of the left in *Plaid Cymru* was confirmed by the election of Dafydd Elis Thomas to the presidency in 1984 in a fight against a candidate primarily identified with the traditional cultural right within the party.[15]

This apparent ideological transformation of the party has, however, been challenged to some extent by events in recent years. The quest for electoral respectability has led to the quietening of some of the party's more left-wing policies in the run-up to the 1987 general election, and discussion in the party was curtailed by Executive directives during the election campaign.[16] In particular, criticism of the electoral alliance with the more right-wing Scottish Nationalist Party was muted, despite misgivings by many members of the party. Perhaps, more importantly, a number of policy decisions have been reversed which have placed question marks over the stability of the relationships formed with other movements.[17]

That *Plaid Cymru* should have embraced socialism at a time when that ideology commands declining electoral support is ironic. If the transition in party thinking had occurred fifteen years previously, the political map in Wales could now look quite different. Instead, *Plaid Cymru*'s electoral future is doubtful despite the 1987 Ynys Môn victory. Yet it should not be forgotten that in the period 1965–79 the course of British politics has been partially determined by the issues of ethnicity and nationality. *Plaid Cymru* has been transformed from a culturally inspired pressure group to an effective political party with an organization and party machinery capable of fighting all the Welsh parliamentary seats, maintaining a considerable body of local government representatives, in addition to supporting up to three Members of Parliament. *Plaid Cymru* had, for a short time, been at the forefront of British politics and the presence of *Plaid Cymru* MPs in Parliament, along with their Scottish colleagues, had forced the British Labour Party to put fundamental constitutional change on the political agenda. *Plaid's* subsequent electoral decline does not detract from the role of ethnic politics in Wales especially during the period 1963–74 and the party has not lost its image as a credible element of the Welsh political structure. It has retained representation in Parliament and its party structure and machinery survives intact.

Additionally, from 1988 onwards, there has been a growing awareness of the pressure on the Welsh-speaking communities from a new wave of English-speaking immigrants. The response has been a fierce debate within the nationalist movement which has once again brought language and cultural factors to the fore. The debate has been epitomized by the exchanges between poet R. S. Thomas and Dafydd Elis Thomas, president of *Plaid Cymru*.[18] The regeneration of interest in national issues that this debate has created has not matched the apparent re-awakening of Scottish nationalism demonstrated by the Govan by-election result. However, it has ensured that Welsh language and culture is part of the mainstream political agenda and is reflected in recent Labour Party discussions of devolution in Wales. Despite the decline of *Plaid Cymru's* attraction to the electorate in recent years, the Pontypridd by-election result demonstrated that it would be a hasty decision indeed to write off either the party or the saliency of ethnicity in Welsh and British politics.

CHAPTER 7

CONTEMPORARY CLASS ANALYSIS

After that brief consideration of the nature and extent of the ethnic and nationalist resurgence in Welsh social and political life during the 1960s and 1970s the process of explanation can begin. In keeping with the earlier analysis of nineteenth-century Welsh nationalism, the theoretical framework developed in Chapters 3 and 4 will be applied to test its relevance to the analysis of contemporary nationalism in Wales. Central to that perspective is the claim that nationalism constitutes an ideological construct, mobilized by classes and class alliances in the context of hegemonic struggle. Nationalism is a class-neutral ideology, appropriated by classes in hegemonic and counter-hegemonic struggle. It provides the ideological cement which facilitates the synthesis of class interests under the political, moral and intellectual leadership of a particular class or fraction of a class. Nationalism is assigned class implications when articulated with the class struggle. As a preliminary to examining that process in twentieth-century Wales, this chapter will establish a theoretical framework in which the constitution of classes in post-war Wales can be analysed.

Moving the site of analysis from the nineteenth century to the twentieth necessitates the recognition of the increased complexity of Welsh society as the advancing development of capitalism has created complex social structures and a division of labour which existed only in embryonic form in the nineteenth century.

> The occupational structure of contemporary capitalist societies is very different from that of the nineteenth century. The range of occupations has greatly increased and considerable differentiation and specialisation has occurred within occupations . . . (Crompton and Gubbay 1977, p. 46)

Coming to terms with this complexity has posed severe problems for all schools of sociology.[1] Particular difficulties have been experienced in explaining the existence and growth of the middle class (Abercrombie and Urry 1983).

Until recently, in British sociology, Weberian class analysis has predominated in attempts to map the modern class structure. Elsewhere, Marxism has had more influence, especially where the outcome of such debates has had greater political significance.[2] However, there has been recently in British social theory a greater reluctance to pose Marx and Weber as irreconcilable figures in the discussion of class and there has developed a stress on their similarities rather than their differences (Abercombie and Urry 1983, Hill 1981, Hyman and Price 1983). Additionally, beginning with Lockwood's *The Blackcoated Worker* (1958), there have been attempts to integrate the Marxist and Weberian perspectives, notably in the work of Giddens (1971, 1973, 1984). Ironically, much of the impetus to develop effective, rather than doctrinal, class analysis has emerged from the Left, faced as it has been with the defeat of its strategies in the arena of British and European politics. Consequently, attempts have been made to develop more sophisticated Marxist class analysis and relinquish the class reductionism of economistic theories of class (Poulantzas 1973, 1975, Wright 1978).[3] These recent contributions have been particularly concerned to analyse the apparent failure of class polarization to emerge in the way predicted by Marx and to explain the related growth of the 'new middle class'. These attempts will be discussed in greater depth below; for now it is sufficient to state that they have tried to analyse the ways in which classes are created in capitalist society by redefining key concepts in Marxist theory.

Despite the reformulation of elements of Marxist theory, critics maintain that the fundamental problem is Marxism itself, in that its central concepts are flawed and its methodology necessarily reductionist. The basic premises of the perspective are said to bind its theorists to an inevitable economism and class reductionism (Parkin 1979, Laclau and Mouffe 1985, Hindess 1987). Cottrell and Roslender (1986) have summarized these various criticisms as: firstly, a tendency of Marxist theory to identify an automatic correspondence between 'economically identifiable classes and their political practice' (p. 13). Secondly, the unwillingness of the Marxist theorists to consider subjective determinants of class, and thirdly the reluctance to acknowledge theories of stratification, 'fearing contamination with Weberian notions such as life chances' (p. 13). Recent Marxist class analyses are dismissed as mere defences of the perspective rather than as contributions to an understanding of modern classes. Not surprisingly, the Marxist perspective has been defended in ways which take on the criticisms outlined above. An increasing number of theorists have attempted to recognize the complexity of the class structure of advanced capitalism and have introduced what have been described as 'neo-Weberian elements' into their theorizing whilst wishing to retain the terminology of the Marxist framework (Cottrell and Roslender 1986, Abercrombie and Urry 1983). Recent contributions to the discussion of class in capitalist society will be referred to in the following pages as clarification of the theory of class to be applied to the analysis of Welsh nationalism in the post-war period.

In describing class in contemporary capitalism it is not proposed here to dwell at any length on what Marx might or might not have said about class. Such discussions have taken place elsewhere (Poulantzas 1973, Wright 1978, Carchedi 1977). Few writers agree on the significance of the various fragments of Marx's writings on class[4] and numerous interpretations are possible (Carter 1985). The present concern is to establish that the methodology of Marxism remains apposite and that the concepts of class and class formation associated with the Marxist perspective remain valuable in the analysis of contemporary capitalism.[5] However, some recognition must be made of the failures of some of Marx's 'predictions' to come true, especially the polarization of classes and the emergence of the proletariat as a 'class for itself'.

Poulantzas (1973), Carter (1985) and Crompton and Gubbay (1977) draw attention to an important distinction between two levels at which Marx can be said to have analysed the capitalist mode of production. The first level can be described as an abstract analysis of 'pure capitalism . . . unimpeded by mediations and competing and contradictory tendencies' (Carter 1985, p. 55). The second level recognizes the complexity of capitalism as it actually exists, in contrast with the more clear-cut characteristics of the pure model. The latter is referred to by Poulantzas as 'a given mode of production' and is contrasted with an analysis of 'a historically determined social formation' (p. 70). For Carter, Marx's discussion of the polarization of classes into two antagonistic camps belongs to the first level of analysis. The second level, however, recognizes the empirical reality of the complexity of the capitalist mode of production and its articulation with alternative modes. In this second level of analysis, class is not reduced to a simple dichotomy. In keeping with this distinction, this chapter will be concerned with developing an abstract analysis of class in contemporary capitalist society. It consists of a review of contemporary theories of class and attempts to contribute to the resolution of some of the difficulties encountered in the theories surveyed. As an abstract analysis it is seen as an essential preliminary to the examination of the specific conditions affecting class relations in post-war Wales. It furnishes the framework within which an analysis of the unique characteristics of the post-war Welsh social formation can take place. In identifying the general tendencies of class development in advanced capitalist societies it is not suggested that each social formation is bound by identical structures. The theoretical framework cannot prescribe the outcome of the interplay between contradictions in specific social formations. It is essential to recognize the constitution of classes as a historical process. Classes are determined by the victories and defeats, the successes and failures of the political and cultural struggles in which they engage. Although brought into existence by relations of production, classes are also the product of the acting out of those relations in the context of the specific conditions of particular nation-states. Bodemann and Spohn (1986) identify this approach with Gramsci's Marxism and more recently the historiography of E. P. Thompson. They write:

> Thompson conceives class, put in Gramsci's terms, as an histori-
> cal phenomenon articulated in experience, action and conscious-
> ness in confrontation wih other classes — not as an isolated, fixed
> phenomenon. (p. 16)

It is this view which underlies the review of class theories in this chapter and is applied to the explanation of ethnicity in post-war Wales in Chapter 9.

Recent contributions to theories of class

The major stimulus to the analysis of class in recent years was the work of Nicos Poulantzas (Johnson 1982b). Poulantzas engaged with the major criticisms which sociological theories of stratification have levelled at Marxist class theory; but more importantly his work was a critique of the position adopted by the French Communist movement in the 1960s (Abercrombie and Urry 1983). In general terms, his writings attempted to explain the absence of class polarization and to analyse the increasing size and political significance of the 'new middle class', termed by Poulantzas the 'new petty bourgeoisie'. To address these issues, Poulantzas engaged in a discussion of the factors which determine classes in capitalist society.

In keeping with the Althusserian perspective, Poulantzas attempts to steer a middle way between economism and voluntarism. In terms of class analysis this necessitates the acceptance of the primacy of structural determinants of class but, in addition, the full recognition of the role of the political and ideological superstructures in that process. Classes are seen not merely as consequences of relations of production but also of the political and ideological struggles which take place over the relations of production. In this way 'political conflict is not reducible to the class struggle between labour and capital', nor can classes be seen as 'homogeneous collective subjects' (Benton 1984, p. 141).

The central argument, then, is that class is not determined by the economic structure alone but by a complex structural determination involving the economic, political and ideological levels of the social formation. Classes are constituted in a unity of political and ideological practices and economic relations.

> A social class can be identified either at the economic level, at the political level, or at the ideological level, and can thus be located with regard to a particular instance. Yet to define a class *as such* and to grasp it in its *concept*, we must refer to the ensemble of levels of which it is the effect. (Poulantzas 1973, p. 64. Author's emphasis)

Thus the objective economic class position of a group of workers, structurally determined by the relations of production, can be overridden by the political and ideological levels, leading to their assignment to an alternative class position specific to the conjuncture. Only an examination of the three levels of the social formation will reveal its class relations fully.

Additionally, this process of overdetermination is further complicated by the articulation of different modes of production in the same social formation. The effect is that a plurality of class structures exist which further prevent the appearance of classes in their pure form. The reality is a complex fusing and fracturing of classes.

> The most important phenomenon in this respect is that *certain distinct classes*, conceivable in the analysis of 'pure' modes of production which compose a formation, often appear in the social formation *dissolved and fused* with other classes, as groups (autonomous or not) of other classes, or even as specific social categories. (Poulantzas 1973, p. 77. Author's emphasis)

Such fractions are in addition to those potentially contained within the 'heart of the same class' (p. 77) as in the example of the 'commercial, industrial and financial bourgeoisie'. How then can we begin to unravel the complexity of class determination in 'a historically determined social formation'? (Poulantzas 1973, p. 77) Poulantzas begins in *Classes in Contemporary Capitalism* (1975) with a consideration of the economic determination of classes. For him the determining criterion is the distinction between productive and unproductive labour. However, he reformulates the orthodox Marxist definition of productive labour (Carter 1986), replacing it with what Hyman (1983) describes as a 'circumscribed (and idiosyncratic) definition' (p. 34). What is different is the way in which Poulantzas ties the definition of productive workers to the physical production of commodities, with 'use values' (p. 216), in addition to the more orthodox criterion of production of surplus value. Consequently, only workers engaged in the actual production of goods are regarded as productive workers, thereby excluding from the working class the service and state sectors (Wright 1978).

The political determination of classes rests for Poulantzas on the relationship of domination and subordination in the capitalist mode of production. If the bourgeoisie dominates the proletariat in the extraction of surplus value and the consequent political structure of the social formation, then any group in society which assists in that process cannot belong to the working class. Nor, however, can they belong to the bourgeoisie. In co-ordinating the labour process managerial and supervisory staff dominate the proletariat yet, at the same time, they are subordinate to capital. For Poulantzas, their political role in the reproduction of the extraction of surplus value is the determining factor in assigning their class place.

> The work of management and supervision under capitalism is the direct reproduction, within the process of production itself, of the political relations between the capitalist class and the working class. (Poulantzas 1975, p. 228)

Consequently, managers and supervisors are members neither of the working class nor of the capitalist class. They are members of the new petty bourgeoisie. Thus, for Poulantzas, the political place of managerial and supervisory workers predominates over economic criteria in the determination of class boundaries.

Finally, Poulantzas describes the ideological determinant of class boundaries. This element of class determination hinges on the distinction between mental and manual labour. Mental labour is defined as labour which utilizes knowledge which is not used by the direct producer. The direct producer either does not possess the knowledge or is denied the opportunity to implement it.[6] The possession of such knowledge by the mental worker may in fact be imaginary: it is sufficient for lower clerical workers to be identified with managerial possession of special knowledge to be considered as supporting the domination of the worker by capital.

Poulantzas offers a number of important insights into the process of class determination and his work has been generally recognized as a significant milestone in the development of class theory (Wright 1978, Johnson 1982). However, such is the nature of some of the solutions to problems of class theory offered by his analysis, his writings have attracted criticisms from all sides. He has been charged with the failure to eliminate economism from his ideas by a number of writers including Hirst (1977), Abercrombie and Urry (1983) and more recently Hindess (1987).[7] In contrast it is the work of Poulantzas which Meiksins Wood identifies as the starting-point for the 'new true socialists' in the 'retreat from class' (1986). For Wood, the autonomization of the superstructures in Althusser, but especially in Poulantzas, paves the way for a reading of politics as a social practice completely disconnected from class, thereby discarding the central tenets of the materialist method.

Less polemical and more penetrating criticisms, however, are made by Wright (1978), and it is these which are most relevant to the discussion here and in the following pages. Wright's primary criticism is of Poulantzas's discussion of the economic determination of classes. The controversial method of defining the working class adopted by Poulantzas has been noted and it is this method which Wright takes issue with. Firstly, he regards the limitation of the definition of productive worker to those involved in 'production of physical commodities' (p. 46) as 'arbitrary' with no effective argument for excluding workers involved in the provision of services and yet still subjected to surplus value appropriation.

Nor, for Wright, does the distinction, as defined by Poulantzas, correspond to 'positions in the social division of labour' (p. 46). Most importantly, the distinction between productive and unproductive workers is not reflected in the existence of different class interests between the classes Poulantzas identifies on the basis of the distinction. To clarify, for Poulantzas's distinction between the working class and the new petty bourgeoisie to be valid, we would have to be able to identify different 'fundamental' class interests between them, that is, that the new petty bourgeoisie did not share an interest in achieving socialism and ending the exploitation they are subjected to in the capitalist mode of production. Wright concludes:

It is hard to see where a fundamental divergence of economic interests emerges from the positions of unproductive and productive labour in capitalist relations of production. Certainly Poulantzas has not demonstrated that such a divergence exists. He has stated that the formal mechanisms of exploitation are different for the two types of workers; but he has not shown why this formal difference generates a difference in basic interests and thus can be considered a determinant of a class boundary. (1978, p. 50)

The consequences of the distinction, coupled with Poulantzas's ideological and political criteria, as Wright illustrates, is the dramatic shrinking of the working class to less than 20 per cent of the American working population whilst the new petty bourgeoisie constitutes 70 per cent. The political consequences of such a conclusion would be extremely debilitating for Marxist theories of class and, consequently, Wright's criticisms of Poulantzas's identification of class boundaries on this basis are valid.

Finally, Wright rejects the arguments Poulantzas presents for the identification of class unity between the old and new petty bourgeoisie. Given their opposed economic interests and their opposed political interests, it lends to the ideological level the capacity totally to determine the relationship between them. This invalidates the claims for the determination of class by all three levels of the social formation — which is precisely what constitutes the distinctive element of Poulantzas's contribution. Wright's conclusion is that the division between the traditional working class and the new petty bourgeoisie does not constitute a class boundary.

The final criticism of Poulantzas addressed here is one aimed more generally at structuralism but with specific consequences for the analysis of class. Althusser's structuralism has been heavily criticized for its decentring of the human subject. Relegated to the status of 'bearer of structures' structuralism has been accused of presenting a world little different from that of the structural functionalist (Thompson 1978). In a shorter and less vitriolic discussion than Thompson's, Johnson (1982b) applies this criticism to the writings of Poulantzas on class.

For Johnson, despite Poulantzas's ready references to the 'class struggle', he fails to break with the deterministic relationship between structure and class associated with Althusser's structuralism. He relegates the role of class struggle in the determination of classes to a discussion of 'class practices' determined by 'class positions' in the division of labour. For Johnson, this is not the exercise of the dialectic but a one-sided emphasis of structural determinants of class which gives no credence to the role of human agents in altering the relations of production through struggle. Johnson writes:

> Any theory that assumes people to be mere 'agents' of overwhelming structures, that negates human agency in history, that poses history 'as a process without a subject', even denies history itself, runs the risk of degenerating into a dehumanized theory both in its content and in its ideological implications. (1982, p. 45)

Whilst Poulantzas has in fact avoided the worst excesses of structuralism in his discussion of political and ideological determination of class boundaries, his work remains open to criticisms such as those made by Johnson. He has failed to push the insights he offers to the point where they introduce subjective dimensions into the analysis and his work remains largely unable to explain subjective determinants of class. The subjective experience of class positions, its effect on class practice and the effect of class practice on the determination of class boundaries remains outside his analysis. The dialectic between base and superstructure is incomplete. Such a dialectic depends on the recognition of the subject acting and bearing influence on the structures which have called the subject itself into existence.

It is therefore important to introduce into class analysis a subjective dimension whilst avoiding conclusions which have characterized recent discussions of class and which have tended to abandon the notion of a connection between class and politics (Laclau and Mouffe 1985, Hindess 1987). Certain fundamental class interests can be identified in capitalist society and they can be demonstrated as having expression in political forces. However, they are never expressed in their true form but in ways which are consequences of a complex process of articulation of classes, which have their origins in different modes of production, as well as of fractions and alliances of the classes identifiable as belonging to the dominant mode of production. It is necessary to recognize the role of the superstructural instances of the social formation in this process, and to substantiate the specificity of their role, particularly that of the ideological instance.

The initial proposal, to obviate some of the difficulties encountered in class theory, is to introduce a greater awareness of the subjective dimensions of class into the analysis. This is not to argue that Marxism has failed to recognize the saliency of subjectivity in understanding class,[8] but that it has taken second place to the analysis of objective economic determinants of class structures and practices. Marxist writers have, too frequently, relegated subjectivism on the part of the working class to the realm of false consciousness, that is, an ignorance on the part of the class of its objective interests. This is clearly reductionist and any coherent theory of class must recognize the effectivity of the political and ideological levels of the social formation on the determination of classes and their practices. Despite Poulantzas's intentions he fails to achieve this and we must look elsewhere.

It is insufficient to explain what Marxists see as the current political passivity of the European working class (Abercrombie and Urry 1983) simply by reference to the power of capitalist ideology. Since Marx argued that the experience of capitalism would produce a revolutionary consciousness, we have to understand why that experience appears to be producing something very different. This necessitates an enquiry into the ways in which subjectively determined class practices emerge, which are distinct from what we may identify, by applying only economic criteria, as the objective practice of a class. This implies the need for an evaluation of the political and ideological effects of material differences experienced by sections of the working class. These differences are not reducible to places in a labour market but are constituted by wide-ranging experiential differences including, for example, race, ethnicity, gender and age. It is theoretically naïve to assume that a miner and a female clerical worker feel themselves to be in the same social situation, sharing similar economic and political objectives, even if social scientists have concluded that objectively they both belong to the working class. It must be recognized that individuals' experiences will predispose them toward different aspects and values of the various class ideologies which interpellate them. Their reaction to competing demands from opposing class practices is as likely to be political vacillation as commitment to working-class radicalism. To understand class the totality of economic, political and ideological relations must be analysed.

An article which moves some way in that direction is *Economic Class, Social Class and Political Forces* (Cottrell and Roslender 1986). They distinguish between three 'class concepts: economic classes, social classes and political forces'. (p. 13).

Economic classes

Cottrell and Roslender point firstly to the various ways in which class has been defined by economic criteria in the work of Poulantzas,

Carchedi and Wright and the problems which have been identified by these schema. They also consider the conclusion of Cutler *et al.* (1977 and 1978) that in advanced capitalism it is the organization that is the true possessor of capital: management are subject to dismissal in the same ways as workers and are consequently all members of the working class. However, Cottrell and Roslender wish to avoid this conclusion by referring to a second criterion for defining economic class in addition to the primary criteria of property relations. This second factor is what they term the 'social division of labour' (p. 18). *Contra* Cutler *et al.* they regard this as of greater significance than a 'mere technical division of labour' (p. 18).

> It is true that managers accomplish technically necessary tasks, nonetheless the specific forms taken by the activities of management and supervision (e.g. democratically accountable or autocratic, devolved onto a special privileged category of employees or 'dispersed' as widely as possible), are socially mutable, open to contest and experimentation by opposed social forces. To this extent the managers/managed division may be legitimately considered a case of *social* division of labour. (Cottrell and Roslender 1986, p. 18. Authors' emphasis)

Thus, they arrive at a 'two-dimensional' conception of economic class, based firstly on the distinction between possessors and non-possessors of the means of production and, secondly, on the distinction between managers and managed. This latter distinction is crucial to the understanding of contemporary class practices and we shall return to it later. Where does this two-dimensional definition of economic class allow the authors to draw class boundaries?

Their concern is to find the place in the class structure of workers who perform managerial functions, those referred to up till now as the new middle class or, for Poulantzas, the new petty bourgeoisie. Firstly, Cottrell and Roslender reject Poulantzas's description of the middle classes as a new petty bourgeoisie, claiming their ideological position is too distinct from that of the traditional petty bourgeoisie to merit the application of the same class nomenclature. They also reject Wright's description of such workers as occupying contradictory class locations, describing his work as an 'ad hoc response to the failure of "orthodox" Marxist class theory' (p. 19). Instead they offer an alternative argument, that their distinction between managers and managed has revealed a new class position:

We are returned therefore, to the 'new class' position. Our view is that it is quite appropriate to speak of a managerial class, distinct from the working class and capitalist class, yet with a quite well-defined place within class relations as outlined above. (p. 19)

This claim will be considered after a brief description of the two remaining class concepts.

Social classes

Cottrell and Roslender regard social class as the product of experiences of individuals and their place in social hierarchies. They hint at an almost infinite number of determinants of social class and continue by identifying the major examples of social classes evident in contemporary capitalism. They do not, however, give details of the criteria for the establishment of the social class boundaries so described, only suggesting a vague mix of cultural values, market positions and status structures. They are certain, however, that there is little or no correspondence between economically defined classes and social classes defined in such ways, nor indeed is there any necessary correspondence between social classes and political forces.

Political forces

This term is applied to organizations and movements which 'aim at influencing state power'. Such forces do not simply express or represent class interests, the link between them being determined by 'constraints and resources and conservation/transformation effects' (p. 23). Restraints exist in the ways in which political parties are obliged to recognize existing class structures in their adoption of policies which secure mass support. Similarly, they have to draw membership and solicit votes from the classes in society, factors described as resources. Finally, political forces, although incapable in themselves of determining classes, nevertheless bear effect on their nature and form, either conserving or transforming them.

This schema has a number of attractive aspects to it, which tackle some of the thorny problems associated with class analysis. Nichols (1986) identifies two responses to the complexity of the issues in the class debate. These are 'simplification' and 'synthesis' (p. 10). He suggests Cottrell's earlier work (1984) is an attempt to simplify matters. In that, it has much to commend it. Firstly, it seems logical to define class primarily in terms of property relations, that is, specifically in terms of the relationship to the means of production. Here it must be repeated that it is possible to analyse capitalism at two levels, firstly in the abstract pure form and secondly in the ways in which it actually manifests itself in specific social formations. Thus to identify the basic abstract economic classes is necessary and a useful preliminary to the actual analysis of the classes as they appear in a given social formation.[9]

Secondly, it is crucial to recognize the ways in which those objectively defined economic classes are transformed and overlaid by ideological cultural and political practices, producing a much more complex mosaic of fractions and alliances of the classes which have been identified economically. In that respect the second determinant of economic class discussed by Cottrell and Roslender sheds light on the construction of social groups in a social formation. The distinction bears further consideration.

In distinguishing between managers and managed they have echoed in many respects the mental/manual divide identified by Poulantzas as an ideological determinant of class. For Poulantzas the distinction is based on the possession and exercise of knowledge of the production process.[10] Carter (1986) regards Poulantzas's claims for this distinction as an insufficient basis for the determination of a class boundary between the working class and the new petty bourgeoisie. Carter recognizes the importance of divisions within the work-force but rejects the idea that this constitutes a class boundary any more than does a division between skilled and unskilled workers (p. 77). It is possible to steer a middle course between Poulantzas and Carter and in doing so modify the claims of Cottrell and Roslender.

Carter's (1986) objection is that Poulantzas's use of the mental/manual divide is not an 'objective ideological relation' but is no more than the 'ideas in people's heads with no necessary relation to reality' (p. 77). Carter's claim represents an important criticism of Poulantzas and substantiates the consequent conclusion that the so-called new petty bourgeoisie is not a new class but remains part of the economically defined working class. This conclusion can be extended to the managers/managed distinction adopted by Cottrell and Roslender; such a distinction is insufficient to constitute one element of a two-dimensional definition of economic class. It would be better to consider the subjective and ideological implications of such distinctions between mental and manual labour or managed and managers. The mental/

manual divide has crucial ideological and cultural significance in both working-class consciousness and capitalist ideology. This distinction has real effects on class consciousness and political practices which can now be outlined.

Whilst this divide is not a sufficient basis for determining separate classes, its role in the fracturing of an economically defined working class should be recognized. In working-class culture the mental/manual divide carries with it many different associations, often dependent on the specific workplace culture.[11] The divide can be identified with frequently expressed dichotomies in work culture, that is, dirty/clean, quiet/noisy, safe/dangerous, salary/wages, knowing/unknowing. Similarly, the division operates as an aspect of bourgeois ideology represented in, for example, the education system (Bowles and Gintis 1976), the hierarchical structures and employment practices of organizations and the physical separation of staff from workers. These divisions represent positions in the division of labour with social, political and ideological consequences.

These divisions do not constitute class boundaries as argued for by Poulantzas and Cottrell and Roslender. Rather, they constitute a fracturing of the economically defined working class along ideological fault-lines. In that the class members have differing evaluations as to their place in the social division of labour, their experience of capitalism is subjectively different. There is no uniform experience and response to capitalist relations of production which can be readily associated with an economically defined class. The phenomenon variously identified as the new middle class or the new petty bourgeoisie is not a separate class but a fraction of the economically defined working class. It is best termed the new working class[12] in that it constitutes an element of the working class brought into existence by the conditions of mature capitalism. As a fraction of a class it is not ideologically consistent with the traditional petty bourgeoisie: Cottrell and Roslender are correct on this point. However, nor is it a new managerial class as they state. The mental/manual division identified by Poulantzas coincides in ideological practice with the managers/managed divide identified by Cottrell and Roslender. However, in contrast with both these positions, the notion that it constitutes a sufficient basis for the determination of separate classes must be rejected. It is, however, a sufficient basis for the production of separate ideological and cultural practices with political consequence for the unity of the working class.

To elaborate, the mental/manual divide constitutes the most significant division in the social hierarchy of the working class. Mental labour, and particularly supervisory labour, even of the lowest order, is seen by both those who perform it and those who are subordinate to it as a clearly distinct separation in subjective class terms.[13] It is consequently a sufficient basis for the determination of what Cottrell and Roslender term *social* classes. It is the division between managers and managed which constitutes the fracturing of the economically defined working class into two distinct *social* classes which we shall term the traditional working class and the new working class. The more limited criteria for the determination of social classes detailed by Cottrell and Roslender are sufficient only to determine social *groups* with common interests limited to narrow dimensions of social and cultural life. The category 'social class' implies more fundamental connections between individuals which express visible, articulated and organized sets of common interests which exist within a unified framework embracing different aspects of social life. They correctly identified the significance of the managers/managed division but wrongly assigned it as a determinant of economic classes. Here it is argued that it is responsible for the determination of a separate *social* class. The relationship between the new working class and the economically defined working class is that it is a fraction of it, but with a relatively autonomous ideological and political existence.

Ideological implications

The terms for the constitution of this social class can be found at the level of ideology. The distinction between managers and managed or between mental and manual labour is an ideological consequence of the physical organization of capitalist production and, in particular, the separation of conception and execution.[14] In reality, of course, conception and execution can never be totally separated and the organizational mental/manual division of labour represents a formal statement of an ideological separation.[15] Its consequences are unfortunately very real in terms of the experience that individuals have of the production process.[16] Their place in relation to that divide determines their rewards, conditions of service, career structure, pension rights and many other factors which affect the life experiences of the individual. Consequently, where the individual stands in relation to the mental/manual divide will to a large extent determine their class consciousness and cultural practice.

What then are the ideological implications of the identification of the new working class? Firstly, because it remains a fraction of the economically defined working class it shares many of the cultural values and ideological constructs of that class. Even if its objective class interests are not fully recognized, elements of them inevitably penetrate its cultural practices. They may appear as particularistic wage-related demands, or passive trade union membership. Secondly, subjectively, members of the new working class are identified with, and identify themselves with, the interests of the capitalist class (Hyman 1980). Thus, they take on some of the values and class practices of the bourgeoisie. The consequence is a 'hybrid' ideological formation. The ideological and cultural practices of both the bourgeoisie and proletariat exist in complex articulation in the new working class. Such an articulation is always present, even for the traditional working class. Pure class ideologies are non-existent and class practices are always developed from opposition to and in conjunction with the practices of other classes. However, for the new working class its workplace experience creates a greater predisposition to link with the dominant values of capitalism than can be found in the traditional working class from which the new working class has experienced a partial ideological severance.

For individuals the quality of that articulation will be determined by the distance that individuals feel themselves to be from the working class. Much of this subjective interpretation may arise from income and status factors determined by that individual's place in the workplace hierarchy. To this extent life chances and status are factors in the determination of the ideology and consequent political practice of this social class: they do not, however, bring it into existence, or contribute significantly to its reproduction. They constitute one of many factors which structure an individual's experience of a social class position.

The articulation of the two ideological practices is further complicated when the implications of social mobility are considered. The development of the new working class is a historical process. It did not spring into existence at the moment it was recognized by sociological investigation. Rather it emerged as a response to the changing patterns of capital accumulation. The growth of a service sector, the enlargement of white-collar employment by the central and local state and the growth of the welfare state are only some of the factors which have produced changes in the occupational structure of advanced capitalism. These trends also have to be coupled with decline in the traditional extractive and heavy manufacturing sectors (Goldethorpe 1980). The consequences are a much enlarged non-manual sector. This changing occupational structure has clearly reflected itself in inter- and intra-generational social mobility, as more individuals cross the mental/manual division in response to the growth of non-manual sectors of employment (Goldethorpe 1980).

The ideological consequences are significant. In the abstract discussions of the new middle class considered earlier, no recognition is given to this historical process. Many of its contemporary membership are 'new arrivals' either in comparison with their parents' occupations or their first occupation on joining the labour market. Consequently in ideological terms they are not raw materials which their new social class position shapes into appropriate class practices. They come wrapped in the culture and class practices of their point of origin. This clearly gives to mobile individuals conceptual and value frameworks through which their new social class position is mediated. This provides a subsidiary path for the introduction of elements of traditional working-class culture into the process of articulation of class practices discussed above. The members of the new working class who arrive there through social mobility arrive with a political and cultural legacy which is itself the product of the historical development of the working class. Cultural practices of this kind are not easily thrown away.

In describing the new working class a complex articulation of working-class and bourgeois ideology has been identified. The outcome of that articulation operates firstly at the individual level and will be determined by the following factors:

1) In ideological terms, whether the individual's location in the work-place hierarchy creates a greater or lesser identification with capital in his/her mind and in the minds of others.
2) The extent of social mobility experienced by the individual. That is, how far has that individual moved across the mental/manual divide. The distance will determine not only attitudes but economic determinants of the ability to adopt bourgeois values and behaviour.
3) The extent to which the individual has experienced geographical mobility, severing family and community connections and thereby weakening association with the class practices of the point of origin.

The individual responses will ultimately coalesce into patterns of political action and social class practice that can be identified with the new working class. These practices will not be the simple sum of the elements of proletarian and bourgeois ideology, but will be the product of a process of articulation, in which those elements themselves will be transformed.

Political implications

We have described a social class with a hybrid ideology, the nature of which is determined by a complex articulation of both bourgeois and proletarian ideology and culture. The political consequences of this are equally complex. At first examination this appears to be an ideal explanation of the vacillation identified with 'middle-class' politics (Klingender 1935). The support, or absence of support, for particular parties can be seen as a simple reflection of the ways in which those parties are ideologically linked with bourgeois or proletarian interests. However, such an interpretation is too simplistic. The concept of a hybrid ideological formation suggests that, rather than contradictory political positions characterizing the new working class at different times producing vacillation, they are experienced at the same time, producing deep inconsistencies in class practice. Consequently, attitudes to specific issues may lead to contradictory political practices, the nature of which will depend on the articulation of the two components of 'new working-class' ideology. This may ultimately reveal itself in electoral swings but will be symptomatic of a much deeper political inconsistency which creates a highly volatile new working class.[17]

This inconsistency was recognized as a general characteristic of the working class by Gramsci in his discussion of the 'ambiguous, contradictory and multiform' (Gramsci 1971, p. 423) nature of working-class consciousness. Gramsci additionally argues that hegemony is never absolute and that the working class displays alternative world views in its actions.

> There exists in the totality of the working masses many distinct wills: there is a communist will, a maximalist will, a reformist will, a liberal democratic will. There is even a fascist will, in a certain sense and within certain limits. (Gramsci 1925, quoted in Boggs 1976, p. 71)

For Femia (1981), at the level of the individual, hegemony is more complete and established for some individuals. The extent of its success is dependent on their 'socio-economic conditions' (p. 45). If individuals experience 'pain', disadvantage, powerlessness and exploitation as consequences of the existing 'distribution of income, power and status' (Femia p. 45), they will be less likely to be totally constituted as subjects by the dominant ideology. They may share in the general value consensus only partially and at the same time display dissent and dissatisfaction with their conditions, thereby demonstrating an 'embryonic revolutionary ideology' (p. 46).

It is argued here that a major determinant of the extent to which an individual identifies with the dominant ideology is the place he or she occupies in the production process. The closer to an economically defined working class position, the more likely will be political, cultural and ideological variance from the hegemonic world view. In contrast, the new working class consists of individuals on a continuum between the poles of working-class 'embryonic revolutionary consciousness' and the dominant ideology. It is in the new working class that the ambiguity and contradiction will be most evident. Consequently, this class constitutes more open ground for ideological struggle. As a class it is interpellated by bourgeois and working-class ideology whilst belonging fully to neither. One consequence can be the mobilization of a synthetic ideology and political praxis which differs from both 'parent' ideologies. This may entail the articulation of non-class differentiae including gender, ethnicity and nationalism. Forms of political movement emerge which do not pursue class politics but which are nevertheless a consequence of the social class position of the new working class.

The above conception of the political process encompasses both the primary determination of political forces by pre-given class structures and the secondary mediation of those structured patterns by contemporary social classes. It is a conception of political life which recognizes the influence of structural determinants of political practice as well as the subjective elements of class consciousness and culture. It reveals the dynamism and fluidity of political change. Political movements remain connected with class and its determination by the economic structure. However, the connection is not necessarily direct and simplistic. The objective interests of economically defined classes remain part of the political process, and elements of the working class and bourgeoisie will follow predictable political patterns on that basis. However, elsewhere in the class structure the ideological determination of social classes creates an articulated political praxis which is a response to the tensions experienced by the new working class in relation to bourgeois and working-class ideological interpellation.

In contrast, the restraints/resources model of political practice offered by Cottrell and Roslender (1986) echoes pluralist theory in its conception of political forces. Parties are constrained to offer political goods which the class-structured market finds feasible (p. 24). This denies the role of the classes themselves in determining the origin and evolution of those political parties, which have their origin in the pursuit of specific interests, identifiable with key economic and social classes. This process of determination of political forces is hinted at in their conception of social classes as resources for parties in the form of 'active membership, leaders, strategists, votes and funds' (p. 24). Unfortunately, their brief discussion of the process of 'working up' these raw materials does not convey the ways in which such human 'resources' actually constitute the political forces. They are not passive resources used by a disembodied party, they *are* the party and the party reflects their concerns and interests. The lack of correspondence between class and political forces demonstrated by the cross-class voting patterns discussed by Cottrell and Roslender is best explained by the effects of subjective and contradictory political beliefs held by fractions of economically defined classes, such as those discussed above.

The new working class and Welsh nationalism

The following chapter will argue that the existence of a new working class in post-war Wales led to the genesis of nationalist support in south Wales in the 1960s and 1970s. Furthermore, this political destabilizing of traditional working-class politics, i.e. labourism, can be seen as pres-aging increasing Conservative support in Wales since 1979 as well as the growth in third party support in the wider British political system. The changes occur as an occupationally and socially mobile section of the working class emerges in Welsh society following the Second World War. The subjective experience of the new social class is highly contradictory. It is an experience torn between origins in archetypal working-class communities and new experiences which are ideologi-cally separated and distanced from those origins. This development of a new social class produced a weakening of the traditional allegiances to the Labour Party but did not create support for the Conservative Party; such a shift constituted too great a cultural and political leap. The elements of traditional working-class practices in the new working-class culture were of too recent an origin and were too powerful to allow a total dominance of the hybrid ideology by bourgeois components. The class and cultural practices of the working class dominated, at least in the short term, but not sufficiently to guarantee the reproduction of traditional patterns of Labour Party support.

The process can best be seen as a gradual destructuring of the traditional working class and the erosion of its political culture and practices. This is particularly true in south Wales where social mobility and consequent emigration has affected the valley communities (Rees 1976). The social mobility alone is sufficient to weaken the links with traditional political practices and where it is accompanied by geographical mobility the effect is enhanced. The ultimate destructuring effect on traditional working-class politics is more profound when it is considered that the emerging political values of the new working class do not remain sealed in a social vacuum but bleed back into the traditional working-class communities through maintained family, peer-group and community associations. One of the characteristics of geographical mobility in the post-war period is the predominance of short-range migration to the coastal plain (Rees 1976). This contrasts with the longer-range migration between the wars. In this way members of the new working class retain social connections with their point of origin and feed their emerging values and political beliefs into traditional working-class culture. The consequences are a gradual erosion and destructuring of the basis of labourism even in the valley heartlands, a process first reflected in the support *Plaid Cymru* gained in parts of south Wales in the 1960s and 1970s. These claims will be elaborated and tested in the following chapter.

CHAPTER 8

CLASS AND NATION IN POST-WAR WALES

In the preceding chapter a theoretical argument was presented for the recognition of the role of the 'new working class' in the nationalist resurgence of the 1960s and 1970s. It was suggested that the major change in Welsh society during that period was the growth of what is generally referred to as the 'middle classes', primarily identified with the growth in the occupational structure of categories of non-manual, white-collar, and supervisory workers. Rather than identifying this group as entirely separated from the working class, it was suggested that it should be recognized as a fraction of an economically defined working class, but distinguished from it at the level of ideology and, as a result, at variance in its political practice.

Additionally, it was suggested that nationalist politics provided an ideological space for political praxis by this social class which has become disconnected from the politics of the traditional working class, of which it is a fraction. The members of this fraction in Wales can be seen as predisposed by ideological conditions to distance themselves from traditional working-class support for the Labour Party and to articulate their political interests with the politics of nationalism, which had acquired greater significance in rural politics during the early 1960s. Bound up within these broad theoretical claims is a wide range of social processes which take place at the economic, political and ideological levels of the social formation. This chapter will attempt to map the complex relationships between these levels. In Chapters 4 and 5 we applied this theoretical framework to the nineteenth-century social formation: now the articulation of class and nation in post-war Wales will be examined.

If it is considered that we are attempting to discover the connection between a social class defined at the level of ideology and its actual existence as a social and political force, we are initially confronted with difficulties in establishing the membership of that class. Whilst, at the level of theory, we can suggest the relationship in the workplace which might lead to this class identity, such arguments do not translate directly into occupational categories, the existence of which can be measured empirically. The 'new working class' exists at the subjective level: in terms of membership it is made up of those who feel themselves to be in a particular relationship to the mental/manual division of labour. Furthermore, once formed, this class begins to interpellate other individuals with its ideology and it 'bleeds' outwards into the social formation, establishing support amongst individuals who do not share the same objective position in the division of labour.

In the theoretical discussion in the previous chapter it was concluded that membership of the 'new working class' hinges on the distinction between mental and manual labour. However, it is the meaning of that distinction in working-class ideology and class practice that gives existence to the new working class. It was suggested that, in popular discourse, routine clerical and low-grade supervisory status are sufficient criteria to identify workers in their own minds, and the minds of others, as an element of managerial structures. This subjective identification will not correspond with their formal place in the organizational hierarchy or with the category such workers occupy in statistical analysis of class structures which employ occupational criteria. Consequently, a direct measurement of the 'new working class', in terms of empirically verifiable occupational categories, is impossible. The new working class exists at the level of ideology and its existence is best verified by reference to the political and ideological levels of the social formation through a study of the political practices and ideological movements which give expression to its values and interests.

Further problems of connecting the theoretical claims of the previous chapter with the empirical reality of the social formation are created by the retrospective nature of this analysis. We are attempting to discover the social basis of a movement which reached its peak nearly fifteen years ago. Directly empirical methods cannot be adopted in such circumstances; methods such as the social survey are impossible to apply reliably in retrospect. It is also important that our attempts at verification confront the process of the development of nationalist politics during this period and thus require a degree of longitudinal analysis (Hechter and Levi 1979). This is an especially difficult objective to achieve and depends on the identification of effective, surrogate measures of ethnicity. Hechter and Levi cite electoral data, newspaper reporting of ethnoregional political mobilization and marriage records as potential sources of information about the connection between ethnicity and class.

The first of these has clear weaknesses. Electoral politics associated with nationalism and ethnicity, by definition, take place in a wider political environment. The issues of ethnicity are articulated with the political, ideological and economic concerns of the wider polity. In Wales the complex relationship between the Welsh dimension of politics and the wider influences of British national politics has many implications for the political practice of nationalism. The often competing concerns of Welsh and British politics present voters in Wales with additional decisions and difficulties in the practice of their political beliefs.

Consequently, general elections and local government elections produce different levels of ethnic activity and support. Much of the support for *Plaid Cymru* in the 1970s was at local level and the party failed to gain equal levels of support at constituency level. Furthermore, electoral statistics inform us only about the political organizations of the nationalist movement and not the social base of the movement in non-political organizations and actions. In the Welsh context, an overemphasis on electoral statistics would fail completely to reveal the activities of *Cymdeithas Yr Iaith Gymraeg* (the Welsh Language Society) and other less vociferous, culturally motivated organizations.

There are similar problems with the second surrogate measure advocated by Hechter and Levi (1979). Newspaper reportage of ethnic political mobilization frequently reflects a centralist perspective. The interpretation of ethnic and regional political events by the media in Wales is generally subordinated to the reportage of the impact of external factors determined by the British political system. Additionally, there is a range of restraints on the reporting of ethnic politics determined by newsworthiness and the status of ethnic politics as a minority political practice. Coverage is consequently selective and subjective and gives little more than an account of the numerical frequency of ethnic political occurrences. If any attempt at evaluation of the content of activity is attempted using this source, a degree of interpretive inaccuracy will be inevitable. Finally, the attempt to measure ethnic cohesiveness by reference to endogamy may have a certain degree of salience in societies clearly divided by race and ethnicity. However, its value in a context such as Great Britain is negligible given the high degree of integration between Celtic and Anglo-Saxon groups and the invisible qualities of the divisions between them.

The discussion above indicates the difficulties of linking the theoretical arguments of the previous chapter with the political practices evident in the Welsh social formation in the post-war period. However, it will be established here that the social, economic, and political conditions necessary for the growth of a new working-class fraction, and its adoption of nationalist politics, were evident in Wales during the post-war period. The conditions which promoted the development of a new working class emerge from changes in the economic and occupational structures of Wales, and the social and political consequences of these changes.

Economic and social restructuring in post-war Wales

The restructuring of the economy in post-war Wales has been well documented (Williams and Boyns 1977, Cooke and Rees 1981, Cooke 1982, Rees and Rees 1983, Edwards 1985).[1] All authors are agreed as to the central characteristics of the restructuring although some have emphasized different aspects of the process. The primary features of this economic reconstruction have been identified by Cooke (1983) as firstly, a reduction of the role of the primary industries in the Welsh economy, secondly, the post-war growth of a 'secondary manufacturing sector' (p. 72) and thirdly, the growth of a service sector. All three developments have potential impact on the class restructuring of the region (Rees and Rees 1983).

The first factor, represented most clearly by the declining significance of coal in the Welsh economy, has been a gradual process evident since the peaks of coal production were achieved in the first two decades of this century.[2] The decline in the coal industry has at times been accelerated by economic crisis and central government policy.[3] The major political consequences of this traditional economic emphasis on heavy and extractive industry was the creation of large work-forces centred on single-occupation industries. Coupled with the commonality of the work experience was the development of a social and cultural experience rooted in the communities of workers living adjacent to their place of employment (Rawkins 1979). The consequences were highly solidary patterns of trade union and Labour Party support.

The decline of the traditional industries was, to some extent, offset by the development of a 'secondary manufacturing sector' during the 1950s and 1960s. This diversification of the economy reflected the core of central government policy on the regional problem expressed in strategies of financial and tax incentives which encouraged industrial development in the region.[4] The jobs created in this sector were seen in policy terms as direct replacements for those lost in the primary sector. However, two factors prevented the achievement of this policy objective. The first was that much of the industry attracted to the area was located on sites of development on the coastal plain and mouths of valleys, some distance from the communities most seriously affected by the decline of coal production (Rees and Rees 1983). The second factor was that the industries which came to the area were in light manufacturing, electrical engineering and later electronics, and textile and clothing manufacture (Edwards 1985). Many of the new jobs created were low-wage and attracted female workers, a pattern reinforced by the recruitment policies of the companies involved. The male labour shed by the traditional primary industries was effectively excluded from the new forms of employment (Town 1978).

This growth of a diversified manufacturing sector, although constituting a major contribution to employment, particularly in south Wales, failed to compensate for the job losses in the traditional industries (Edwards 1985). Furthermore, the primary characteristic of this developing diversification was the extent to which it was controlled by companies with their centres outside Wales (Tomkins and Lovering 1973). Edwards (1985) suggests that the secondary status of these branch plants within company structures contributed to the rapid collapse of this sector in Wales during the economic crisis of the late 1970s and early 1980s.[5]

Despite the crucial importance of the growth and rapid decline of this sector, the most signicant shift in the pattern of employment, particularly in south Wales, is identified by Cooke (1983) and Rees and Rees (1983) as the growth of a service sector throughout the post-war years, but especially from the late 1960s onwards. For Cooke, this sector has consistently grown in size and significance in the Welsh economy.

> It is this sector which, to a considerable extent, is responsible for revolutionising the occupational patterns of workers in the diverse areas of Wales. (Cooke 1983, p. 73)

The service sector was initially the product of the developing role of the state in the post-war period as its increasing activities in the provision of education, health and welfare services created large bureaucracies. From the 1960s onwards the pattern of state activity also included a devolution of administratve functions to the regions. There has also been in the late 1980s the emergence of a commercial and financial service sector centred on Cardiff. The key impetus of this process was established by the creation of the Welsh Office (Randall 1972) and the relocation of a number of government departments during the 1960s and 1970s.[6]

Cooke shows that this 'tertiarisation' of the economy has 'almost offset the loss of manufacturing jobs throughout Wales as a whole during the period 1976–1981' (p. 79). This considerable growth in the service sector is significant in the emergence of the 'new working class' in Wales during the post-war years, in that it is the service and administrative sector which is most likely to produce the different ideological orientations to work and society which will characterize the 'new working class'.

The net effects of these three patterns of change in the occupational structure of the Welsh economy have been a destabilizing of the political practices and social forces derived from traditional patterns of class relations and their gradual replacement by alternative political and social formations. The decline of the primary and extractive industries has had considerable effect on the class structure of south Wales. The shared work and communal experience engendered by single-occupation communities has been eroded by the decimation of employment in coal production during the 1950s and 1960s and again in the 1980s and 1990s, and in steel and metal manufacture in the 1970s and 1980s. As a result the social and economic basis of the reproduction of labourism has diminished. Whilst those already stamped with the work and community experience of the mining valleys are likely to retain their political loyalties to the Labour Party, emerging cohorts of voters no longer experience a reinforcement of familial, political socialization in their work and community experience. The totality of socialization in Labour politics has been broken.

The effects of the decline of male manual employment opportunities have been exaggerated by the nature of the alternative forms of employment which have developed. The location of much of the new employment opportunities at the valley-mouth and coastal-belt locations has imposed difficult choices on the members of valley communities. For Rees and Rees (1983) the response by the working class has been varied. Of some significance to the argument presented here is their belief that a section of the working class are able to take advantage of these structural changes by becoming geographically and socially mobile. An element of the younger, and more educationally qualified, population relocate themselves on the coastal belt and take advantage of the employment opportunites offered by the developing industrial and service-sector enclave.

What is happening is that those working class who are able to 'make out' in the changing world of post-war south Wales are distancing themselves from the less fortunate members of working class communities, not only in terms of the material conditions of their lives, but also in a literal, spatial sense. (Rees and Rees 1983, p. 119)

For Rees and Rees, the consequence is the erosion of working-class solidarity in the Labour heartlands of the valleys and a weakened working-class resistance to capitalist restructuring of the Welsh economy. Migration also results in a weakening ideological identification with working-class community identity and the political values that such an identity has historically carried. The geographically/socially mobile emigrants become severed from their political and cultural environment, opening a space for alternative ideological elements to interpellate them. One of the initial effects of this social and geographical mobility is a weakening of the correspondence between Labour Party ideology and the political, moral and social values of this mobile section of the working class.

An additional source of destabilization of working-class politics can also be identified in the growth of the service sector. Whilst at one level it is clear that this growth provides opportunity for managerial and supervisory employment, the extent to which such opportunities have been filled by indigenous workers or English immigrants, the latter identified by Williams (1981) as 'spiralists' (p. 299), is not clear. Such spiralists are highly geographically and socially mobile and rarely settle in Wales for sufficient time to enable integration with the wider community and culture. This, for Williams, 'approximates a cultural division of labor'(p. 300); key supervisory and decision-making posts in the service sector, and to a similar extent in the industrial sector, are increasingly occupied by a 'foreign bourgeoisie' (p. 301). Williams argues that this serves to add an ethnic dimension to class divisions in the workplace.

As such institutions become established, however, they recruit local labour to positions of higher authority, promoting the growth of an indigenous group of managerial and supervisory workers who experience the dislocation from traditional political, community and cultural influences already identified. Indeed, for Day (1981), the growth of the service sector in Wales has been marked by the Welsh character of many of the institutions established, especially in the post-war period. This has created employment opportunities for a

Welsh-speaking middle class which has grown numerically and in significance as a result. Day claims:

> Cardiff has become the home of a tight-knit, and sizeable, Welsh middle class involved in administration, education and the media. (1981, p. 32)

Electorally, this group has not had the effect Day's analysis might at first suggest. *Plaid Cymru* has never secured even its national average levels of support in the Cardiff constituencies (Balsom and Birch 1980). The significance of this group is perhaps more in its capacity to accelerate and reinforce the development of the 'regional consensus' identified by Rees and Lambert (1981). This consensus is shared by state officials, business organizations and trade unions and is reproduced in the state agencies with special responsibilities for Welsh affairs. For Day, this Welsh middle class allies itself with the traditional nationalism of the intellectual, culturalist wing of the nationalist movement, in a shared attempt to secure the 'means of administration, and the means of cultural reproduction' (p. 37).

These effects of the development of the service and administrative sector of the economy in south Wales are clearly of considerable significance in the restructuring of class in the region. However, the number of managerial and higher supervisory jobs created for an indigenous labour force, by the growth of the service sector, are small in comparison with the large number of jobs created at thc lower levels of the occupational structure. Primarily the employment created has been low-paid and female work, much of it part-time. Consequently, for Cooke this creates a 'proletarian' (p. 83) work experience. However, Cooke's conclusion represents a reading of their class position from limited, objective economic criteria, and does not consider ideological factors which may influence the experience such employees have of their work and their political attitudes. Whilst many of the jobs are routine clerical work, of low pay and status, they are, however, on the mental side of the mental/manual divide and consequently can be identified with a bourgeois class position to varying degrees.

The theoretical justification of this statement in the previous chapter hinges on the distinctions made in traditional working-class ideology between mental and manual labour and the association of the former with the management of capital. It was argued that this distinction represents a factor which can constitute the basis of the formation of a social class; a fraction of a basic class which behaves differently at the level of politics and ideology. It is therefore suggested that, despite the objective economic class position of routine clerical, administrative and certain service-sector workers, an ideological division has developed between this and the more traditional, manual-labouring sectors of the working class. The immediate consequence is a disarticulation of the experience of the workplace from the political discourse of labourism. Again, the resulting social and geographical mobility, as workers move to the centres of administration and service provision, furthers the breakdown of traditional political socialization and the erosion of the traditional social base of labourism in south Wales.

To summarize, in post-war Wales there has been gradual erosion of the industrial and occupational basis of Labour Party domination of the formal political structure. The primary determinant of this change has been the net effects of the transformation of economic activity, constituted by a collapse of heavy extractive and primary industries and the evolution of a light manufacturing and service sector as the prime source of economic activity. This has been accompanied by a resettlement of economic activity on the coastal plain and a consequent pattern of migration to this area from the valley communities. This changing structure of economic activity has created considerable change in the occupational structure, with consequences for class relations and the nature of political practice in south Wales. The most obvious consequence of this economic reconstruction is the erosion of the conditions which reproduce labourism, permitting the emergence and reproduction of alternative political and ideological practices.

Nationalism can be seen as the ideological response of a mobile section of the working-class to the failure of labourism to respond to the changing social and political climate of the region. It offered a radicalism and a conception of social justice which was not bound within working-class imagery and culture but was not entirely alien to it.

Nationalism connected with a sense of Welsh identity which had survived in Welsh working-class culture from the nineteenth-century influence of Welsh radicalism and Nonconformism. Corrado (1975) and Balsom et al. (1982) suggest that, whilst Welsh-language use is the most clear indicator of ethnic identification and nationalist aspirations, we must also recognize the influence of a sense of Welsh identity which is not dependent on the medium of speech. Corrado (1975) identifies the existence of 'social communalism' which is a general 'desire of individuals to retain certain social habits' (p. 363) associated with Welshness but not necessarily linked to Welsh language and its corresponding culture. In its simplest form this 'social communalism' is represented by support for 'Welsh athletic teams' (p. 364). In a more detailed survey Balsom *et al.* (1982) found that 62 per cent of 'Welsh identifiers' (p. 4) were not Welsh speakers. The authors distinguished between 'Cymrics' who spoke Welsh and identified themselves as Welsh, and the 'Welsh', who spoke only English but, nevertheless, also identified themselves as Welsh. The latter group constituted 34 per cent of the survey sample. Whilst the survey revealed no clear link between Welsh identification and nationalist support, it did conclude that such an identity can be mobilized by different political movements leading to support for both the Welsh Labour Party and *Plaid Cymru*. Their findings suggest that Welsh identity is a sedimented element of Welsh working-class consciousness which, in the nationalist resurgence of the 1970s, provided the basis of support for *Plaid Cymru* from monoglot English-speaking, Welsh identifiers. However, in the 1980s the same sense of Welsh identity has led to a greater identification with the Labour Party, which seems to them to represent the clearest source of opposition to a centralist Conservative government

In examining the post-war economic reconstruction in Wales this chapter has established that the conditions for the emergence of what has been identified as the 'new working class' were promoted by the changes in the class structure of the region, especially in the industrialized areas of south and south-east Wales. It has been suggested that the economic restructuring of this period created a class restructuring, determined by a growth of the occupational categories which constitute a fraction of the working class which seeks an alternative political practice consonant with its ideological position. It has been argued that the ideology of labourism failed to correspond with the subjective class images of the new working class and that nationalism provided an alternative form of political expression by the 1960s and 1970s. Consequently our next objective is to establish whether the impact of this class fraction on Welsh nationalist politics can be identified in the post-war period.

The social base of nationalist politics

In determining the social base of nationalism during the 1960s and 1970s our primary concern will be with identifying the emergence of nationalist support in the industrialized south-east of Wales. Primacy is given to this region because it will be suggested that the most significant element of the nationalist resurgence in Welsh politics is the recruitment of increasingly large numbers of traditional Labour Party supporters in the Labour-dominated constituencies of the south. It is the emergence of this increasing working-class support in the industrialized south which signals a conjuncture during which nationalist politics were to have considerable impact on the politics of Britain as a whole. It also represents a fundamental shift in the social basis of support for *Plaid Cymru* and results in a concomitant change in party ideology and policy.

It was suggested in Chapter 7 that *Plaid Cymru* and nationalism had little effect on the path of British politics during the inter-war and early post-war years (Butt Philip 1975). Nationalism remained the political reserve of the Welsh-speaking intelligentsia and literati, concerned primarily with cultural and linguistic maintenance and relatively indifferent to the achievement of nationhood (Davies 1983). However, *Plaid Cymru*'s participation in the Parliament for Wales Campaign of the early 1950s indicated some belief in the objective of independence on the part of the party leadership, although no popular support for the movement was mobilized (Morgan 1981). The resurgence of nationalism and ethnicity began in the opening years of the 1960s as concern mounted for the declining use of the language and the increasing threat to Welsh culture and life-style posed by industrialization, English immigration into Welsh-speaking areas and the growing cultural imperialism of English-language media.

Such fears had been present throughout the 1950s[7] but were brought to a head by the proposal to flood the valley of Tryweryn (Madgwick *et al.* 1973). The growing concern was given influential voice by Saunders Lewis in his radio lecture *Tynged Yr Iaith* (1962). These fears for the future of Welsh language and culture initially gained support from the traditional nationalist base in the rural Welsh-speaking communities. This initial stage in the resurgence of nationalism in post-war Wales derived from the vestigial form of nationalism which had its origin in nineteenth-century Wales and was still intimately connected with Nonconformist worship and the Welsh tenantry and farming communities. Rawkins (1979) refers to this form of nationalism as 'fortress nationalism' (p. 443) and identifies it with a rural middle class, educated primarily in the Welsh University colleges. 'Fortress nationalism' mounts a defence of the rural community against external pressures which make inroads into the integrity of the rural Welsh culture and life-style. Rawkins identifies it primarily with the inter-war generation of nationalists but emphasizes its continued influence over the post-war nationalist movement.

In response to the growing concern over linguistic and cultural decline, the threat to flood Tryweryn and the call to action from

Saunders Lewis, increasing criticism emerged of *Plaid Cymru*'s parliamentarianism (Butt Philip 1975). The result was increasing political protest and the formation of *Cymdeithas Yr Iaith Gymraeg* (the Welsh Language Society) which was dedicated to a programme of non-violent direct action. Increasingly militant and radical in the forms of protest adopted, this developing political practice constituted for Rawkins (1979) the emergence of 'militant cultural nationalism' (p. 449).

'Militant cultural nationalism' existed in uneasy alliance with the 'fortress nationalists' of the pre-war movement. Ironically, many of them were from the same social background in the rural middle class. For Rawkins (1979), Madgwick (1973) and Grant and Preece (1968), it is the comparative youth of this element of nationalist support which is its outstanding feature, prompting some explanation by reference to the wider phenomenon of student and youth unrest (Madgwick 1973).[8] However, for Rawkins (1979), more important are the family connections between the 'fortress nationalist' and the 'militant cultural nationalist'. The latter were often the sons and daughters of the former.

> The majority had grown up in families for whom Welsh cultural and religious life was the core of their existence, though a few had grown up in homes where only one parent was Welsh-speaking, and where the use of the language was not encouraged. Most came from comfortable, middle-class, highly literate backgrounds in rural Wales. (Rawkins 1979, p. 450)

Of equal importance was the education of this generation of nationalists in the Welsh colleges, especially at Aberystwyth (Rawkins 1979).

This rural configuration of support for nationalism can clearly be linked to the linguistic and cultural concerns of a rural middle class. Additionally, it can be analysed as a reaction to the threat to its primacy in the rural class structure constituted by Anglicization and secularization of the rural communities. This basis of support was sufficient to secure the election of *Plaid Cymru* candidate Gwynfor Evans in the July 1966 Carmarthen by-election when a number of specifically local factors created an opportunity for a Plaid victory.[9] However, as a basis for a resurgence of nationalist politics these, primarily rural, factors were of insufficient political magnitude. The ability of the rural middle class significantly to affect the course of Welsh politics was severely limited by the narrow basis of its appeal to popular democratic politics. Its political platform was limited to linguistic and cultural concerns and was the product primarily of rural conditions, with little obvious relevance to an industrial working class. As in the instance of the nineteenth-century development of nationalism, we have to consider factors in the industrial regions of the Welsh social formation to understand fully the resurgence of nationalist political activity. The basis of support in the rural conditions outlined above were of crucial significance in heightening ethnic awareness and recruiting a new generation to a more vigorous form of cultural nationalism. However, it was the emergence of nationalist sympathies amongst key sections of the urban working and middle classes which was to form the basis of the domination of Welsh politics by nationalist demands, evident by the mid 1970s.

Rawkins (1979) identifies the emergence of what he describes as the 'modernists' (p. 452) in the Welsh national movement from 1966 onwards. Modernists were distinguished from other forms of nationalist by their location in the urban and industrial communities of south and south-east Wales. For Rawkins, these nationalists were less concerned with the survival of culture and more motivated by 'radical political commitment to economic and social justice' (p. 453). Largely middle-class, university-educated and English-speaking, it was this section which was to articulate a form of nationalism which could appeal directly to the 'new working class' in south Wales. As branches multiplied in the industrial valleys and as 'modernists' increasingly penetrated party organization, the ideology of cultural nationalism, which for so long had constituted the identity of *Plaid Cymru*, was challenged by an increasingly economistic interpretation of the problems of Welsh society (Rawkins 1979, Butt Philip 1975, Davies 1985). The result was a gradual movement of the party to the left of the political spectrum, establishing a socialist ideology and party policy (Davies 1985). This transformation from a linguistic/culturalist nationalism to a socialist nationalism represented the culmination of conflicts and struggles in the party throughout the 1970s. Nor is such a transformation ever total and there has been resistance to the socialist objectives of the party from cultural nationalists, expressed initially by the Hydro group.[10]

It is clear, however, that the transition from a limited cultural nationalism in the early 1960s to a thoroughly economistic appraisal of Welsh politics by the early 1970s represented an ideological shift brought about by the participation of an increasing membership in the industrial south (Butt Philip 1975). The policies of *Plaid Cymru* moved rapidly from a culturalist protectionism to a radical, campaigning, social democracy. Whilst a content analysis of party publications is beyond the scope of this chapter, it is clear from even a brief review of the period that a major ideological transformation had occurred. This is perhaps most clear in major party publications such as *The Economic Plan For Wales* (Plaid Cymru 1969) and the *Report of the Commission of Enquiry* (Plaid Cymru 1981). In reading such publications we can see a transition to a party which regards its own future, and the future of Wales, as being secured in the industrial south and south-east. Whilst it has not forsaken entirely its commitment to language and cultural issues, it has left such areas increasingly to *Cymdeithas Yr Iaith Gymraeg* and other cultural institutions (Davies 1985).

It has been suggested in this and the previous chapter that it is the interpellation, by nationalist ideology, of an industrialized, 'new working' class and sections of the urban middle classes which constituted the grounds of the nationalist resurgence of the 1960s. Without this emergence of an urban basis for nationalist politics the rural forces would not in themselves have constituted a sufficient social basis for the resurgence of nationalist politics in post-war Wales. The application of the theoretical framework developed in Chapters 3 and 4 suggests that the nationalism of this period can only be understood by referring to the articulation of nationalism and ethnicity with the class-based politics of the period. We must consider the ways in which the rural middle class and an urban, 'new working' class come together in an alliance which was opposed to the domination of Welsh politics not only by a centralized British state but also by a monolithic Labour Party which was, for all intents and purposes, the political establishment of the region.

The Labour Party can be seen to have been hegemonic in the Welsh social formation and to have established a political and moral leadership which was becoming increasingly out of tune with popular feeling and aspirations. Bound within the political framework of inter-war politics and practising an increasingly out-of-date and irrelevant conception of the class strucure of Wales, the Labour Party remained wedded to a political orthodoxy which no longer corresponded to the experience of key sections of the working class. Social and geographical mobility was beginning to sever the community associations of occupation, life-style and politics and create the basis for a more open ideological terrain.

This process was felt most of all by the 'new working class'. Geographically and socially mobile, this social class finds itself interpellated by the competing ideologies of its objective working-class membership and by its ideological connection with bourgeois subject positions. Separated from full acceptance of working-class ideas and values by the mental/manual division of labour, it finds itself interpellated by bourgeois values and ideology. However, given the origins of many of its members in the traditional working class and, given the minimum distance such members have moved across the mental/manual divide, the transition to support for bourgeois political objectives is limited.

In south Wales, support for the Conservative Party was not forthcoming in the initial stages of this destabilization of the traditional basis of Labour Party support. Yet neither could the new working class maintain its commitment to the domination of politics in south Wales by the Labour Party. Although this class shared some of the objectives and values of labourism, the Labour Party was rejected as a fit vehicle for the achievement of those objectives. Instead, the new working class found itself on an open ideological terrain which enabled articulation with the class-independent ideology of nationalism. Nationalist ideology provided a potentially radical alternative to the ideologies of Conservatism and labourism, neither of which directly corresponded to the position of the new working class.

Unable to distance itself from its immediate labourist past to an extent that would permit Conservative support, the mobile section of the working class attached itself to the nationalism of the rural classes. It quickly became the hegemonic force within the nationalist movement, establishing its concerns and policies as the platform on which the political wing of the nationalist movement appealed to the people of Wales. Increasingly, that appeal drew a response from the Welsh working class in the Labour Party heartlands, reaching beyond the 'new working class' into the traditional sections of the working class. A socially mobile and primarily young, urban, nationalist movement successfully challenged the hegemony of the Labour Party in the south Wales communities and reconstructed Welsh nationalism in the process. It was the articulation of socialistic concepts of economic organization and social justice, wedded to a sense of national identity which was not dependent on Welsh-language use (Balsom *et al.* 1982) which was to form the basis of a serious challenge to the Labour Party in Wales, as well as to the centralism of the British state.

Plaid Cymru support in the industrial south and south-east of Wales has considerable significance for the analysis of Welsh politics; working-class nationalist support cannot be dismissed as a protest vote prompted by Labour Party failures in the early 1970s. The strategy of protest voting suggests that, having made the protest, the electorate would eventually return to a support of the party which most clearly represents their objective interests. It has here been suggested instead that the emergence of *Plaid Cymru* as a political force in the Labour heartlands is indicative of a declining basis of social support for the Labour Party. It reflects significant changes in the structure of class and the ideological and political effects of those changes.

The emergence of support for *Plaid Cymru* in the industrial south of Wales in the 1970s can be seen as the first stage in the destabilizing of Welsh politics, reflecting a declining traditional working-class political base and an increasing social class differentiation. Such changes eventually created the basis of support for SDP/Liberal alliance candidates in local government and general elections, but more importantly has allowed a growth of Conservative Party support after 1979. This is not to suggest that the individual electors who first moved their support from Labour to *Plaid Cymru* completed their political odyssey by voting for Conservatism. Rather this demonstration of working-class support for *Plaid Cymru* signalled the decline of the social basis of Labour support, a decline which has accelerated in the 1980s. The electoral cohort which first supported *Plaid Cymru* would have either maintained that support or reverted to traditional Labour allegiance. It is subsequent voters, who find themselves more distanced from traditional working-class political culture, who have been more socially mobile than the previous cohort, and who have made the final transition to Conservative Party support. It is no coincidence that the Conservative inroads into Welsh politics have occurred in the coastal towns and dormitory constituencies most clearly associated with the sunrise industries and the increasing affluence of this part of south Wales.

The resurgence of Welsh nationalism in the 1970s was indicative of fundamental changes in the political structure of Great Britain as well as of Wales. The changing occupational structure experienced in south Wales during the post-war period has also been experienced in other regions. However, in other regions the absence of ethnic differentiation prevented such early opportunity for the new working class to give voice to its increasing alienation from labourism and the Labour Party. The consequences were a delay in the expression of the alternative political aspirations of this social class until the political climate favoured the emergence of a third party in the context of British politics. Welsh politics in the 1970s gave an indication of the likelihood of third-party interventions in traditional Labour heartlands throughout Britain in the elections of 1979, 1983 and 1987.

CONCLUSION

In this study an attempt has been made to analyse and explain the genesis of Welsh nationalism in the nineteenth century and its resurgence in the twentieth century. To achieve this objective a theoretical framework has been developed which employs the concepts of ideology and hegemony to discover the role of nationalist political practice in the economic, ideological and political relations of the social formation. These concepts have been central to the development of Marxist social and political theory in the post-war period and have permitted the emergence of a less economistic and reductionist form of Marxism than is conventionally identified with the perspective. In applying these concepts to the study of nationalism the framework has remained consistent with the paradigm which extends from the thought of Marx and Engels on the national question, through the work of Lenin and reaching its most coherent expression in the writings of Antonio Gramsci.

In adopting this paradigm the attempts of Kedourie, Gellner and Smith to explain the national question were rejected. Kedourie's analysis is regarded as idealistic and lacking any grounding in the real world of human social and political practice. By contrast, Gellner's work, and to a lesser extent Smith's, offers a far more sociological analysis in which nationalism is formed by the social relationships of a world divided by the effects of modernization. Unfortunately, in Gellner's analysis, a limited conception of the process of modernization creates an ahistoricism which restricts the capacity of his theory to explain both pre-capitalist expressions of nationalism, and the wave of nationalist resurgences in the developed world in the post-war period. Similarly, Smith fails to identify and explain the conditions under which the responses to modernization identified by his theory occur.

Nationalism is manifest in many contexts and in many different forms; any useful theory of nationalism must come to terms with both its universality and its diversity. A theory capable of analysing and explaining nationalism must uncover the underlying, causative factors which give nationalism its universal qualities. It must also have the capacity to evaluate the unique qualities of different social formations, which determine the nature and form of each expression of nationalism. From recent developments in the usage of the concepts of ideology and hegemony, a theoretical framework has been developed here which is capable of both these requirements.

The universality of nationalism, as a political practice, can be explained by examining its role in hegemonic struggle. As suggested here, nationalism provides an ideological cement which binds classes together in 'historical blocs' providing the common ground for a synthesis and transcendence of particularistic class interests. The class neutrality of nationalist ideology gives it a 'free floating' quality which permits its appropriation by any class, class fraction or combination of classes. Struggles between such elements of the social structure are universal and, consequently, nationalism and national identity are articulated universally as elements of political and ideological discourse. This class-neutral quality of nationalist ideology is the point at which this study deviates most fundamentally from orthodox Marxist accounts of the national question.

Nationalism is not a bourgeois ideology. This is not to argue that it does not have an important role to play in bourgeois ideology and the maintenance of a ruling class hegemony. Nor is it simply a proletarian ideology, although it may provide the ideological cement binding proletarian political movements to other subordinate classes. Nationalism has to be recognized as a class-independent and neutral ideology which is given its class significance by a process of articulation with class practices and ideologies. Nationalism can equally be an element of bourgeois or of proletarian ideology. In nineteenth-century Wales, the class-neutrality of nationalism is evident in its presence in the political practice of a rural tenantry, with its origins in the feudal mode of production, and in the political practice of an indigenous urban bourgeoisie. It bound these classes together in an attack on the landed class in the rural sector and provided the basis of a bourgeois hegemony in the industrial sector.

In twentieth-century Wales the class-neutrality of nationalism is demonstrated by its mobilization by both a rural middle class and a fraction of the industrial working class. The result is an alliance and synthesis of their separate and particularistic class interests under the moral and intellectual leadership of an urban, 'new working class'. This demonstrates that nationalism operates as an ideology within the context of a general process of struggle between all social classes, not only the primary economic classes. We can recognize that the important features of class struggle are not always limited to an open conflict between a ruling and a subordinate class. Hegemonic conflict also occurs between subordinate classes. In Wales in the 1960s the struggle was not simply between labour and capital, but was a struggle over which social class should be the hegemonic force amongst the subordinate classes in Wales. This suggests that any social formation must be seen as layered with a hierarchy of hegemonic conflicts in which social classes compete for places in a structure of class relations. Such a structure is more complex than is indicated by reference to a simple, dichotomous relationship between a ruling and a subordinate class. The complex internal structure of hegemonic and counter-hegemonic movements must be recognized.

The final feature of nationalism, indicated by a recognition of its class-neutrality, is that its existence is not limited to certain stages in the development of a social formation. One of the difficulties associated with the western origin of theories of nationalism has been an inability to analyse pre-capitalist expressions of nationalism. The effect has been an ethnocentrism which was discussed in Chapter 2. Given recognition of the class-neutrality of nationalist ideology and its universal role in hegemonic struggles, the universality of such struggle transcends capitalist and pre-capitalist divisions and, consequently, nationalism can constitute an element of hegemonic struggle in pre-capitalist societies.

It was also suggested earlier that, as well as explaining the universality of nationalism, an adequate theory of nationalism must be capable of analysing the particular forms it takes. The opening chapter brought attention to the diversity of nationalism and the many ways in which nationalist aspirations are expressed. Its articulation with conservative, liberal and revolutionary movements has posed serious difficulties for the analysis of nationalism. It has been impossible to place nationalism on any political spectrum of left and right, or identify any universal characteristics such as an inherent conservatism or radicalism. The variety in the expression of national identities is best explained by reference to the role that the ideology performs in hegemonic struggle within each specific social formation. Nationalism is articulated with class ideologies in the context of class struggle and its characteristics will be dependent on which class mobilizes the ideology or alternatively which class is the moral and intellectual leader of any classes brought together under the nationalist banner.

The first factor which will determine the character of nationalism is whether the nationalist movement is hegemonic or counter-hegemonic. Is the nationalism mobilized to establish the interests of a ruling class as a general will within the social formation? Or does it provide the basis for a hegemonic unification of the interests of a plurality of classes, attempting to undermine and destroy a ruling class-hegemony? These considerations will have an effect on the characteristics of a national movement.

Furthermore, if the nationalism provides the ideological cement for an alliance of classes and class fractions, the quality of the nationalism will depend on which class or class fraction dominates the hegemonic alliance. Within any such social movement groups compete for power and control within the organizations of the movement and at the level of its ideology. The outcome of such struggles establishes a moral and intellectual leadership within the movement, which gives voice to the interests of the leading element over and above other elements. In Wales in the nineteenth century this process of internal struggle within a counter-hegemonic movement resulted in the domination of that movement by an indigenous bourgeoisie. In twentieth-century Wales the alliance between the rural middle class and the urban 'new working class' produced a movement dominated by the latter and which adopted an ideological and political stance consonant with their class interests and objectives. The consequences were a demotion of the importance of language and cultural issues in the programmes of the nationalist party after the mid 1960s.

The nature of a nationalist movement is determined firstly by the class or combination of classes which is expressing the nationalism. Secondly, it will be determined by whether it is an element of a dominant ideology or an oppositional ideology, that is, whether it is hegemonic or counter-hegemonic. Finally, the form a nationalism takes will depend on which class is dominant in the hegemonic alliance and succeeds in establishing its interests as the primary moral and intellectual values of the movement.

To summarize, nationalism is a class-neutral or 'free-floating' ideology which gains its class significance when articulated with class practices and ideologies. The process of articulation takes place within the general and universal process of hegemonic conflict. The particular form of expression nationalism assumes is dependent on the unique features of the specific social formation in which it is expressed. Its form and content will depend on the specific class, combination of class or class fractions which have articulated nationalist ideology with their class practice.

It is hoped that these general conclusions have been substantiated by the analysis of Welsh nationalism in both its nineteenth- and twentieth-century expressions. It is also hoped that this book will contribute to an understanding of nationalism in Wales and its role in the political processes of the region. Previous attempts to theorize Welsh nationalism and the nationalism of the Celtic fringe of Great Britain have not been considered in any detail up to this point in this study. This omission has been deliberate and analysis of specific theories of Celtic nationalism has been suspended until the value of the theoretical perspective adopted in this study was established. In the light of the application of the theory to Welsh nationalism we are now in a position to consider theories of Celtic nationalism from an informed basis.

The explanation of Celtic nationalism during the 1970s was dominated by the work of Michael Hechter and Tom Nairn, representing two distinctive attempts to theorize the resurgence of nationalism in the Celtic regions of Great Britain. Following the collapse of the appeal of nationalism in the late 1970s, academic endeavour has centred on the explanation of the success of 'New Right' political discourse and the analysis of nationalism has considered its complex role in 'New Right' popular interpellations. Hechter's and Nairn's explanations of Celtic nationalism have not been superseded and consequently must be addressed within the context of this study.

Hechter and the internal colony thesis

The publication of Hechter's *Internal Colonialism: The Celtic Fringe in British National Development* (1975) was of considerable significance in the development of sociology in Wales. Uncritically accepted by the nationalist movement[1] it prompted considerable reaction in academic circles and was criticized and rejected as theoretically flawed (Lovering 1978). Yet it had served to introduce into the sociology of Wales a thoroughly internationalist perspective which introduced theories of underdevelopment into the analysis of Welsh society (Berry 1977). In considering Hechter's analysis in the light of the preceding examination of Welsh nationalism little will be added to already existing criticisms of his work, but many of those criticisms will be substantiated.

Hechter's analysis employs a marriage of neo-Marxist and neo-Weberian concepts in an attempt to assess the role of the Celtic nations, Scotland, Ireland and Wales, in the process of British national development. He borrows the core-periphery distinction from Marxist theories of underdevelopment, and from Gellner (1964) the Weberian notion of a cultural division of labour or social closure. The core/

periphery distinction is primarily associated with the work of Andre Gunder Frank (1969a, 1969b, 1978) and describes the process of incorporation of the Latin American economies into the structure of Western capitalism. For Frank, the development of the peripheral economy is the product of a process of penetration by capitalism and the consequent relations it has with the metropolitan centre. The development of the capitalist nations and the underdevelopment of Latin America are seen as the two sides of the same coin (Frank 1969a). The peripheral or satellite economy is developed in the interests of the core or metropolitan centre as surplus production in the periphery is extracted and appropriated by the core in a relationship of exploitation. Furthermore, these relationships penetrate every level of the satellite economy, creating an internal structure which secures the flow of surplus from the remotest enclaves of the periphery through to the core. In this sense, internal regions of the periphery are seen as internal colonies of a centre within the satellite economy. It is this conception of an internal colony which Hechter adopts to describe the status of the Celtic fringe in British national development.

> It must not, however, be assumed that this type of colonial development is to be found only in those areas subjected to nineteenth-century overseas imperialism. Simultaneous to the overseas expansion of Western European states in the fifteenth and sixteenth centuries were similar thrusts into peripheral hinterlands. (Hechter 1975, p. 31)

Consequently, for Hechter, in Britain the Celtic fringe nations have been subjected to a process of annexation and imperialism and their economies have been developed to further the economic interests of the centre. Wales, Scotland and Ireland are internal colonies of the English state.

To this economic relationship, Hechter adds an ethnic and cultural dimension. He argues that the periphery is also characterized by different cultural and ethnic groups who are deliberately held in a state of 'backwardness' (p. 32) and denied the rewards of modernization. In much the same analysis as Gellner, Hechter maintains that élites, belonging to the core culture, monopolize the command and control positions in the internal colony and prevent the advancement of members of the peripheral culture. Within the internal colony there is thus a 'cultural division of labour' (p. 38) in which key posts in social, commercial and state institutions are held by personnel from the core culture.

Ultimately, it [the core] seeks to regulate the allocation of social roles such that those roles commonly defined as having high status are generally reserved for its members. Conversely, individuals from the less advanced group tend to be denied access to these roles. Let this stratification system be termed the cultural division of labour. (Hechter 1975, p. 39)

Hechter's model is based on neo-Marxist theories of capitalist exploitation and is reinforced by Weberian notions of social closure. Criticisms of his work have centred on the ambiguity of many of his arguments and in the application of key concepts such as class and exploitation (Day 1978, Lovering 1978). For Day (1978), Hechter confuses the Marxist conception of class with the Weberian concept of status group and at key points in the text it is unclear which Hechter is referring to.[2] For Lovering (1978), Hechter's analysis of the exploitative relationship between the English core and the Welsh periphery is 'descriptive' and 'seriously flawed' (p. 57). In criticizing Hechter's theory of internal colonialism, Lovering considers five definitions of exploitation, current within contemporary theories of underdevelopment, and demonstrates that Hechter fails to establish the existence of any of them in the relationship between Wales and England.[3]

The aspect of Hechter's theory which is of greatest relevance to this study is his belief that the existence of a 'cultural division of labour' promotes the persistence of ethnic identification in the periphery:

However, if the unequal distribution of resources is based on observable cultural differences there is always the possibility that the disadvantaged group in time will reactively assert its own culture as equal or superior to that of the advantaged group. (Hechter 1975, p. 38)

The analysis of Welsh nationalism prsented in this book has suggested very different origins of nationalism in both the nineteenth and twentieth centuries and has presented argument which suggests that many of Hechter's claims are doubtful. Aspects of the discussion which point to different explanations of the emergence and persistence of nationalism in Wales will be briefly summarized.

The analysis of nineteenth-century Wales is particularly difficult to integrate with Hechter's analysis. The speed and degree of industrial development in nineteenth-century Wales is indicative of its central place within the British economy. Williams (1985) demonstrates the role of Welsh production in the British Atlantic economy and sees the region as an element of the core British economy rather than a periphery within it.[4] Hechter's analysis would suggest a process of capital flow outwards to England during this period, together with a monopolization of commercial activity by members of the core culture.

> Commerce and trade among members of the periphery tend to be monopolized by members of the core. Credit is similarly monopolized. When commercial prospects emerge, bankers, managers and entrepreneurs tend to be recruited from the core.

The conditions of capitalist development in nineteenth-century Wales differ significantly from this picture. Whilst the English origins of capital in the initial stage of industrial development were noted it was also recognized that there was increasing indigenous entrepreneurial activity during the second phase of industrialization in the coal fields (Minchinton 1969).[5] Indeed, it has been suggested that it is the emergence of a local bourgeoisie which is central to the emergence of nationalism at this time. The development of the Welsh economy during this period had clear effects on the pattern of capital accumulation in Wales: it is not simply a picture of outward flows to the English economy, even if these were characteristic of the period. The development of the coastal plain and the transport and shipping networks represent the centrality of Welsh steel and coal in the world economy, rather than the route through which Welsh capital flowed to England, as suggested by Hechter's analysis. Rather than Wales being maintained as 'backward' by this development of her economy, it created clear advances in the economic, social and political structure of the region. Morgan (1963, 1981) paints a picture of a vibrant economic, social and cultural life with vast accumulations of capital on the part of Welsh entrepreneurs and industrialists. This pattern is revealed in the considerable investment in land and sea transport facilities and in the growth of prestigious cities and towns on the coastal belt.

The benefits of this development were not limited to the indigenous bourgeoisie. Morgan also describes the growth of a local middle class, the administrators and managers of this industrial growth. Finally, he describes the high wages of the Welsh work-force during this period, creating a 'labour aristocracy' in the British context. Consequently, Wales in the latter half of the nineteenth century was characterized by significant class divisions and cannot be envisaged as a homogeneous, culturally defined region, permanently held in a state of under-development and 'backwardness'.

This discussion also suggests that the concept of a 'cultural division of labour' is difficult to apply to this particular period. The emergence of local entrepreneurs and the development of a Welsh bourgeoisie and middle class suggest that there were few barriers to the entry of Welsh people into 'roles commonly defined as having high status' (Hechter 1975, p. 39). In fact, Chapter 4 showed that Welsh people occupied the command positions in Wales. The existence of a Welsh-speaking Nonconformist élite dominating the political and cultural institutions of the region was seen as the primary characteristic of the period (Morgan 1963). Nor were these key figures restricted in their achievements to the Welsh context. Welsh politicians and Welsh affairs were central in the context of British politics during the latter half of the nineteenth century.

In Hechter's analysis nationalism and ethnicity emerge as a response to economic and cultural exploitation of an ethnic group. Such relations of exploitation are impossible to identify in nineteenth-century Wales. The social group which mobilized an ethnic identity and formulated a political nationalism were a dominant class in the Welsh social formation: they had not been denied the benefits of industrialization but had reaped them in full. Wales cannot be seen as populated by a culturally homogeneous Celtic people held in subjection by an alien English élite. It was an internally class-divided society, the conditions of which promoted the emergence of nationalism as a hegemonizing ideology. It is the internal conditions of the Welsh social formation which promoted the development of nationalism, rather than the existence of an exploitative relationship with the English state. Finally, if there was an exploited group in the Welsh social formation, it was the industrial work-force which, as the century progressed, increasingly rejected nationalism and ethnic identity in exchange for a class identity.

Similar problems are encountered in introducing Hechter's analysis to contemporary nationalism. Despite the attractiveness to nationalists of the internal colony model in describing the 'branch plant economy' of post-war Wales, evidence of a cultural division of labour is difficult to establish. Although key personnel in branch plants are frequently brought into the region from outside (G. Williams 1981), this is also true of branch plants in other areas of Britain. This reflects the general geographical mobility of skilled, expert and managerial personnel and the outward flow of such personnel from Wales is the other face of this coin (Berry 1977). It is also a feature of the innovative nature of much of the industrial restructuring of the post-war years. The emphasis on light fabrication, electronics and textiles could not draw solely on an indigenous pool of skills, given the historical emphasis on primary and extractive industries in the region.

Additionally, it was shown in Chapter 8 that nationalism in twentieth-century Wales has been identified with an alliance between a rural middle class, a Welsh-speaking, urban middle class and the new working class. None of these social classes can be described as the victims of policies of ethnic discrimination practised by the British state. They can be shown to derive comparative benefits from Wales's economic relations with England. Both the rural and urban Welsh-speaking middle class owe much of their status and economic position in Wales to post-war language and cultural policy and to the general process of devolution which has established a range of managerial and professional opportunities in the media, education and civil service. Similarly the 'new working class' is a product of the economic restructuring of the Welsh economy for which the English state is partially responsible through its regional aid policies.

Hechter's analysis is not only theoretically flawed (Lovering 1978) but cannnot be substantiated by historical analysis of the Welsh social formation. Welsh nationalism in both its nineteenth- and twentieth-century expressions results from relations between classes within the Welsh social formation. The analysis of nationalism is dependent on the recognition of the role of nationalism as an ideological cement in hegemonic and counter-hegemonic political movements within the context of the Welsh social formation. This is not to deny the relevance of 'external' relations; responses to 'external' conditions by elements of the Welsh social formation are a fundamental aspect of the general process of class conflicts in Wales. The social, political and economic structure of Wales is inseparable from that of England. However, the articulation of a Welsh national identity is 'unique' and represents the major site of investigation here. This observation is also important when considering the contribution of Nairn (1977) to the analysis of Welsh nationalism.

Nairn and the 'break-up of Britain' thesis

In turning to the work of Nairn (1977), we find a general perspective closer to that adopted in this study than is evident in the work of Hechter. However, despite Nairn's application of Marxist methods of analysis, the specific points of his explanation of Welsh nationalism share some of the misconceptions of Hechter's model. Furthermore, Nairn fails to distance himself from the conventional Marxist conception of nationalism as an ideology bound irretrievably to the bourgeoisie.

Nairn locates the resurgence of nationalism in post-war Britain as a reflection of the political decline and economic collapse of the British state. For Nairn, the historical experiences of peripheral bourgeoisies differ from those of their English counterparts, permitting their recognition of the 'twilight of the British state' in advance of the 'English intelligentsia or the English working class' (Nairn 1977, p. 70). At the same time nationalism in the Celtic fringe is a reaction to the consequences of uneven development expressed in linguistic/cultural terms.

> In the case of the British Isles, the factors of internal uneven development are clear. They were of course clear in the older example of Southern Irish nationalism; but essentially the same kind of dilemma, 'under-development' and ethnic-linguistic exclusion has continued in North and West Wales, and furnished the basis for the more politicized and state-orientated nationalism of the present day Plaid Cymru. (Nairn 1977, p. 72)

This internal process of British underdevelopment is enhanced by Britain's state of imminent collapse caused by the uneven development of the world economy. Neo-nationalism is the peripheral bourgeois response to the knowledge of this process.

Nairn, however, is aware of the problem of seeing the periphery simply in terms of 'relative underdevelopment'. He sees the role of 'relative overdevelopment' in the formulation of peripheral nationalism (p. 202). He sees the Basque country, Catalonia, Protestant Ulster and Scotland as relatively overdeveloped regions. Of these Scotland and Catalonia can be classified as 'historic' nations in the sense that they have enjoyed a history of independent government prior to annexation and that many of their social, cultural and political institutions survived annexation. Scotland, for Nairn, is the most 'intact' (p. 207) of the historic nations. As a consequence, Scotland developed its own bourgeoisie and maintained a strong identity without a dependence on a visible cultural, literary or linguistic base.

In contrast, for Nairn, Wales occupies a place midway between 'historic' and 'non-historic' national status. Wales possesses the characteristics of both a 'forced underdevelopment' (p. 208) and a relative overdevelopment. It was overdeveloped in the extent of its industrialization, yet underdeveloped in the nature of the development process.

> However, this industrialization was like that of such periphery regions in being overwhelmingly guided from outside: it was not the work of a native entrepreneurial bourgeoisie accumulating

capital for itself (as in Scotland or the Basque country) but much
more like an invasion from outside. (Nairn 1977, p. 209)

Consequently, Wales had no independent institutional and political
basis for national identity and has created an identity 'evoked over-
whelmingly by literary and musical culture, and having as its
mainspring the language question' (Nairn 1977, p. 208).

This volume has presented an explanation of the origins of Welsh
nationalism in the nineteenth century and its resurgence in the twentieth
century which is at some variance with Nairn's work. The nineteenth-
century genesis of Welsh nationalism must be seen as the ideological
cement of a rural tenantry and an indigeneous bourgeoisie. It facilitated
the development of a bourgeois hegemony by breaking the domination
of the rural sector by a landed élite and, through the ideologies of Welsh
liberalism and Nonconformity, dominated the industrial working class.
The key difference from Nairn's analysis is that we have identified a
more active role played by an indigenous bourgeoisie. The primacy of
Welsh culture in the ideology of this class rested on its integrative role
which permitted the bringing together of diverse social classes within a
single social movement; Welsh, Nonconformist radicalism. The
increasing emphasis on culture and language was a response to the
increasing secularization, Anglicization and organization of the working
class in Wales. In response to these pressures on its hegemony the Welsh
Nonconformist bourgeoisie emphasized its ideological components:
language, culture, religion and Liberalism (Stead 1980).

Similarly, in considering the resurgence of Welsh nationalism in the
twentieth century, Nairn overemphasizes the role of culture and
language in the national movement. Whilst his arguments may be true
for a brief period in the 1960s, it is clear by the early 1970s that the
character of political nationalism in Wales was increasingly articulated
with working-class interests in the industrial south. The pure culturalism
of the early years of the resurgence was being replaced in nationalist
ideology by increasingly economic and material demands. It has been
suggested here that this represents the articulation of nationalist
ideology by the 'new working class' in south Wales. Nor can this
mobilization of a nationalist ideology by the 'new working class' be
seen as an echo of a 'peripheral bourgeois ideology'. The 'new working
class' in Wales was the leading moral and intellectual force in Welsh
nationalism by the mid 1970s. Nairn failed to recognize this because of
his reductionist identification of nationalism as a strictly bourgeois
ideology.

To summarize, the causes of nineteenth- and twentieth-century nationalism have been identified with the presence of internal class struggles in the Welsh social formation. It is the relations between indigenous classes and class fractions which have promoted the articulation of nationalist ideology with the class struggle. Nationalism in Wales cannot be identified simply as an element of bourgeois discourse. In the 1970s it was articulated with the interests of a fraction of the working class in a direct attempt to counter the hegemony of a centralist Labour Party which it felt no longer reflected its lived experience of capitalist social relations. In that particular instance it led to a counter-hegemonic alliance with a rural and urban, culturally motivated, middle class. In establishing its leadership in that movement it reconstructed nationalism and created a direct threat to the centralist British state.[6]

That threat was survived by the state which moved on to a period of increasing centralism. Ironically, as the awareness of a North/South divide has entered popular consciousness, regionalism, if not nationalism, has re-entered British electoral politics. The highly visible basis of opposition to the Conservative Government in Scotland and Wales in the 1987 election suggests that peripheral identities may not be as extinct as has been thought. Furthermore, the 1989 Govan by-election result and the part played by *Plaid Cymru* in the 1989 Pontypridd constituency by-election clearly demonstrates that nationalist politics can arise quickly and forcefully from the ashes of the devolution debate of 1979. Balsom *et al.* (1982) have suggested that in recent years the sense of Welsh identity, pervasive in Wales, has benefited the Labour Party, which is seen as the obvious source of resistance to the effects of contemporary state policies in Wales. National identity may not yet have played its full role in British politics.

NOTES

Introduction

(1) This belief was particularly influential in American and Canadian analyses of ethnic conflict and reflects the more powerful hold that theories of 'post capitalism' had on American sociology. See for example the proceedings of the Joint Seminar on 'After the Referenda: The Future of Nationalism in Britain and Canada' (University College of North Wales, Bangor, 1981).

(2) Full consideration is given to Hechter's work in the Conclusion where its value as an explanation of Celtic nationalism is considered in the light of the theory of Welsh nationalism developed in this book.

(3) For a literature indicative of the work of this group see Rees and Rees (1980) and G. Williams (1983).

(4) The pressure to become 'historically informed sociologists' (Stedman Jones 1983, p. 74) was not limited to the study of Wales but was indicative of a general coming together of historical and sociological research (Stedman Jones 1983).

(5) The most influential of Althusser's works were *For Marx* (1969), *Reading Capital* (1970, with Balibar) and *Lenin and Philosophy and Other Essays* (1971a).

(6) For discussions of recent controversies in the debate on methodology in Marxism, see Laclau (1977a) and Benton (1984).

Chapter 1

(1) Nationalism is an important element of fascist ideology (Seton-Watson 1977, Mosse 1973) but, equally, has established liberal democratic states, e.g. India, and has contributed significantly to revolutionary movements, as in China and Vietnam (Amin 1980). Schwarzmantel (1987) suggests a distinction between left and right nationalism as useful in analysing the contradictory nature of nationalism.

(2) The archetypal attempt to create a typology of nationalist movements is Louis Wirth's *Types of Nationalism* (1936). Smith (1971) also identifies this approach with numerous writers on nationalism including Deutsch (1953) and Seton Watson (1965).

(3) See Smith (1971) for a review of the modernization theory of Eisenstadt

and Smelser whose work underpins Gellner's analysis.

(4) Kedourie is not alone in periodizing the birth of nationalism in this way. The eighteenth century is almost universally accepted as the period when nationalism became a central force in European societies, e.g. Kohn (1965), Kamenka (1973b), Minogue (1967), Seton Watson (1977).

(5) Both concepts play a major role in the writings of Hechter (1975). Similarly, Gellner's arguments about the need for innovative sources of identity experienced by members of modernizing societies is echoed in the work of Elton Mayo (1974) on post-war European ethnic movements.

(6) Gellner draws here from a considerable body of thought on uneven development and its consequences. However, he is the first non-Marxist writer to use the concept as an element of an explanation of nationalism (Orridge 1981).

(7) This argument, in many ways, reflects Bauer's discussion of 'nations without history' and the emergence of what he termed 'national hate'. Herod (1976) writes, 'Bauer also said that the strongest nationalism would occur among a nationally conscious minority in situations where the minority did not occupy positions of privilege and the right to exploit, but lived in the life style of a servile and exploited class. In such cases, nationalism developed among the exploited class out of hate for the exploiters' (p. 95).

(8) Gellner clearly employs Weber's ideas on 'social closure' in outlining this element of his theory (Weber 1968, p. 342). Weber points to a process whereby social groups maximize their access to scarce resources by restricting group membership. Parkin (1974, 1979) develops the concept further, recognizing the power of 'exclusion' and the reactive power of 'solidarism' as the principal forms of social closure which structure the nature of collectivities in social formations (1974, p. 3 or 1979, p. 44).

(9) This statement draws on a wide-ranging discussion about the definition of modes of production and the nature of transition between them. See Amin (1976, 1980) for a valuable contribution to this debate. See also Foster-Clarke (1978) and Hindess and Hirst (1975).

(10) Kiernan (1976), in discussing the link between industrialization and nationalism sees nationalism as growing alongside capitalism in a period of 'four centuries of preparation for the big leap of the Industrial Revolution' (p. 111).

(11) Modernization theory is not unique in its ethnocentrism. For a similar critique of western Marxism, see Amin (1980). Amin argues that the Marxist attachment to the concepts of feudal and Asiatic modes of production creates a 'West centred perspective' (p. 6). Lele (1980) criticizes Gellner and Nairn (1977) for their 'Eurocentrism'. He identifies in Gellner the 'narcissism of Western thought' (p. 204).

(12) Amin (1980) identifies Italian unification as a consequence of the actions of a 'northern agrarian bourgeoisie' in alliance with 'elements of a southern feudalism' (p. 115).

(13) Aarebrot (1982) suggests that 'peripheries can be rich relative to their centres' (p. 72) and puts forward three types of periphery classified by economic status.

i) Industrial peripheries — enjoying real wealth creation.

ii) Service peripheries — e.g. tourism-based and lacking real wealth creation.

iii) Deprived peripheries — lacking employment and general wealth creation.

For a brief discussion of the Basque region's disproportionate contribution to the Spanish economy, see Greenwood (1977).

(14) Controversy breaks out periodically over whether Wales is a net contributor to, or beneficiary of, the British state. Scottish nationalism, in recent years, has been able to claim that oil revenue has been appropriated from the Scottish people (Esman 1977b). For a discussion of the viability of an independent Welsh economy see Kohr (1971).

(15) See Cummins (1980) for an elaboration of this point. He analyses Marx's argument that anti-Irish sentiment contributed to the 'false consciousness' of the English proletariat 'acclimatizing' them to 'bourgeois ways' (p. 114).

(16) This remains true of his more recent contribution *Culture, Identity and Politics* (1987). His theoretical discussion maintains its dependence on the distinction between 'structure' and 'culture' (see pp. 6–46). Additionally, he argues for the need for 'linguistic and cultural homogeneity' (p. 14) created by industrialization and the complex division of labour which results from that process. Finally, he repeats the argument of 1964 and 1983 by identifying the need for 'universal literacy' (1987, p. 15) in societies founded on a principle of permanent growth. If anything, in this later work, we lose the contribution of his earlier discussion of uneven development which constituted a major element of his theory of nationalism.

(17) See bibliography for full details.

(18) Elsewhere (Adamson, 1988) I have shown the consequences of Smith's underemphasis of economic issues for his system of categorizing national movements.

Chapter 2

(1) Amin (1980) suggests Marx and Engels 'sometimes substituted nations for classes' consequently identifying 'progressive and reactionary nations' dependent on their 'contribution to bourgeois revolution' (p. 106).

(2) For a brief but informative discussion of the Austro-Marxists, see Lowy (1976). For more detailed consideration, see Bottomore and Goode (1978). For an analysis of Otto Bauer's contribution, see Herod (1976).

(3) Overemphasis on the arguments in *The Communist Manifesto* have led to a simplistic identification of Marxism with a reductionist position which sees nationalism as a bourgeois ideology counterbalanced only by the internationalism of the proletariat. For an example see Vogler (1985). This is neither a reasonable evaluation of the ideas of Marx and Engels on the national question nor a recognition of the diversity of opinion of different Marxists, e.g. Lenin and Luxemburg.

(4) For detailed discussion of Marx and Engels on Irish nationalism, see Cummins (1980).

(5) Given the paucity of translations of Luxemburg's writings on the national

question, this account is dependent on Nettl's (1966) discussion. Many of his references are to 'The question of nationality and autonomy', *Przeglad Socjaldemokratyczny*, August 1908, No. 6, reprinted in *Wybór Pism*, Vol. II, pp. 114–66.

(6) For informative discussions of the meaning of the term 'hegemony' and its place in Gramsci's work, see Boggs (1976) and Femia (1981). More recently Bocock (1986) subjects the concept to critical analysis and traces its evolution up to its controversial application in recent 'post-Marxist' writings.

(7) Although Gramsci makes this distinction it does not constitute a separation. Both forms of domination are always present in the social formation. 'The political is not defined by, it cannot be understood in terms of, only one of its attributes, of force or consent. It is *both* force *and* consent, authority *and* hegemony, violence *and* civilta.' (Sassoon 1980, p. 112. Author's emphasis)

(8) For Gramsci's discussion of the concept of Jacobinism and his applicaticn of it to the Italian context, see *Notes on Italian History* (in Gramsci 1971) especially pp. 63–81. See also Sassoon (1980, pp. 125–8).

(9) For a full discussion of the meaning of this term see Gramsci (1971) footnote, p. 58.

(10) For a discussion of the Risorgimento as a 'passive revolution', see Femia (1981), pp. 47–9.

(11) For Laclau and Mouffe (1985) this chained Gramsci to economic determinism as closely as previous Marxists. Despite his recognition of the full role of the political superstructure, they claim his conception of hegemony was underpinned by a causal link between class and political practice.

Chapter 3

(1) Althusser's endeavours can best be seen as an attempt to eliminate economism in Marxist theory by recognizing the 'relative autonomy' of the superstructures. For a number of critics Althusser fails in this attempt and they have offered alternative methods of achieving Althusser's objective, e.g. Poulantzas (1973, 1974, 1975), Laclau (1977a), Laclau and Mouffe (1985) and Urry (1982). In this way Althusser opened a debate which has secured more rigorous analysis of ideology than was previously possible (Boswell *et al.* 1986).

(2) See Chapter 4 for a full discussion of the articulation of modes of production within the social formation.

(3) Althusser's work can be seen as an attempt to rescue Marxism from the stultifying economism of Stalinist orthodoxy (Benton 1984, Callinicos 1976).

(4) This use of the term ideology has been particularly influential in the sociology of knowledge (Larrain 1979).

(5) This conception of ideology has recently been referred to as 'the dominant ideology thesis' (Abercrombie *et al.* 1980).

(6) See Abercrombie *et al.* (1980) for a full discussion of the concept of a dominant ideology. They reject the existence of a dominant ideology as

explanation of the political passivity of the working class, preferring the explanation offered by the economic compulsion inherent in capitalist relations of production.

(7) The acceptance of certain elements of Althusser's theory does not represent here an uncritical acceptance of his work. However, the concepts examined have contributed significantly to our understanding of the social formation and the relations between its different levels and their value does not necessarily depend on the overall perspective of which they are part. Callinicos (1976) writes: 'I have been puzzled by a persistent objection to the effect that there is a contradiction between accepting elements of a theory and refusing to subscribe to it as a whole. Logically this is certainly not the case.' (p. 9)

(8) Craib (1984) sees this as an extension of the architectural metaphor of base and superstructure to an analogy of a three-storey building, each floor representing a level of the social formation. In the analogy, the work carried out on the second floor and the lives of the residents of the third floor are independent of the business concern carried out on the first but are inevitably conditioned by it.

(9) He supports this argument by reference to Lenin's analysis of pre-revolutionary Russia and Mao's discussion of principal and secondary contradictions as evidence of the complexity of the social formation and Marxism's awareness of it (Benton 1984).

(10) For a discussion of these epistemological issues, see Benton (1984, Chapter 2), McLennan *et al.* (1978), Callinicos (1976, Chapter 1) and Craib (1984, Chapter 8).

(11) For brief discussions of the political circumstances which promoted this self-criticism, see Benton (1984, pp. 80–1) and Callinicos (1976, pp. 94–5).

(12) Althusser illustrates the 'Subject/subject' relationship through the example of Christian ideology in which God is 'Subject'. In capitalism it is the dominant ideology which is 'Subject' and the interpellated individual is 'subject'.

(13) In Althusser's distinction between the ISAs and RSAs, Benton (1984) and McLennan *et al.* (1978) record his debt to Gramsci — as indeed does Althusser (1971, p. 137). However, Benton regards Althusser's application of the coercion/consent distinction as more mechanical than Gramsci's which recognized more fully the 'specific *combination* of consent and coercion, the two being understood as inseparable aspects of a single process' (Benton 1984, p. 102).

(14) Callinicos (1976), writing of Althusser's contribution, argues: 'His critique of Hegelian Marxism and his attempt to think, in the concepts of overdetermination and structural causality, a materialist dialectic that is radically non-teleological and that captures the complexity of contradiction are achievements of lasting value' (p. 103).

(15) This discussion of class ideologies as the consequence of lived experience represents something of a contradiction in his arguments given his objective of refuting the 'humanism' of Lukacs which indicates a direct reading of class and class consciousness from economic positions (Boswell 1987). For Clarke *et al.* (1978) Poulantzas at first distinguishes

between ideology and lived experience but in his discussion of ideology and its place in the social formation conflates them.

(16) Meiksins Wood (1986) sees in this greater autonomization of the superstructures in Poulantzas's work, the 'embryo' (p. 25) form of the 'new true socialism' which she sees as departing from central tenets of Marxism.

(17) See Meiksins Wood (1986, pp. 3–4) for a list of the basic premises of Marxism which the 'new True Socialists' such as Laclau and Mouffe have rejected. Also see Geras (1987, pp. 43–4).

(18) See footnote 32, p. 101, Laclau (1977b).

(19) See Geras (1987, p. 65–7) for a discussion of the problems of relativism and theoretical confusion which arises from the privileging of discourse.

(20) See particularly Geras (1987) and Meiksins Wood (1986).

(21) See Chapter 2 for a full discussion.

Chapter 4

(1) The discussion of the articulation of modes of production is introduced initially in Balibar's footnote on p. 207 (Althusser and Balibar 1970).

(2) The inherent teleology in Marxist theories of historical change is identified by Hindess and Hirst (1975).

(3) For a detailed discussion of the process of transition between modes of production which captures the positions adopted by various writers, see Benton (1984, pp. 126–34).

(4) The exception to this tendency has been the work of Williams (1950 and 1955) and more recently of Llafur, the Welsh labour historians.

(5) This view is encapsulated in the writings of Gwynfor Evans who projects an unbroken 'two to three thousand years' (1973, p. 9) of Welsh nationhood in which the tribal period of Hywel Dda represents the zenith of cultural achievement.

(6) For Morgan (1973a) the Act of Union was a culmination of a process in which 'Welsh independence was lost by stages, in fact, first of all religious autonomy, then, from the eleventh to thirteenth centuries, political autonomy, leaving only cultural independence.' (1973, p. 16)

(7) The belief that tenants lived as harsh a life as their labourers is argued by a number of historians (Williams 1950, Dodd 1951, Morgan 1963) who are probably influenced by Rhys and Jones (1900) who after some discussion of the common poverty of tenant and labourer conclude: 'Nay in some instances the farmer in a small way lives quite as hard as his labourer (p. 551).

(8) Writing of Anglesey in the eighteenth century Evans (1936) could conclude: 'It may seriously be doubted whether there was any considerable class of labourers. References to them, except in the more or less theoretical rates of wages, are exceptional.' (p. 165). Fortunately, more information has become available for the latter part of the nineteenth century through the work of Pretty (1989).

(9) Similar losses of traditional land rights resulting from enclosure are identified in England by Thompson (1968).

(10) Opposition to tithe also characterized English rural politics (Thompson

1968). However, in Wales the economic and religious objections were supplemented by the linguistic and cultural difference between tenants and the Church.

(11) This is particularly true of the work of Morgan (1963 and 1981).

Chapter 5

(1) The reader should refer to the discussion of the concept of mode of production and the relationships between its elements, in Chapter 4.

(2) The consequences of identifying two levels of analysis of the capitalist mode of production in the work of Marx are discussed by Carter (1985). Full consideration of the distinction between an abstract analysis and an analysis of the empirical reality of capitalism follows in Chapter 8.

(3) This is, of course, a feature of many third-world economies which have a modernized manufacturing centre and peripheral agricultural production. In this way the wage structure of the peripheral capitalism is supplemented by the peasant production of the rural economy (Foster-Carter 1978).

(4) See also the collection of essays edited by Glanmor Williams (1966).

(5) The initial is employed here to distinguish the work of L.J. Williams from that of G.A. Williams of the same date. Both are published in Smith (1980).

(6) For Jones (1973) the events of the Merthyr rising severed the tenuous links between the 'radical middle classes' and the working class in Merthyr Tydfil. Unable to control the 'forceful methods' (p. 141) adopted, the former withdrew from the actions taken.

(7) Davies (1965) gives the example of a sermon by Thomas Revel Guest, brother of the Dowlais ironmaster.

(8) Such societies included the Iforites, Ancient Britons and Antediluvian Buffaloes, all demanding secular oaths and usually meeting in public houses (Davies 1965).

(9) A Thomas Thomas of the Baptist College at Pontypool denied any connection between the ideals of Chartism and the principles of civil and religious liberty of Nonconformism in an article in the *Standard* in 1839 (Davies 1965).

(10) L.J. Williams (1980) writes of the local origin of many coalowners. Initial capital outlay was quite small in many instances and easily raised by the local 'shopocracy spawned by the growing iron industry' (p. 100).

(11) G.A. Williams (1980) suggests that Welsh participation at such significant levels in the Atlantic economy created a labour aristocracy, happy to take on the Liberal Nonconformism of their employers as long as they benefited from it.

(12) This was discussed in full in the previous chapter.

(13) There had been a visit earlier in the year to Merthyr Tydfil by the Owenite orator William Twiss, giving some factual basis for Wilkins's statement.

(14) The mythology of the English agitator does have some substance. Williams (1980) points to the incorporation of Welsh working-class leaders into the ideology and institutions of Nonconformism. Radical working-class leadership was left, in many instances, to English organizers. This does

not deny the existence of a ready audience and willing participation of indigenous Welsh workers.

(15) An interchange between two candidates in the 1908 general election reveals the ultimate conclusion of this schism which had been developing in Welsh society since 1831. On the eve of election the Revd J. Hughes, the Nonconformist candidate, published the following remarks in a pamphlet entitled *What is Socialism*:

> It is crying for the moon. What are its fruits in Mid Glamorgan. Look around our churches. What is depleting them of young men. Socialism!

In reply, his opponent V. Hartshorn, a miners' agent, stated:

> Clothed in the garb of religious rectitude and wearing the nationalist colours you hide the grinning skeleton of a political hack.

(both quoted in Stead 1980, p. 156)

Chapter 6

(1) For a discussion of the demise of nationalist politics after the turn of the century, see Butt Philip (1975, p. 3).
(2) These contributions were part of a considerable literature which developed to describe and explain nationalism in Wales and similar developments in Scotland and elsewhere in the Celtic fringe. The debate was generally referred to as 'the break-up of Britain thesis'.
(3) Most of these contributions concentrate on the emergence of *Plaid Cymru* as the major manifestation of nationalism and ethnicity at this time, to the detriment of other movements and organizations which were equally part of the resurgence. The exception to this is Butt Philip (1975). For detail of the development of *Plaid Cymru* and its policies, see Dewitt Combs Jnr. (1978), Davies (1985). For the pre-war years of *Plaid Cymru*, see Hywel Davies (1983). For detailed discussion of the devolution debate and referendum, see Osmond (1979) and Foulkes, Jones and Wilford (1983). Finally, for examples of partisan nationalist-orientated literature, see Thomas (1971), Evans (1973 and 1975), Hearne (1975 and 1977), Betts (1976) and Clews (1980).
(4) The 1962 radio address by Saunders Lewis entitled 'The Fate of the Language' has been credited as instigating the formation of *Cymdeithas Yr Iaith Gymraeg*. In reality the speech captured a mood that had arisen out of the campaigns at Tryweryn and the failure of *Plaid Cymru* to lead in acts of civil disobedience.
(5) This was even more true of the bombings campaigns associated with *Mudiad Amddiffyn Cymru* (Movement for the Defence of Wales) and the activities of the Free Wales Army. Both organizations raised the spectre of a scale of violence more associated with Irish than Welsh politics. See Clews (1983) for a highly partisan account of both movements. In the 1980s it has been the actions of *Meibion Glyndŵr* which *Plaid Cymru* has been careful to separate itself from.
(6) Concessions include numerous extensions of Welsh-language use on official forms and in state institutions, improvements in Welsh-language

broadcasting and media provision and extension of Welsh-medium education provision, especially in English-speaking areas of south-east Wales.

(7) See Davies (1985, pp. 141–6).

(8) This general argument can be identified with the thinking of the National Left and has been most frequently argued by Dafydd Elis Thomas (Davies 1985).

(9) Davies (1985) cites 'the upgrading of the Welsh Development Agency, the commitment to the establishment of a Welsh-language television channel and the payment of compensation to quarrymen suffering from silicosis' (p. 141) as the primary concessions achieved during this period.

(10) The label attached by 'Yes' vote campaigners to the Welsh Labour MPs who vociferously opposed the devolution proposals of the 1978 Wales Act and campaigned for a 'No' vote in the referendum. The most outspoken of the six was Neil Kinnock.

(11) The five were Eurfyl ap Gwilym, Emrys Roberts, Owen John Thomas, Dafydd Wigley and Dr Phil Williams: a group generally representative of the spectrum of party opinion.

(12) In private correspondence in 1982 a leading member of the National Left points to the failure to establish a meaningful discussion of socialist ideas at the grass-roots level of the party.

(13) Attendance at several recruitment drive meetings at this time revealed basic doubts as to the role of multinational capital, small businesses, the financial institutions and the organization of labour in a decentralist socialist Wales on the part of the majority of speakers at branch level.

(14) See Davies, Lord Gifford and Richards (1984) for a full account of the trial and its findings which failed to convict all of the defendants except one.

(15) That candidate was Dafydd Iwan who had been chairman of *Cymdeithas Yr Iaith Gymraeg* during its most active campaigns in the 1960s. His identification in the party was primarily with the language issue and he had not involved himself to any extent with the more economic arguments for nationalism which had been emerging in the party throughout this period.

(16) This has been revealed in discussion with two leading activists, one of whom has stood for the party in the last general election and as candidate in a recent by-election.

(17) Recent changes have lost women an automatic 50 per cent of seats on *Plaid Cymru*'s national Executive. Dafydd Elis Thomas has dropped his unequivocal opposition to nuclear power, arguing instead that a review of energy policy is necessary. Finally, the close relationship between *Plaid Cymru* and striking miners in the 1984 dispute has failed to materialize in a more permanent shift of political allegiance on the part of trade unionists in Wales.

(18) Dafydd Elis Thomas has repeatedly advocated that the crisis of rural immigration can only be solved by redressing the economic imbalances between England and Wales (see *Western Mail*, Thursday 9 June 1988). He has rejected the anti-immigration stance of people such as R. S. Thomas as similar to the policies of the French National Front leader, Jean

Le Pen. For an effective summary of the issues involved in this debate see
Thomas (1988).

Chapter 7

(1) The classical sociology of Marx, Weber and Durkheim recognizes the
increasing complexity of capitalism compared with traditional society,
although they describe and analyse the process differently. Their insights
have been developed by those writing within their respective paradigms,
e.g. Althusser (1969), Giddens (1973), and Parsons (1951).

(2) For example in Germany between the wars and in France after the Second
World War where the outcome of such debates was of crucial significance
in determining the political strategies of left parties (Carter 1985,
Abercrombie and Urry 1983).

(3) For some critics these attempts have opened a way for a new form of
'revisionism' which has relinquished Marxism rather than contributed to
it. See the discussion of Laclau in Chapter 3. Also see Meiksins Wood
(1986) and Geras (1987). For an evaluation of the development of this
tendency in the work of one writer, see Elliot (1986).

(4) For a discussion which argues that Marx recognized the diversity of class
in advanced capitalism and the role of the middle class, see Carter (1985).
For a discussion which claims that Marx only discussed the middle class in
relation to a dichotomous class structure, see Hyman and Price (1983). For
generally informative accounts, see Crompton and Gubbay (1977), Hall
(1977).

(5) For a defence of Marxism against Weberian models of stratification, see
Crompton and Gubbay (1977). They argue convincingly for the primacy
of relations of production over market relations and conclude: 'We wish to
argue that Marx's theory, even at this very abstract level, gives a better
understanding of the class structure of capitalist societies than that of
Weber.' (p. 17)

(6) This distinction has considerable importance in Marxist analysis of
capitalist relations of production. Braverman (1974) places the mental/
manual division of labour as the most significant component of Tayloristic
forms of capitalist organization.

(7) Their major concern is to demonstrate the failure of Poulantzas to describe
effectively the ways in which class boundaries are determined by the
political and ideological levels of the social formation. Nor, they argue,
does he map the ways in which class struggle changes the nature of class.

(8) Marx's class 'in itself' and 'for itself' distinction and Lenin on 'trade
union consciousness' implicitly recognizes that the economic interests of
classes are overlaid by other elements in the determination of class
consciousness.

(9) See the discussion earlier in this chapter.

(10) See discussion on page 242.

(11) Hyman and Price (1983) claim 'in popular discourse the distinction
between "manual" and "non-manual" labour relates closely to that
between working and middle classes'. (p. 15)

(12) The selection of this term does not convey any connection with the

'technicist' discussion of the 'new working class' associated with theories of post-capitalism and the end of ideology. See Oppenheimer (1982) for a discussion of that application of the term.

(13) For an expression of this subjective division in the language of the workplace, see the contrasting accounts of working life by Wheeler Stanley and Gary Bryner in Terkel (1985, p. 166–78)

(14) This division is most clearly visible in Tayloristic organizational principles and represents the appropriation of workers' skills by management. For Braverman (1974) this represented the principal mechanism by which management deskilled the work-force and achieved control of the workplace (Braverman 1974, Hill 1981).

(15) For a discussion which reveals the impossibility of a meaningful separation of mental from manual labour, see Bain and Price (1972).

(16) See Hyman (1980) for an account of the subjective significance of the mental/manual division of labour. Hyman points to its recognition in labour law, official statistics, employer practice, wage and salary structures and 'staff and works' distinctions. He also points to the effects of the division in influencing 'attitudes and actions' (p. 4).

(17) Potential examples of contradictory political beliefs are endless. We could identify in recent years individual trade union members who support reduction of trade union rights. Similarly, there is support for reduced state expenditure and at the same time distaste for cuts in housing, education and health care. Such contradictions amount to more than a simple failure to see the consequences of particular policies: they represent inconsistency brought about by competing ideological interpellations.

Chapter 8

(1) The references are only representative of a considerable literature on the economic restructuring which has taken place in Wales since the Second World War. There is a broad consensus within the literature as to the form of that restructuring and the theoretical explanation of it. Generally, a framework of uneven development and a spatial division of labour have contributed to the analysis of the period. Of particular influence has been the work of Doreen Massey (1978, 1979).

(2) Coal production peaked in 1913 at 56 million tons per annum (Minchinton 1969).

(3) Cooke (1983) cites the example of the 'modernization' of the coalfield in the 1960s as a period of accelerated decline resulting from the policies of the Wilson Government. Similarly, steel capacity was drastically reduced in the early 1980s by the policies of the Conservative administration.

(4) For Glyn Williams (1981), such state strategies represented nothing more than a state subsidization of capital accumulation. 'What these policies seek to do is to lower the price of labour and capital by means of taxation and subsidies in order to make locating in the periphery more attractive to private enterprise. In other words, it involves subsidizing private enterprise in order to attract it to the periphery where there is a a ready workforce whose labour can be exploited.' (p. 285).

(5) Edwards (1985) gives a detailed statistical analysis of the decline of this

period epitomized by the loss of employment caused by the rationalization of steel production. Additionally there was a 23.3% loss of employment in 'secondary manufacture of metals and and engineering' and 25.9% 'lighter industrial categories'. The only exceptions to this decline were in the 'Food, Drink and Tobacco sectors' which experienced a '14.7% increase in the 1975–1985 period' (p. 95). For a discussion of the general characteristics of branch plants see Watts (1981).

(6) The most significant of the relocated state departments have been the DVLC at Swansea, the Royal Mint at Llantrisant, Companies House at Cardiff and the Business Statistics Office at Newport. There has also been an expansion of the state as an employer in Wales determined by its increasing role in post-war society generally. This has been matched until recently by a growth in the provision of services and the level of employment by local government.

(7) Most authors cite the efforts of the Beasley family to secure Welsh-medium rate demands throughout the 1950s (Thomas 1971, Madgwick 1973). Saunders Lewis drew attention to their efforts, in his 1962 radio speech, as typical of the attempts to stem the tide of language decline.

(8) The connection between the nationalist resurgence in Wales and the student and youth protest throughout the western world during this period is also drawn by Hechter and Levi (1979) and Birch (1978). Hechter and Levi also comment on the almost universal resurgence of 'ethnoregionalism' in the major European nations during this period. For Hechter and Levi this is explained by reference to 'changes in the international system', including *détente* and increased national security. I would prefer to recognize a general role for the development of the class structures of such nations along similar lines to those discussed in Chapter 7.

(9) See Butt Philip (1975) for a full discussion of the circumstances of this by-election. Important contributory factors to *Plaid Cymru*'s victory included the candidates' personalities, of which Gwynfor Evans's was notable. In addition, he was the only candidate resident in the constituency. *Plaid Cymru* funds had also been swelled recently by a considerable bequest, enabling an effective campaign to be launched. Butt Philip (1975) also regards the timing of the election as of crucial significance, by allowing a greater consideration of local issues than national issues on the part of the electorate.

(10) The Hydro group emerged out of the conflicts of the 1981 *Plaid Cymru* Conference and the discussions of the acceptance of the socialist strategies recommended by the 1981 Committee of Enquiry. No single group currently exists within the party which represents and organizes cultural nationalist opinion.

Conclusion

(1) Nairn (1977) discusses the ideological significance of the concept of cultural exploitation for the Welsh nationalist movement. 'It fits many aspects of Welsh experience rather well, obviously. And as an ideology it

probably appeals directly to the strong cultural dimension of the Welsh national movement.' (Nairn 1977, p. 200).

(2) The problematic usage of the concept of class in Hechter's application of the theory of internal colony is perhaps inevitable given the origins of the concept. The criticisms of Ander Gunder Frank's early application (1969a) of the dependent development model concentrate on his definition of capitalism and the centrality of market relations in his definitional criteria, rather than relations of production. See Laclau (1971) and Brenner (1977). This ambiguity is resolved to some extent in a later paper (Hechter 1978) in which he is clear about the centrality of the Weberian concept of status group in formulating the concept of an 'ethnic division of labour'.

(3) The five forms of exploitation considered by Lovering (1978) are: 'Economic Exploitation' (p. 57), 'Unequal Exchange' (p. 57), 'Marxian Class Exploitation' (p. 58), 'Exploitation as Dependence' (p. 59), and 'Cultural Exploitation' (p. 59).

(4) This view is substantiated by Evans (1983) who argues: 'The economic cores in the nineteenth century were precisely areas of heavy industry like South Wales.' (p. 2).

(5) Hechter's oversights are perhaps inevitable given the minimal attention he pays to the industrialization process in Wales. Evans (1983) writes: 'The century of the industrial revolution is passed over in silence. The standard works on Welsh industrialization rate four mentions between them.' (p. 2)

(6) Nairn describes the 'neo-nationalism' of the 1960s and 1970s as the 'gravedigger of the old state in Britain' (1977, p. 89).

BIBLIOGRAPHY

Aarebrot, Frank H. 1982. On the structural basis of regional mobilization in Europe. In B. De Marchi & A. M. Boileau (eds.), *Boundaries and Minorities in Western Europe*, pp. 33–92 Franco Angeli Editore: Milan.

Abercrombie, Nicholas & Urry, John. 1983. *Capital, Labour and the Middle Classes*. George Allen & Unwin: London.

Abercrombie, Nicholas, Hill, Stephen, & Turner, Bryan S. 1980. *The Dominant Ideology Thesis*. George Allen & Unwin: London.

Adamson, David L. 1984. Social class and ethnicity in nineteenth century rural Wales. *Sociologia Ruralis* XXIV, 3/4: 202–15.

Adamson, David L. 1986. Cultural imperialism and economic exploitation. *Radical Wales* 12: 20–1.

Adamson, David L. 1988. Modes of Production, Social Class Structure and the Development of Welsh Nationalism. PhD Thesis: University of Wales.

Adamson, Walter L. 1980. *Hegemony and Revolution. A Study of Antonio Gramsci's Political and Cultural Theory*. University of California Press: Los Angeles.

Alavi, Hamza & Shanin, Teodor (eds.). 1982. *Introduction to the Sociology of Developing Societies*. Macmillan: London.

Alcock A. E., Taylor, B. K. & Welton, J. M. 1979. *The Future of Cultural Minorities*. St Martins Press: New York.

Althusser, Louis. 1969. *For Marx*. Allen Lane: London.

Althusser, Louis & Balibar, Étienne. 1970. *Reading Capital*. New Left Books: London.

Althusser Louis. 1971a. *Lenin and Philosophy and Other Essays*. New Left Books: London.

Althusser, Louis. 1971b. Ideology and ideological state apparatuses. (Notes Towards an Investigation). January – April 1969. In Louis Althusser, *Lenin and Philosophy and Other Essays*, pp. 121–73. New Left Books: London.

Amin, Samir. 1976. *Unequal Development. An Essay on the Social Formation of Peripheral Capitalism*. Monthly Review Press: London & New York.

Amin, Samir. 1980. *Class and Nation. Historically and in the Current Crisis*. Monthly Review Press: New York.

Anderson, Benedict. 1983. *Imagined Communities. Reflections on the Origin and Spread of Nationalism*. Verso: London.

Anon. 1911. *The Faith of a Nationalist. A Memorandum Addressed to Young Wales*. The Welsh Publishing Co. Ltd.: Caernarfon.

Arjomand, Said Amir (ed.). 1984. *From Nationalism to Revolutionary Islam*. Macmillan: London.

Armstrong, Peter, Carter, Bob, Smith, Chris & Nichols, Theo. 1986. *White Collar Workers, Trade Unions and Class*. Croom Helm: London.

Bain, George Sayers & Price, Robert. 1972. Who is a white collar employee? *British Journal of Industrial Relations*, X, 3: pp. 325–38. Reproduced in Richard Hyman & Robert Price, *The New Working Class? White-Collar Workers and Their Organizations. A Reader*, pp. 46–51. Macmillan: London.

Balsom, Denis & Burch, Martin. 1980. *A Political and Electoral Handbook for Wales*. Gower: Farnborough.

Balsom, Denis. 1979. *The Nature and Distribution of Support for Plaid Cymru*. Studies in Public Policy No. 36. Centre for the Study of Public Policy, University of Strathclyde: Glasgow.

Balsom, Denis, Madgwick, Peter & Van Mechelen, Denis. 1982. *The Political Consequences of Welsh Identity*. Studies in Public Policy No. 27. Centre for the Study of Public Policy, University of Strathclyde: Glasgow.

Bankowski, Zenon & Mungham, Geoff. 1980. Political trials in contemporary Wales: cases, causes and methods. In Zenon Bankowski & Geoff Mungham (eds.), *Essays in Law and Society*, pp. 53–70. Routledge & Kegan Paul: London.

Barrington Moore Jnr., J. 1967. *Social Origins of Dictatorship and Democracy*. Allen Lane: London.

Beer, William R. 1977. The social class of ethnic activists in contemporary France. In Milton J. Esman, *Ethnic Conflict in the Western World*. Cornell University Press: Ithaca & London.

Bell, P. M. H. 1969. *Disestablishment in Ireland and Wales*. SPCK: London.

Benton, Ted. 1984. *The Rise and Fall of Structural Marxism: Althusser and His Influence*. Macmillan: London.

Berrisford, Ellis P. 1968. *Wales. A Nation Again! The Nationalist Struggle for Freedom*. Tandem Books: London.

Berry, David. 1977. *Wales. The Myth of Internal Colonialism*. Paper presented to the British Sociological Association, Sociology of Wales Study Group, Annual Conference. Gregynog.

Betts, Clive. 1976. *Culture in Crisis. The Future of The Welsh*

Language. The Ffynnon Press: Wirral.
Birch, A. H. 1978. Minority nationalist movements and theories of political integration. *World Politics* 30, 3:325–44.
Birch, A. H. 1977. *Political Integration and Disintegration in the British Isles*. Allen & Unwin: London.
Blackburn, Robin (ed.). 1978. *Revolution and Class Struggle. A Reader in Marxist Politics*. Harvester Press: Brighton.
Bocock, Robert. 1986. *Hegemony*. Horwood: Chichester.
Bodemann, Michael Y. & Spohn, Willfried. 1986. The organicity of class and the naked proletarian. Towards a new formulation of the class conception. *The Insurgent Sociologist* XIII, 3: pp. 10–19.
Boggs, Carl. 1976. *Gramsci's Marxism*. Pluto Press: London.
Boswell, Terry E., Kiser, Edgar V. & Baker, Kathryn A. 1986. Recent developments in Marxist theories of ideology. *The Insurgent Sociologist* XII, 4: pp. 5–22.
Bottomore, T. 1965. *Classes in Modern Society*. George Allen & Unwin: London.
Bottomore, T. 1979. *Political Sociology*. Hutchinson: London.
Bottomore, T. & Goode P. 1978. *Austro Marxism*. Clarendon Press: Oxford.
Bourhis, Richard Y. (ed.). 1984. *Conflict and Language Planning in Quebec*. Multi-Lingual Matters Ltd: Clevedon.
Bowles, Samuel & Gintis, Herbert. 1976. *Schooling in Capitalist America*. Routledge & Kegan Paul: London.
Bradley, Ian. 1982. *The English Middle Classes are Alive and Kicking*. Collins: London.
Braverman, Harry. 1974. *Labour and Monopoly Capital. The Degradation of Work*. Monthly Review Press: New York.
Brenner, Robert. 1977. The origins of capitalist development: a critique of Neo-Smithian Marxism. *New Left Review* 104: 25–92.
Buci-Glucksman, Christine. Translated by David Fernbach. 1980. *Gramsci and the State*. Lawrence & Wishart: London.
Butler, David & Sloman, Anne. 1980. *British Political Facts* (5th ed.). Macmillan: London.
Butler, D. E. & Stokes, D. 1974. *Political Change in Britain* (2nd ed.). Macmillan: London.
Butt Philip, Alan. 1975. *The Welsh Question. Nationalism in Welsh Politics*. University of Wales Press: Cardiff.
Buttel, Frederick H. & Newby, Howard (eds.). 1980. *The Rural Sociology of the Advanced Societies. Critical Perspectives*. Croom Helm: London.
Callinicos, Alex. 1976. *Althusser's Marxism*. Pluto Press: London.
Carchedi, Gugliemo. 1977. *On the Economic Identification of Social Classes*. Routledge & Kegan Paul: London.

Carney, J. & Lewis, J. 1978. Accumulation, the regional problem and
    nationalism. In P. W. J. Batey (ed.), *Theory and Method in Urban
    and Regional Analysis,* pp. 67–81. Pion: London.
Carr, Edward Hallet. 1945. *Nationalism and After.* Macmillan: London.
Carter, Bob. 1985. *Capitalism, Class Conflict and the New Middle
    Class.* Routledge & Kegan Paul: London.
Centre for Contemporary Cultural Studies. 1978. *On Ideology.*
    Hutchinson: London.
A Celt. 1895. *Cymru Fydd.* Welsh National Press: Caernarfon.
Chappell, Edgar L. 1943. *Wake Up Wales! A Survey of Home Rule
    Activities.* Foyle's Welsh Co. Ltd.: London.
Clammer, John. 1978. *The New Economic Anthropology.* St Martin's
    Press: New York.
Clarke, John, Connell, Ian & Macdonough, Roisin. 1978. Misrecog-
    nizing ideology: ideology in political power and social classes. In
    Centre for Contemporary Cultural Studies, *On Ideology,* pp. 106–22.
    Hutchinson: London,
Clews, Roy. 1980. *To Dream of Freedom. The Struggle of M.A.C and
    the Free Wales Army.* Lolfa: Talybont.
Coleman, William. 1984. Social class and language policies in Quebec.
    In Richard Y. Bourhis, *Conflict and Language Planning in Quebec,*
    pp. 130–47. Multi-Lingual Matters Ltd.: Clevedon.
Combs Jnr, Thomas Dewitt. 1978. *The Party of Wales, Plaid Cymru.
    Populist Nationalism in Contemporary British Politics.* University of
    Connecticut (PhD Thesis).
Committee, Welsh Land Enquiry. 1914. *Welsh Land.* Hodder &
    Stoughton: London.
Cooke, Philip N. 1981. Dependent development in the United Kingdom
    with particular reference to Wales. *Progress in Planning* 15, 1: pp.
    1–63.
Cooke, Philip N. 1982. Class interests, regional restructuring and state
    formation in Wales. *International Journal of Urban and Regional
    Research* 6, 2: pp. 187–204.
Cooke, Philip N. 1983. The regional division of labour. In Glyn
    Williams (ed.), *Crisis of Economy and Ideology. Essays on Welsh
    Society, 1840–1980,* pp. 72–87. SSRC/BSA Sociology of Wales
    Study Group: London.
Cooke, Philip N. & Rees, Gareth. 1981. *The Industrial Restructuring of
    South Wales. Papers in Planning Research. No. 25.* Dept of Town
    Planning, UWIST: Cardiff.
Corrado, Raymond R. 1975. Nationalism and communalism in Wales.
    Ethnicity 2: pp. 360–81.
Cottrell, Allin. 1984. *Social Classes in Marxist Theory and in Post War
    Britain.* Routledge & Kegan Paul: London.

Cottrell, Allin & Roslender, Robin. 1986. Economic class, social class and political forces. *International Journal of Sociology and Social Policy* 6, 3: 13–27.

Craib, Ian. 1984. *Modern Social Theory. From Parsons to Habermas.* Wheatsheaf: Brighton.

Crewe, Ivor. 1986. On the death and resurrection of class voting: some comments on 'How Britain Votes'. *Political Studies* XXXIV, 4: 620–38.

Crompton, Rosemary & Jones, Gareth. 1984. *White Collar Proletariat. Deskilling and Gender in Clerical Work.* Macmillan: London.

Crompton, Rosemary & Gubbay, Jon. 1977. *Economy and Class Structure.* Macmillan: London.

Cummins, Ian. 1980. *Marx, Engels and National Movements.* Croom Helm: London.

Cutler, A., Hindess, P., Hirst, P. & Hussain, A. 1977/8. *Marx's Capital and Capitalism Today.* Vols. 1 & 2. Routledge & Kegan Paul: London.

Davies, E. T. 1965. *Religion in the Industrial Revolution in South Wales.* University of Wales Press: Cardiff.

Davies, D. J. 1958. *Towards Welsh Freedom.* Plaid Cymru: Cardiff.

Davies, Horace B. 1967. *Nationalism and Socialism. Marxist and Labor Theories of Nationalism to 1917.* Monthly Review Press: New York & London.

Davies, D. Hywel. 1983. *The Welsh Nationalist Party 1925 – 1945. A Call to Nationhood.* University of Wales Press: Cardiff.

Davies, John. 1985. Plaid Cymru in transition. In John Osmond (ed.), *The National Question Again. Welsh Political Identity in the 1980s,* pp. 124–54. Gomer Press: Llandysul.

Day, Graham. 1981. *Development and Regional Consciousness. The Welsh Case.* Paper presented to the Symposium on the Social Anthropology of Europe. Inter-Congress: Amsterdam.

Day, Graham & Sugget, Richard. 1983. *Conceptions of Welshness: Aspects of Nationalism in Nineteenth-Century Wales.* Paper presented to British Sociological Association, Annual Conference; Cardiff.

Day, Graham. 1978. Underdeveloped Wales? *Planet* 45/6: 102–10.

De Marchi, Bruna & Boileau, Ann M. (eds.). 1982. *Boundaries and Minorities in Western Europe.* Franco Angeli Editore: Milan.

Debray, Regis. 1977. Marxism and the national question. *New Left Review.* 105: 25–41.

Deutsch, Karl W. 1953. *Nationalism and Social Communication. An Enquiry into the Foundations of Nationality.* M.I.T Press: Massachusetts.

Dodd, A. H. 1951. *The Industrial Revolution in North Wales.*

University of Wales Press: Cardiff.

Dofny, Jacques & Akiwowo, Akinsola. 1980. *National and Ethnic Movements.* Sage: London.

Dunleavy, Patrick & Husbands, Christopher T. 1985. *British Democracy at the Crossroads. Voting and Party Competition in the 1980s.* Allen & Unwin: London.

Edwards, Ness. 1924. *The Industrial Revolution in South Wales.* Labour Publishing Co: London.

Edwards, Arwel J. 1985. Manufacturing in Wales: a spatial and sectoral analysis of recent changes in structure, 1975–85. *Cambria* 12, 2: 89–115.

Elliot, Gregory. 1986. The odyssey of Paul Hirst. *New Left Review* 159: 81–107.

Elton Mayo, Patricia. 1974. *The Roots of Identity. Three National Movements in Contemporary European Politics.* Allen Lane: London.

Esman, Milton J. (ed.). 1977a. *Ethnic Conflict in the Western World.* Cornell University Press: Ithaca & London.

Esman, Milton J. 1977b. Scottish nationalism, North Sea oil and the British response. In Milton J. Esman (ed.), *Ethnic Conflict in the Western World,* pp. 251–86. Cornell University Press: London.

Evans, E. D. 1976. *A History of Wales 1660 – 1815.* University of Wales Press: Cardiff.

Evans, Nesta. 1936. *Social Life in Mid-Eighteenth Century Anglesey.* University of Wales Press: Cardiff.

Evans, Neil. 1983. *Interpreting the Industrialization of Wales. Internal Colony, Imperial Node – or Uneven Development?* Paper presented to the British Sociological Association, Annual Conference: Cardiff.

Evans, Neil (ed.). 1989. *National Identity in the British Isles.* Coleg Harlech Occasional Paper No. 3. Coleg Harlech: Harlech.

Evans, Gwynfor. 1973. *Wales Can Win.* Christopher Davies: Llandybïe.

Evans, Gwynfor. 1975. *A National Future For Wales.* Plaid Cymru: Cardiff.

Femia, Joseph V. 1981. *Gramsci's Political Thought. Hegemony, Consciousness and the Revolutionary Process.* Clarendon Press: Oxford.

Feuer, Lewis S. 1975. *Ideology and the Ideologists.* Basil Blackwell: Oxford.

Flakser, David. 1971. *Marxism, Ideology and Myths.* Philosophical Library: New York.

Foster-Carter, Aiden. 1978. Can we articulate 'articulation'? In John Clammer (ed.), *The New Economic Anthropology,* pp. 210–49. St Martin's Press: New York.

Foster-Clarke, Adrian. 1978. The mode of production controversy. *New Left Review* 107: 47–77.

Foulkes, David, Jones, J. Barry & Wilford, R. A. 1983. *The Welsh Veto. The Wales Act 1978 and The Referendum.* University of Wales Press: Cardiff.

Foweraker, J. W. 1978. The contemporary peasant: class and class practice. In Howard Newby (ed.), *International Perspectives in Rural Sociology*, pp. 131–58. John Wiley & Sons: Chichester.

Frank, Andre Gunder. 1969a. *Capitalism and Underdevelopment in Latin America.* Monthly Review Press: New York.

Frank, Andre Gunder. 1969b. *Latin America. Underdevelopment or Revolution.* Monthly Review Press: New York.

Frank, Andre Gunder. 1978. *Dependent Accumulation and Under-development.* Macmillan: London.

Franklin, S. H. 1969. *The European Peasantry. The Final Phase.* Methuen: London.

Gellner, Ernest. 1964. *Thought and Change.* Weidenfeld & Nicolson: London.

Gellner, Ernest. 1983. *Nations and Nationalism.* Blackwell: Oxford.

Gellner, Ernest. 1987. *Culture, Identity and Politics.* Cambridge University Press.

Geras, Norman. 1987. Post-Marxism? *New Left Review* 163: 41–82.

Giddens, Anthony. 1971. *Capitalism and Modern Social Theory.* Cambridge University Press.

Giddens, Anthony. 1973. *The Class Structure of the Advanced Societies.* Hutchinson: London.

Giddens, Anthony. 1982. *Profiles and Critiques in Social Theory.* Macmillan: London.

Giddens, Anthony. 1984. *The Constitution of Society. Outline of the Theory of Structuration.* Polity Press: Cambridge.

Giddens, Anthony & Held, David (eds.). 1982. *Classes, Power and Conflict. Classical and Contemporary Debates.* Macmillan: London.

Goldethorpe, John H. 1980. *Social Mobility and Class Structure in Britain.* Clarendon Press: Oxford.

Goodman, David & Redcliffe, Michael. 1981. *From Peasant to Proletarian: Capitalist Development and Agrarian Transition.* Basil Blackwell: Oxford.

Gorz, André. 1982. *Farewell to the Working Class: An Essay on Post-Industrial Socialism.* Pluto: London.

Gottman, Jean (ed.). 1980. *Centre and Periphery: Spatial Variation in Politics.* Sage Publications: London.

Gramsci, Antonio. 1971. *Selection from The Prison Notebooks.* Edited and translated by Quinton Hoare & Geoffrey Nowell Smith. Lawrence & Wishart: London.

Gramsci, Antonio. 1925. La Volontà delle Masse. *L'Unità (24 June 1925), Scritti Politici:* 620–1.

Gramsci, Antonio. 1977. *Selections from Political Writings, 1910-1920.* Selected and edited by Q. Hoare. Translated by J. Mathews. Lawrence & Wishart: London.

Gramsci, Antonio. 1978. *Selections from Political Writings, 1921–1926.* Edited and translated by Q. Hoare. Lawrence & Wishart: London.

Grant, W. P. & Preece, R. J. C. 1968. Welsh and Scottish nationalism. *Parliamentary Affairs* XXI, 3: 255–63.

Greenburg, William. 1969. *The Flags of The Forgotten. Nationalism on the Celtic Fringe.* Clifton Books: Brighton.

Greenwood, Davydd J. 1977. Continuity in change. Spanish Basque ethnicity as a historical process. In Milton J. Esman (ed.), *Ethnic Conflict in the Western World,* pp. 81–102. Cornell University Press: London.

Hall, Stuart. 1977. The political and the economic in Marx's theory of classes. In A. Hunt (ed.), *Class and Class Structure,* pp. 15–60. Lawrence & Wishart: London.

Hearne, Derrick. 1975. *The Rise of the Welsh Republic: Towards a Welsh Theory of Government.* Lolfa: Talybont.

Hearne, Derrick. 1977. *The Joy of Freedom: Towards an Ideology of Welsh Liberation.* Lolfa: Talybont.

Heath, Anthony, Jowell, Roger & Curtice, John. 1985. *How Britain Votes.* Pergamon Press: Oxford.

Hechter, Michael. 1975. *Internal Colonialism: The Celtic Fringe in British National Development.* Routledge & Kegan Paul: London.

Hechter, Michael & Levi, Margaret. 1979. The comparative analysis of ethnoregional movements. *Ethnic and Racial Studies* 2, 3: 260–74.

Hechter, Michael. 1978. Group formation and the cultural division of labour. *American Journal of Sociology* 84, 2: 293–318.

Herod, Charles C. 1976. *The Nation in the History of Marxian Thought: The Concept of Nations with History and Nations without History.* Martinus Nijhoff: The Hague.

Hill, Stephen. 1981. *Competition and Control at Work.* Heinemann: London.

Hindess, Barry & Hirst, Paul Q. 1975. *Pre-Capitalist Modes of Production.* Routledge & Kegan Paul: London.

Hindess, Barry. 1987. *Politics and Class Analysis.* Basil Blackwell: Oxford.

Hirst, Paul Q. 1977. Economic classes and politics. In A. Hunt (ed.), *Class and Class Structure,* pp. 125–54. Lawrence & Wishart: London.

Hirst, Paul Q. 1976. Althusser and the theory of ideology. *Economy and Society* 5, 4: 385–412.

Hoare, Tony. 1983. *The Location of Industry in Britain.* Cambridge University Press.

Hobsbawm, Eric. 1977. Some reflections on 'The Break-up of Britain'. *New Left Review* 105: 1–23.

Hobsbawm, Eric. 1977. La Scienza Politica. *Rinascita,* 50–1, 23 Dec.

Hoffman, John. 1975. *Marxism and The Theory of Praxis. A Critique of Some New Versions of Some Old Fallacies.* Lawrence & Wishart: London.

Howell, David W. 1977. *Land and People in Nineteenth-Century Wales.* Routledge & Kegan Paul: London.

Humphries, Graham. 1972. *Industrial Britain: South Wales.* Charles: Newton Abbot.

Hunt, Alan (ed.). 1977. *Class and Class Structure.* Lawrence & Wishart: London.

Hyman, Richard & Price, Robert. 1983. *The New Working Class? White-collar Workers and Their Organizations. A Reader.* Macmillan: London.

Hyman, Richard. 1980. White collar workers and theories of class. In Richard Hyman & Robert Price (eds.), *The New Working Class? White Collar Workers and Their Organizations. A Reader,* pp. 3–45. Macmillan: London.

Jackson, Robert H. 1984. Ethnicity. In Giovanni Sartori, *Social Science Concepts. A Systematic Analysis.* Sage Publications: London.

John, A. H. 1950. *The Industrial Development of South Wales 1750 – 1850. An Essay.* University of Wales Press: Cardiff.

Johnson, Terry. 1977. What is to be known? The structural determination of class. *Economy & Society* 6: 194–233.

Johnson, Dale L. (ed.). 1982a. *Class and Social Development. A New Theory of the Middle Class.* Sage: Beverly Hills.

Johnson, Dale L. 1982b. Toward a historical and dialectical social science. In Dale L. Johnson (ed.), *Class and Social Development: A New Theory of the Middle Class,* pp. 29–48. Sage: Beverley Hills.

Jones, David. 1973. *Before Rebecca: Popular Protest in Wales 1793–1835.* Allen Lane: London.

Jones, Ieuan Gwynedd. 1980. Language and community in nineteenth-century Wales. In David Smith, *A People and a Proletariat. Essays in the History of Wales 1780–1980,* pp. 47–71. Pluto Press: London.

Jones, R. Mervyn. 1982. *The North Wales Quarrymen, 1874–1922.* University of Wales Press: Cardiff.

Jones, J. Barry. 1983. The development of the devolution debate. In David Foulkes, J. Barry Jones & R. A. Wilford, *The Welsh Veto: The Wales Act 1978 and the Referendum,* pp. 19–33. University of Wales Press: Cardiff.

Kamenka, Eugene (ed.). 1973a. *Nationalism. The Nature and Evolution of an Idea.* Edward Arnold: London.

Kamenka, Eugene. 1973b. Political nationalism: the evolution of an idea. In Eugene Kamenka (ed.), *Nationalism: The Nature and Evolution of an Idea.* pp. 2–20. Edward Arnold: London.

Kedourie, Elie. 1960. *Nationalism.* Hutchinson: London.

Khlief, Bud B. 1980. *Language, Ethnicity and Education in Wales.* Mouton: The Hague, Paris & New York.

Kiernan, V. G. 1972. Gramsci and Marxism. In Ralph Miliband & John Saville (eds.), *The Socialist Register 1972.* Merlin Press: London.

Kiernan, Victor. (1976). Nationalist movements and social classes. In Anthony D. Smith (ed.), *Nationalist Movements,* pp. 110–133. Macmillan: London.

Kitching, Gavin. 1982. *Development and Underdevelopment in Historical Perspective. Populism, Nationalism and Industrialization.* Methuen: London & New York.

Klingender, F. D. 1935. Clerks as Proletarians. From, *The Condition of Clerical Labour in Britain* (London: Martin Lawrence), pp. xi–xii, 17–19, 58, 61–3, 98–9. Reproduced in Richard Hyman and Robert Price. 1983. *The New Working Class? White Collar Workers and Their Organizations. A Reader,* pp. 52–7. Macmillan: London.

Kohn, Hans. 1945. *The Idea of Nationalism. A Study in its Origins and Background.* Macmillan: London.

Kohn, Hans. 1965. *Nationalism. Its Meaning and History.* Van Nostrand: New York.

Kohr, Leopold. 1971. *Is Wales Viable?* Christopher Davies: Llandybïe.

Laclau, Ernesto. 1971. Feudalism and capitalism in Latin America. *New Left Review,* 67: 19–38.

Laclau, Ernesto. 1977. *Politics and Ideology in Marxist Theory.* New Left Books: London.

Laclau, Ernesto. 1977b. Fascism and ideology. In Ernesto Laclau, *Politics and Ideology in Marxist Theory,* pp. 31–42. New Left Books: London.

Laclau, Ernesto & Mouffe, Chantal. 1985. *Hegemony and Socialist Strategy. Towards a Radical Democratic Politics.* Verso: London.

Landsberger, Henry A. (ed.). 1974. *Rural Protest: Peasant Movements and Social Change.* Macmillan: London.

Larrain, Jorge. 1979. *The Concept of Ideology.* Hutchinson: London.

Lawner, Lynne. 1979. *Letters from Prison by Antonio Gramsci.* Quartet Books: London.

Lazonick, William. 1974. Karl Marx and enclosures in England. *Review of Radical Political Economics* 6, 2: 1–32.

Lele, Jayant. 1980. The two faces of nationalism: on the revolutionary potential of tradition. In Jacques Dofny and Akinsol Akiwowo,

National and Ethnic Movements, pp. 201–16. Sage: London.
Lenin, V. I. 1964. *Collected Works.* Lawrence & Wishart: London & Progress Publishers: Moscow.
Lewis, E. D. 1958. *The Rhondda Valleys: A Study in Industrial Development, 1800 to the Present.* Phoenix House: London.
Lewis, H. Elvet. 1904. *Nonconformity in Wales.* National Council of Evangelical Free Churches: London.
Lewis, Saunders. 1962. *Tynged Yr Iaith.* Translated as *The Fate of the Language.* In Alun R. Jones & Gwyn Thomas (eds.), *Presenting Saunders Lewis* (1973), pp. 127–41. University of Wales Press: Cardiff.
Lockwood, David. 1958. *The Blackcoated Worker.* George Allen & Unwin: London.
Lovering, John. 1978. *Dependence and the Welsh Economy.* Institute of Economic Research, Economic Research Papers No. 22, U.C.N.W: Bangor.
Lovering, John. 1978. The theory of the 'internal colony' and the political economy of Wales. *Review of Radical Political Economists* 10: 55–67.
Lowy, Michael. 1976. Marxists and the national question. *New Left Review* 96: 81–100.
MacAllister, Ian & Rose, Richard. 1984. *The Nationwide Competition for Votes. The 1983 General Election.* Francis Pinter: London.
Madgwick, P. J. 1973. *The Politics of Rural Wales: A Study of Cardiganshire.* Hutchinson: London.
Makarius, Raoul. 1974. Structuralism: science or ideology? In Ralph Miliband & J. Saville (eds.), *The Socialist Register,* pp. 189–225. Merlin Press: London.
Mandel, Ernest. 1971. *The Formation of the Economic Thought of Karl Marx.* Monthly Press: London.
Manners, Gerald (ed.), 1964. *South Wales in the Sixties: Studies in Industrial Geography.* Pergamon Press: Oxford.
Manning, D. J. (ed.). 1980. *The Form of Ideology.* George Allen & Unwin: London.
Marx, K. & Engels, F. 1974. *Collected Works.* Lawrence & Wishart: London.
Marx, K. & Engels, F. 1967. *The Communist Manifesto.* Introduction by A. J. P. Taylor. Penguin: Middlesex.
Massey, Doreen. 1976. In what sense a regional problem. *Regional Studies:* 13, 233–44.
Massey, Doreen. 1978. Regionalism: some current issues. *Capital and Class* 6: 106–25.
McCarney, Joe. 1980. *The Real World of Ideology.* Harvester Press: Brighton.

McIntyre, Steve. 1985. National film cultures: politics and peripheries. *Screen* 26, 1: 66–76.

McLellan, David. 1973. *Karl Marx. His Life and Thought.* Macmillan Press Ltd: London.

McLennan, Gregor, Molina, Victor & Peters, Roy. 1978. Althusser's theory of ideology. In Centre for Contemporary Cultural Studies, *On Ideology,* pp. 77–105. Hutchinson: London.

Meiksins-Wood, Ellen. 1986. *The Retreat from Class. A New 'True' Socialism.* Verso: London.

Mensah, Ebow. 1980. Expulsion and secession: towards a model for the analysis of minority formation. In Jacques Dofny & Akinsola Akiwowo. *National and Ethnic Movements,* pp. 217–31. Sage: London.

Meszaros, Istvan. 1972. Ideology and social science. In Ralph Miliband & John Saville (eds.), *The Socialist Register,* pp. 35–81. Merlin Press: London.

Migdal, Joel S. 1974. *Peasants, Politics and Revolution: Pressures Toward Political and Social Change in the Third World.* Princeton University Press.

Minchinton, W. E. 1969. *Industrial South Wales, 1750–1914.* Frank Cass: London.

Minogue, K. 1967. *Nationalism.* Batsford: London.

Monière, Denis. 1981. *Ideologies in Quebec: The Historical Development.* University of Toronto Press.

Montague Jnr, Joel B. 1963. *Class and Nationality: English and American Studies.* Vision Press Ltd: London.

Morgan, Kevin. 1980. *State Regional Interventions and Industrial Reconstruction in Post War Britain. The Case of Wales.* Working Paper. Urban and Regional Studies No. 16. University of Sussex.

Morgan, Prys. 1973. Welsh national consciousness — the historical background. In W. J. Morgan (ed.), *The Welsh Dilemma,* pp. 14–34. Christopher Davies: Llandybïe.

Morgan, W. J. (ed.). 1973. *The Welsh Dilemma.* Christopher Davies: Llandybïe.

Morgan, Kenneth O. 1963. *Wales in British Politics, 1868–1922.* University of Wales Press: Cardiff.

Morgan, Kenneth O. 1981. *Rebirth of a Nation: Wales 1880–1980.* Clarendon: Oxford and University of Wales Press: Cardiff.

Morris, R. J. 1979. *Class and Class Consciousness in the Industrial Revolution 1780–1850.* Studies in Economic and Social History. Macmillan: London.

Mosse, George L. 1973. Mass politics and the political liturgy of nationalism. In Eugene Kamenka (ed.), *Nationalism. The Nature and Evolution of an Idea,* pp. 38–54. Edward Arnold: London.

Mouffe, Chantal (ed.). 1979. *Gramsci and Marxist Theory.* Routledge & Kegan Paul: London.

Nairn, Tom. 1977. *The Break Up of Britain: Crisis and Neo-Colonialism.* New Left Books: London.

Neale, R. S. (ed.). 1983. *History and Class. Essential Readings in Theory and Interpretation.* Blackwell: Oxford.

Nettl, J. P. 1966. *Rosa Luxembourg.* Vols. 1 & 2. Oxford University Press.

Newby, Howard (ed.). 1978. *International Perspectives in Rural Sociology.* John Wiley & Sons: Chichester.

Newby, Howard, Bell, Colin, Rose, David & Saunders, Peter. 1978. *Property, Paternalism and Power. Class and Control in Rural England.* Hutchinson: London.

Nichols, Theo. 1986. Introduction. In Armstrong, Carter, Smith & Nichols, *White Collar Workers: Trade Unions and Class,* pp 1–16. Croom Helm: London.

Nimni, Ephraim. 1985. Marxism and nationalism. In Martin Shaw (ed.), *Marxist Sociology Revisited. Critical Assessments,* pp. 99–142. Macmillan: London.

Nyström, Kerstin & Rönnquist, Ralf. 1982. Regions in upheaval. Notes on social change and ethnic conflict in contemporary Europe. In B. De Marchi & A. M. Boileau (eds.), *Boundaries and Minorities in Western Europe,* pp. 93–110. Franco Angeli Editore: Milan.

Oppenheimer, Martin. 1982. The political mission of the middle strata. In Dale L. Johnson (ed.), *Class and Social Development: A New Theory of the Middle Class,* pp. 109–32. Sage: Beverley Hills.

Orridge, A. W. 1981. Uneven development and nationalism. *Political Studies* XXIX, 1 (pp. 3–15) & 2 (pp. 182–90).

O'Shea, Alan. 1984. Trusting the people: how does Thatcherism work? In T. Bennet *et al., Formations of Nation and People,* pp. 19–41. Routledge & Kegan Paul: London.

Osmond, John. 1979. *Creative Conflict. The Politics of Welsh Devolution.* Routledge & Kegan Paul: London.

Osmond, John (ed.). 1985. *The National Question Again. Welsh Political Identity in the 1980s.* Gomer Press: Llandysul.

Paige, Jeffrey M. 1975. *Agrarian Revolution. Social Movements and Export Agriculture in the Underdeveloped World.* The Free Press: New York.

Parekh, Bhikku. 1982. *Marx's Theory of Ideology.* Croom Helm: London.

Parkin, Frank (ed.). 1974. *The Social Analysis of Class Structure.* Tavistock: London.

Parkin, Frank. 1979. *Marxism and Class Theory: A Bourgeois Critique.* Tavistock: London.

Parsons, Tolcott. 1951. *The Social System*. Free Press: New York.
Plaid Cymru. 1969. *Economic Plan for Wales*. Plaid Cymru: Cardiff.
Plaid Cymru. 1981. *The Report of the Commission of Enquiry*. Plaid Cymru: Cardiff.
Plaid Cymru. 1983. Editorial. *Radical Wales* 1: 3.
Poulantzas, Nicos. 1973. *Political Power and Social Classes*. Verso: London.
Poulantzas, Nicos. 1974. *Fascism and Dictatorship. The Third International and the Problem of Fascism*. New Left Books: London.
Poulantzas, Nicos. 1975. *Classes in Contemporary Capitalism*. New Left Books: London.
Pretty, David A. 1989. *The Rural Revolt that Failed: Farm Workers' Trade Unions in Wales, 1889–1950*. University of Wales Press: Cardiff.
Randall, P. J. 1972. Wales in the structure of central government. *Public Administration* 50: 352–72.
Rawkins, Philip M. 1978. Outsiders as insiders: the implications of minority nationalism in Scotland and Wales. *Comparative Politics* 10, 4: 519–34.
Rawkins, Philip M. 1979. An approach to the political sociology of the Welsh nationalist movement. *Political Studies* XXVII, 3: 440–57.
Rees, Alwyn D. 1951. *Life in A Welsh Countryside*. University of Wales Press: Cardiff.
Rees, Gareth & Lambert, John. 1981. Nationalism as legitimation? Notes toward a political economy of regional development in south Wales. In M. Marloe (ed.), *New Perspectives in Urban Change and Conflict*, pp. 122–37. Heinemann: London.
Rees, Gareth & Rees, Teresa. 1983. Migration, industrial restructuring and class relations: an analysis of south Wales. In Glyn Williams (ed.), *Crisis of Economy and Ideology. Essays on Welsh Society, 1840–1980*, pp. 103–19. SSRC/BSA Sociology of Wales Study Group: London.
Rees, Gareth & Rees, Teresa (eds.). 1980. *Poverty and Social Inequality in Wales*. Croom Helm: London.
Rees, Gareth & Rees, Teresa. 1981. *Migration, Industrial Restructuring and Class Relations. The Case of South Wales*. Papers in Planning Research, No. 22. UWIST: Cardiff.
Rees, Teresa. 1976. *The Origin and Destination of Migrants to and from the South Wales Valleys, with special reference to the Upper Afan Valley*. Home Office/West Glamorgan CDI Research Team. Working Paper No. 16. Department of Town Planning, UWIST: Cardiff.
Rhys, John & Jones, David Brynmor. 1900. *The Welsh People*. Fisher Unwin: London.

Roberts, K., Cook, F. G., Clark, S. C., & Semenoff, E. 1977. *The Fragmentary Class Structure*. Heinemann: London.

Rose, Richard. 1982. *Understanding the United Kingdom. The Territorial Dimension in Government*. Longman: London.

Sarlvik, Bo & Crewe, Ivor. 1983. *A Decade of Dealignment: the Conservative Victory of 1979 and Electoral Trends in the 1970s*. Cambridge University Press.

Sartori, Giovanni. 1984. *Social Science Concepts. A Systematic Analysis*. Sage Publications: London.

Sassoon, Anne Showstack. 1980. *Gramsci's Politics*. Croom Helm: London.

Sathyamurthy, T. V. 1983. *Nationalism in the Contemporary World. Political and Sociological Perspectives*. Frances Pinter: London.

Scase, Richard (ed.) 1977. *Industrial Society: Class, Cleavage and Control*. George Allen & Unwin: London.

Schwarzmantel, J. J. 1987. Class and nation: problems of socialist nationalism. *Political Studies* XXXV, 2: 239–55.

Seers, Dudley. 1983. *The Political Economy of Nationalism*. Oxford University Press.

Seliger, Martin. 1977. *The Marxist Conception of Ideology: A Critical Essay*. Cambridge University Press.

Seton Watson, Hugh. 1965. *Nationalism, Old and New*. Methuen: London.

Seton Watson, Hugh. 1977. *Nations and States: An Enquiry into the Origins of Nations and the Politics of Nationalism*. Methuen: London.

Shanin, Teodor. 1966. The peasantry as a political factor. *The Sociological Review* 14, 1: 5–27. Reproduced in Teodor Shanin (ed.), *Peasants and Peasant Societies. Selected Readings*, pp. 238–63. Penguin: Harmondsworth.

Shanin, Teodor (ed.). 1971. *Peasants and Peasant Societies. Selected Readings*. Penguin: Harmondsworth.

Shaw, Martin (ed.). 1985. *Marxist Sociology Revisited: Critical Assessments*. Macmillan: London.

Simon, Roger. 1982. *Gramsci's Political Thought: An Introduction*. Lawrence & Wishart: London.

Smith, David (ed.). 1980. *A People and a Proletariat: Essays in the History of Wales 1780–1980*. Pluto Press: London.

Smith, Anthony D. 1971. *Theories of Nationalism*. Duckworth: London.

Smith, Anthony D. (ed.). 1976a. *Nationalist Movements*. Macmillan: London.

Smith, Anthony D. 1976b. Introduction: the formation of nationalist movements. In Anthony D. Smith (ed.), *Nationalist Movements*, pp.

1–30. Macmillan: London.
Smith, Anthony D. 1979. *Nationalism in the Twentieth Century*. Martin Robertson: Oxford.
Smith, Anthony D. 1981. *The Ethnic Revival in the Modern World*. Cambridge University Press.
Smith, Anthony D. 1983. *State and Nation in the Third World. The Western State and African Nationalism*. Wheatsheaf: Brighton.
Snyder, Louis L. 1954. *The Meaning of Nationalism*. Greenwood Press: Connecticut.
Snyder, Louis L. 1964. *The Dynamics of Nationalism: Readings in its Meaning and Development*. Van Nostrand: New York.
Spring, David. 1977. *European Landed Elites in The Nineteenth Century*. John Hopkins University Press: London.
Stead, Peter. 1980. The language of Edwardian politics. In D. Smith (ed.), *A People and a Proletariat: Essays in the History of Wales, 1780–1980*, pp. 148 – 65. Pluto Press: London.
Steadman-Jones, Gareth. 1983. From historical sociology to theoretical history. In R. S. Neale (ed.), *History and Class: Essential Readings in Theory and Interpretation*, pp. 73–85. Blackwell: Oxford.
Terkel, Studs. 1985. *Working*. Penguin: Harmondsworth.
Texier, Jacques. 1979. Gramsci, theoretican of the superstructures. In Chantal Mouffe (ed.), *Gramsci and Marxist Theory*, pp. 48–79. Routledge & Kegan Paul: London.
Therbon, Goran. 1978. *What Does the Ruling Class Do When It Rules?* New Left Books: London.
Therbon, Goran. 1980. *The Ideology of Power and the Power of Ideology*. Verso: London.
Thomas, Dafydd Elis. 1983. Freud Cymru. *Radical Wales* 1: 18. Plaid Cymru: Cardiff.
Thomas, Edgar. 1927. *The Economics of Small-Holdings. A Study Based on a Survey of Small-Scale Farming in Carmarthenshire*. Cambridge University Press.
Thomas, Hugh. 1972. *A History of Wales, 1485–1660*. University of Wales Press: Cardiff.
Thomas, Ned. 1971. *The Welsh Extremist. A Culture in Crisis*. Gollancz: London.
Thomas, Ned. 1989. Can Plaid Cymru survive until 1994? *Planet. The Welsh Internationalist* 70: 3–10.
Thompson, E. P. 1968. *The Making of the English Working Class*. Penguin: Harmondsworth.
Thompson, E. P. 1978. *The Poverty of Theory and Other Essays*. Monthly Review Press: New York & London.
Tilley, C. 1975. *The Formation of Nation States in Western Europe*. Princeton University Press: New Jersey.

Tomkins, Cyril & Lovering, John. 1973. *Location, Size, Ownership and Control Tables for Welsh Industry*. Welsh Council: Cardiff.

Town, Stephen W. 1978. *After the Mines: Changing Employment Opportunities in a South Wales Valley*. University of Wales Board of Celtic Studies: Cardiff.

Urry, John. 1982. *The Anatomy of Capitalist Societies*. Macmillan: London.

Vincent, J. E. 1896. *The Land Question in North Wales: A Brief Survey of the History of Agitation and of the Nature and Effect of the Proceedings of the Welsh Land Committee*. Longmans, Green & Co: London.

Vogler, Carolyn M. 1985. *The Nation State: The Neglected Dimension of Class*. Gower: Aldershot.

Wanhill, Stephen. 1980. *An Econometric Model of Wales*. Bangor Occasional Papers in Economics, No. 18. University of Wales Press: Cardiff.

Ward, Barbara. 1967. *Nationalism and Ideology*. Hamish Hamilton: London.

Watts, H. D. 1981. *The Branch Plant Economy. A Study of External Control*. Longman: London.

Weber, Max. 1930. *The Protestant Ethic and the Spirit of Capitalism*. Allen & Unwin: London.

Weber, Max. 1968. *Economy and Society. An Outline of Interpretive Sociology*. Bedminster Press: New York.

Welsh Office. 1967. *Wales: The Way Ahead*. Cmnd 3234, HMSO: Cardiff.

Wenger, G. Clare. 1980. *Mid Wales: Deprivation or Development. A Study of Patterns of Employment in Selected Communities*. Board of Celtic Studies Social Science Monograph, No. 5. University of Wales Press: Cardiff.

Wilkins, Charles. 1867. *The History of Merthyr Tydfil*. Harry Wood Southey: Merthyr Tydfil.

Wilks, Ivor. 1984. *South Wales and the Rising of 1839*. Croom Helm: London.

Williams, Colin H. 1982a. *National Separatism*. University of Wales Press: Cardiff.

Williams, Colin H. 1982b. Ethnic regionalism in the Celtic periphery: the Welsh experience. In B. De Marchi & M. Boileau, *Boundaries and Minorities in Western Europe,* pp. 111–48. Franco Angeli Editore: Milan.

Williams, David. 1950. *A History of Modern Wales*. John Murray: London.

Williams, David. 1955. *The Rebecca Riots*. University of Wales Press: Cardiff.

Williams, G. 1981. *Power and Conflict in Change. Toward a Political Economy of Wales.* Routledge & Kegan Paul: London.
Williams, Glanmor (ed.). 1966. *Merthyr Politics: The Making of a Working Class Tradition.* University of Wales Press: Cardiff.
Williams, Glyn. 1978. *Social and Cultural Change in Contemporary Wales.* Routledge & Kegan Paul: London.
Williams, Glyn. 1981. Economic development, social structure and contemporary nationalism in Wales. *Review* 2: 275–310.
Williams, Glyn (ed). 1983. *Crisis of Economy and Ideology. Essays on Welsh Society, 1840–1980.* SSRC/BSA, Sociology of Wales Study Group: London.
Williams, Gwyn A. 1966. The Merthyr of Dic Penderyn. In Glanmor Williams (ed.), *Merthyr Politics: The Making of a Working Class Tradition,* pp. 9–27. University of Wales Press: Cardiff.
Williams, Gwyn A. 1978. *The Merthyr Rising.* Croom Helm: London. Reprinted by University of Wales Press (1988).
Williams, Gwyn A. 1980. Locating a Welsh working class: the frontier years. In David Smith (ed.), *People and a Proletariat: Essays in the History of Wales, 1780–1980,* pp. 16–46. Pluto Press: London.
Williams, Gwyn A. 1985. *When Was Wales? A History of the Welsh.* Penguin: Harmondsworth.
Williams, L. J. 1980. The coal owners. In David Smith (ed.), *A People and A Proletariat. Essays in the History of Wales, 1780–1980,* pp. 94–113. Pluto Press: London.
Williams, L. J. & Boyns, T. 1977. Occupations in Wales, 1851–1971. *Bulletin of Economic Research* 29: 71–83.
Williams, W. Llewellyn. 1919. *The Making of Modern Wales: Studies in the Tudor Settlement of Wales.* Macmillan: London.
Wirth, Louis. 1936. Types of nationalism. *American Journal of Sociology* 41, 6: 723–37.
Wolf, E. R. 1969. On peasant rebellions. *International Social Science Journal* 21: Reproduced in Teodor Shanin, *Peasants and Peasant Societies. Selected Readings,* pp. 264–76. Penguin: Harmondsworth.
Wright, Erik Olin. 1978. *Class, Crisis and the State.* New Left Books: London.
Wright, Erik Olin. 1985. *Classes.* Verso: London.
Young, David. 1893. *Origin and History of Methodism in Wales.* Charles Kelly: London.

INDEX